continued...

AGGRO RAG
FREESTYLE MAG!

PLYWOOD HOODS ZINES '84–'89:
THE COMPLETE COLLECTION

by Mike Daily

Dale Mitzel

STOVEPIPER BOOKS MEDIA
http://stovepiperbooks.com

Edited & Art Direction by Mike Daily

Visit us on the web at **aggrorag.com** & **stovepiperbooks.com**

ISBN 978-0-9642339-2-8

Copyright © 2013 by Mike Daily

All Rights Reserved. No part of this book may be reproduced, scanned or distributed in any printed or electronic form, including information storage and retrieval systems, without the written consent of the publisher, Stovepiper Books Media.

Printed in USA

Hoy! Hi. Fatherhood and grinding 40+ hours a week leaves limited time to do what I love: write and ride. Sound familiar? Sure must…

Karl Rothe wrote in a recent email:

Hey Mike:

I've put some serious thought into a nugget for your 'zine [Issue 13.5], but I've come up with nothing at all. It seems my energy and spirit for freestyle gassed off many moons ago. Nowadays I'm content being an occasional, quiet observer of the mix.

Word up,

Karl

Word.

Aggro Rag Freestyle Mag! Plywood Hoods Zines '84-'89: The Complete Collection had to exist. I hope you enjoy the read. I'm especially grateful to Chip Riggs for his invaluable contribution in graphic design, and to Ron Bonner and Ryan Sher at Subrosa Brand for collaborating with Riggs and me on the 2013 Subrosa DTT *Aggro Rag* Limited Edition frames. Thanks also to Raybo and Jim Dellavalle for access to their video tapes.

Thank you for reading. Thank you for riding.

As ever, "Ride First, Read Later,"

Mike Daily

FOREWORD

I met Mike Daily at Madison Square Gardens in New York at an AFA contest. It was 1986. He was distinctive in that he was a shy teenager who wore his curly hair in a sort of new wave pompadour.

As we sat in the stands watching practice, he handed me a smallish yet thick booklet. He looked at me with a timorous expression and asked me to share it with as many people as possible. "It's my zine, *Aggro Rag*," he told me. He went on to tell me he constructed it in York, Pennsylvania, and it featured the exploits of a two-wheeled gang he called the Plywood Hoods.

My memory gets a little hazy here—hell, it was almost 27 years ago. But I do remember telling as many people as I could about *Aggro Rag*. And it just got thicker and thicker with each passing issue—it became a giant over-sized burger when most other bike zines of the time were simple Hors d'Oeuvres. It was thick and dense and East Coast greasy. You were never sure if you could even get your mouth around it, let alone eat the entire thing. *Aggro Rag* was a big sloppy mess of words and photos. A delicious tome to freestyle BMX and friendship.

Put on your bib and enjoy.

—**Andy Jenkins**

FREESTYLIN'
September 1985

Summer 2012,
Ron Wilkerson sent this to me.

My guess was:

Wilkerson Airlines (WAL) fork dropout.

I was wrong.

Bottema.

Mark "Lungmustard" Eaton &
Unidentified Bottema Forks Guy
Thunderdohm Skatepark
York, PA
1983

INTRODUCTION

Spring break road trip circa 2010. Shopping with teenage daughters in North County San Diego at a high-end outlet mall nestled amidst the monoculture and endless stucco sprawl. We're in a cool youth brands chain store. My kids compete in a game of who can find the cutest espadrilles or flip-flops. I wander the aisles like a ghost, recognizing labels that grew out of acquaintances' garages and bedrooms, then warehouses, then bigger warehouses, then Chinese garment factories. And I come across a brand on a rack with a handscrawled-esque typeface on the hang tag: Zine. The garment bearing the Zine moniker is an unassuming tank top in circus peanut orange—no graphics or features whatsoever—and a retail price $38. For a fucking tank top? At an outlet mall?

The first time I visited this zip code was 1985, doing photo shoots with Pete Augustin and Jason Parkes. When freestyle was new. The sport felt like it moved so fast you could feel it shifting under your feet. Paradoxically, the information moved as slowly as the pace of a monthly magazine or an AFA contest; between these events, BMX kids were left to their own devices to fill in the gaps and write their own history. Some were better at it than others. Back in 1985, the word "zine" brought to mind something much different than overpriced tank tops.

I met Daily through the US mail, appropriately. The son of a magician, he chronicled the east coast scene, taking particular care to stoke a white hot fire around the epicenter of York, PA. *Aggro Rag*'s reputation for sticky content steadily grew. Along with the VHS sister media, *Dorkin' In York*, A-Rag became a national underground phenomenon and within 3 years it was the, uppercase italics, premier Xeroxed freestyle publication.

Equal parts daredevil and starving artist, with a dash of naiveté: That's the recipe for making something that's still savory, 25 years later. Thank you, Mike, for those toner-blackened fingers typing out the drumbeat of the times.

Long live *Aggro Rag*.

—**Mark Lewman**

ABOUT THE COVER

Mike Daily: Can I get some info about this photo, man? It's incredible.

Kevin Jones: [Laughs.] Why do you like that photo so much?

Well, it's a Polaroid, for one thing. And you're looking at the camera. And you're riding your tricked-out CW with all the pink parts on it. What is this trick?

It's a Squeakerson, or whatever. Wheelchair Walk, sittin' on the handlebars. I don't really remember what it would have been called. Or if it was even a main trick then. That's what it looks like to me: the tire walk. Squeakerson. Squeakerson Walk. I have a hard time remembering where it was. I don't place the spot. I'm not sure who would have taken that photo.

How about the bike? Do you remember this bike?

I loved that bike. My CW. Awesome. I loved the kicked-back seat angle with tons of distance space for the top tube, between the stem and the seat post. That's why I have that laid-forward seatpost—the layback turned around, so that the seat would actually meet up close to the grip for the side glide position. The seat angle was so far back. That made it awesome for the decades. That's actually the bike that I did the triple decade on.

Was that the first triple decade you ever did?

Yep. On the CW, the chrome one. It was all by accident. I was just tryin' to do a double and ended up gettin' lucky. I hadn't even fidged "triple decade," you know? I hadn't even thought it in my mind at that point yet. I'd only done the double maybe like less than ten times.

That's great. The other thing that stands out about this photo—besides the short shorts—are the Pumas.

[Laughs.] I had some leftover stock from the breakdancin' era.

That's what I was gonna ask you: You said in the *Freestylin'* **book that when you got back into flatland, you "started trying all the tricks and incorporating a little bit of the breakdance knowledge into the bike." Can you talk more about that?**

Oh, yeah. Well, I guess from doin' all the physical things in the breakdancing: you're constantly holding yourself up with your arms—a lot of power-type moves—so I wanted to try to get that in there. I probably didn't do it as much as I should have. I wanted to learn, like, handstands and stuff—try to throw a boomerang handstand and stuff like that—but after getting' hurt a few times, I kind of didn't want to try that way as much. I did get a couple straight-up handstands, but once you get a couple slams on it, it's not so good. The boomerangs, they're kind of like breakdancing…the way that you would use your legs to get momentum was kind of similar to a flair. I tried to spend a lot of time on those. And the decade, that's a pretty quick power move. And bar hops and stuff. I'm just staring at this picture, thinkin' about the shit.

You've got the ACS Rotor on there…

Yep, I got the terrible Rotor. I'm trying to look close, make it a little bigger.

It looks like you have a little yellow thing on your lever. Do you know what that is?

I'm not sure. I'm trying to get it zoomed in. Probably…it's just like a little rubber-coated end off of something. I'm not really sure what it would be off of. Maybe I put it on the end of the lever so it wouldn't hurt my finger that much, maybe? But I don't remember it at all. I actually didn't notice that before you said that. I'm seeing that I got the tiniest little pegs that you can barely even see. And I have the stander, and the seat post clamp holdin' the coaster brake. There's no pegs on the front, only the pink GT flip-down standers. I don't really remember havin' it that dialed—like, with the pink. I don't remember those pink standers at all. I must've got rid of those quick after that and put pegs on or something. Seems strange.

What's interesting is the fact that you're riding Tuff Wheels here, and you went on to ride for Skyway and run Tuffs later as a sponsored rider.

Yeah. I loved the Tuffs. I'm looking at it now, with the super knobby tire. Like Comp III or something. [Laughs.] Kashimax seat. I spent so much time with the Tuffs that it just seemed normal to me. Back then the weight didn't matter, so it was kind of something that looked cool. You didn't have to mess with 'em too much and they were relatively cheap.

I noticed online somewhere that somebody was asking you about Mushroom grips and you said the newer ones weren't as good as the originals. Right here, you're running the originals. They must be really hard to find now.

Oh, those? Yeah. On that bike, those were II's. Shortly after, I started finding the Mushroom I's, just because the ends were so hard—the plastic ends on the two-piece ones. I still to this day, still have been runnin' Mushroom I's. I just manage to find 'em all the time. Or at least enough to keep goin'. I have three left now; I got orange ones. I did try the new ones, but they're not quite as good. Something seems a little different, like the rubber's not as soft.

How did you get the old school ones?

I get lucky and find 'em on eBay for cheap. When people aren't noticing 'em. You just have to look into it. They can be 50 to 70 bucks—whatever, too much. But most of the ones I got were maybe 15 dollars for a pair, so…not bad.

Do you use eBay a lot, or any of the message boards, to find old parts nowadays?

I usually just go straight to eBay if I'm lookin' for something, unless it comes up somewhere else. I've never bought anything off of anywhere other than eBay, as far as old school stuff. I guess whatever I'm lookin' for I never see, or if it is on one of these other sites, it's too much. Like, I want it, but I don't want it that bad. I'm not willing to pay hundreds of dollars for something. I pretty much find what I want, or what I need—old school stuff—cheap. If you keep looking, eventually you'll find it.

Is there anything besides the grips that you really do want, or look for?

The only main thing that I like that isn't old school is the Peregrine rims. And I have a hard time finding brakes and brake pads that work properly and don't make any kind of noise and are just right. The silver Super Pros are the best rims for me. They work in all conditions, as well. Even if it's kind of damp out, they don't slip or squeal. That's about the only part really that I desperately look for. I have enough to last me for several years, so I'm not worried about it right now.

Kevin Jones, 1986

Jeff Watert, 1983

BMX RAG (1984)
Red Lion, PA
6" x 8"

"Jeff Watert and my brother [Brad] built the first ramp. I don't think there was any plan. They saw what it looked like in the magazine and just sort of built one. It was pretty thin plywood—I landed from an air one time and my front wheel actually stuck through the plywood at the bottom of the ramp."—**Brian Peters, Plywood Hoods**

1st ISSUE

Lawrence Weber, 1982
Thunderdohm Skatepark
York, PA

Dale Mitzel & Mark Eaton
The Cardboard Lords
Cable 4 York Talent Show
February 1985

In early '84, breakin' was everywhere—York, PA, even.

Mike Daily: What got you guys into breakin'?

Dale Mitzel: Mark [Eaton] did. I think he saw it on TV. We actually took a class. Did you ever know we took a class?

Was that with Joyce Freeman?

Yeah, Joyce Freeman Studio. She was teachin' some basic moves like runarounds and coffee grinders. Downtown at Zakie's, we picked up some moves like backspins and other ways of doin' backspins—not just from a certain stand-up position. I think the third week or so, we were kind of learnin' more than she was teachin' so we stopped goin'.

Interesting. You guys became obsessed quick.

Yeah. I mean, just like anything else we were into: We were just into doin' more and more—practicin' to get better at it. Back then, we didn't have the Internet, so we didn't have YouTube to see: "Now…what are the moves?" There were a lot of music videos and commercials that were showin' little clips of breakin', so we saw the main moves that way.

How about the movies? *Breakin'*…

Yeah: *Breakin'*…then *Breakin' 2*. They were good. They were great. I remember the Presidential inauguration had breakdancin' on—Ronald Reagan. I think he had the New York City Breakers on, if I'm not mistaken. We taped that. Certain things we knew ahead of time were going to be on and then we would tape it.

Kevin Jones, Headspins.

FREE
(and thas' cheap)

FIRST EVER BMX RAG

EDITORIAL

What is a BMX RAG the cross eyed aardvark asked? Now listen up you turkeys out there in freestyle land 'cause I'm only gonna say this once. This rag will be like your basic local updater, with listings of local ramps, cool stories, what's hot, some fake drawings, and maybe a few interviews. And don't forget, tons of jammin' photos of local dudes shreddin' their ramps.

If you're readin' this rag, then you're probly not a geekball, cause these are gonna be hard ta get.

SO READ ON, YOUNG HEROES.......

FREESTYLERS EDGE

Who dat?
Who dat say who dat?
Who dat say who dat say who dat?
Aw cut it out.
Allright already. It's me.

What does that lead have to do with the article? Absolutly nothing, but I had to use it somewhere in this rag.

I'm gonna tell you chowderheads how to liven up your spare bodiddlin' time. Number one on on the ol' list is to build a quarter pipe ramp. But I don't have to tell YOU guys to.... What's that? You don't have one? Make one. It's the most bitchen set-up ever.

Numero dos is DON'T JUST RIDE, WAKE UP! Don't get wrapped up in the same old humdrum riding routine. THINK! Push yourself! It's all mental. Be positive!

Number three is a lil' safety precaution. Wear protective gear to help salvage your bod from a heavy bail. Remember, one serious wack on the bean and you'll be drooling all over your bib when mommy feeds you for the rest of your life. Now go on out and have a heavy shredding session on your fave ramp. Gnarly? Yup.

A THRASHERS' LIFE

Okay dudes, Picture this:

Your basic thrasher dude is ridin' his ped sled home from school when suddenly he gets an ultra rad sensation, like he just HAS to get rad. As he's gliding down the road he does two fluid 360 bunnyhops, followed by a couple of sano rock walks, then finishes up with a purty gnarly gut lever.

"Well ain't that just too cool!", gawked one of the football players at the nearby football field, where the entire school football team was practicing.

"Yeah," another added, "That's for those geeks who can't play a real sport, Football!" The team laughed in approval.

Now buds, as you know, all BMX'ers can take a little shuckin' and jivin', but being called a geek is pretty low on the ol' list.

Just as our hero was about to come back with a possible obcene remark or gesture, the coach breaks it up.

"Okay guys, let's go, enough of this foolin' around or you'll be doin' one arm push ups on your knuckles!", the coach bellowed out over the field.

The team groaned and started walking away with the coach.

"Yeah, get to work you bozos", our fearless bike berserko yelled, "If that's what you call what you're doin', 'cause everyone knows that I could play better than all of you squids even on my scoot!"

(CONTINUED)

The coach stopped dead in his tracks. He slowly turned around and looked at the punk sitting on his bike with his arms crossed.

"Okay scumbag, we'll see what you can do", the coach growled, "I'll hike the pigskin back to you, stuff it in your handlebars, and we'll see if you can (snicker, chort, chuckle) score a touchdown."

Well, our thrasher dude, being the suave and debonair guy he is, accepted the challenge and casually rode his bike to the middle of the football field.

A crowd of about 17 football players line up snarling and drooling, fiendishly laughing, ready to destroy and mutilate.

Our main freestyler dude positions himself behind the coach and sets up his pedals.

"Hike, terdball!",the biker yells.

The football is hiked back, the mega-rad BMX'er jams it through his bars, and starts pedalling furiously toward the mountain of golden helmeted monsters, his bike leaping forward with every pedal stroke.

In their haste to mash our hero, the football jocks get kind of clumped up, and our fearless gladiator sees a perfect launching pad;a shoulder pad!

The BMX'er, dodging flailing arms and shoulders, impacts off the shoulder pad from the downed player and sails blithly through the air. With a lil' kickout, he manages to knock one of the charging robots silly with a masterful smash to the head!(Yea!Clap! Cheer!Go for it!)

(CONTINUED)

parking lot surfing.

Totally shredding grass and roosting all over the clods, and bunnyhopping over downed players, our skater raider totally out manuevers the scrambling meatheads.

Everything is really jammin' now, but just as our moto man thinks he's home free, one of the players knocks the ball out of it's wedge hold between the handlebars and the football goes tumbling out in front of the BMX'ers charging bike.

The quick thinking rider leans off the side of the bike down to ground level, his head just inches away from the ground and from the fast stomping cleats of the frenzied football players.

The Kawabonzical Kid scoops up the ball and stuffs it under his arm, the grass appearing to be a blur.

The biker then hops up on the seat and handlebars and balances his fast moving machine like a surfboard, grasping the football tightly. 30........ ..25......20....The rider tucks down cutting wind resistence.....15....10....The football players straining and grunting.....5..4...3...2....He did it!!!! As he speeds through the end zone he reaches up and slam dunks the football over the field goal!!

Allright fellow BMX'ers, I guess the moral to this story is : When some squids start raggin' on ya, or if they start actin' real lame, DON'T GET MAD, GET RAD!!!!

KEEP RIPPIN' !!

WHAT'S HOT

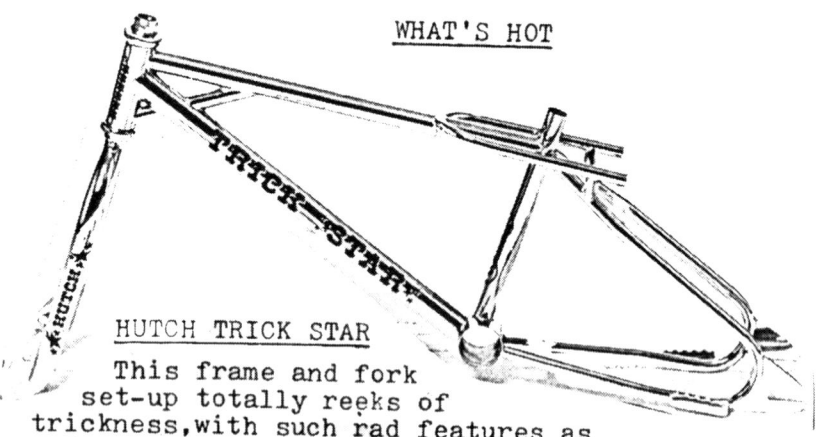

HUTCH TRICK STAR

This frame and fork set-up totally reeks of trickness,with such rad features as a frame standing platform (Add grip tape and you got it rear chain stay serrated(That means SHARP!)cages great for grasshoppers,pogos,etc.,and a weird steering configuration which allows exceptional front brake clearance.These red hot jewels are available in candy apple red and high lustre show chrome.So stroll on down to your local bike shop and check 'em out.They're HOT!!!!

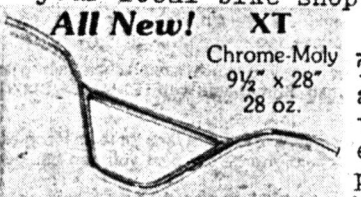

POWERLITE XT BARS

These bars are 9 1/2 in. high, and are 28 in. wide.The cool thing about these bars is they have contoured ends,which helps alot in pulling power.Excellent freestyle stuff here,gang.Get'em at your local bike shop or write directly to Powerlite.

THAT'S: POWERLITE INDUSTRIES
1035 Armando,Unit D
Anaheim, California 92806

MDP BOLT-ON FOOTSTEPS

Turn your current ho-hum scoot into a freestyle machine in just a few minutes.How,you ask?Simple.Just install these MDP footsteps on your rear axle bolts and then start doing tricks as wild as YOU can imagine.They come in CHROME and WHITE.

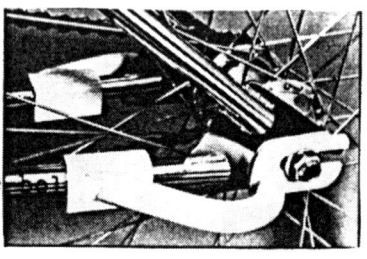

MDP
14116 Whittier Bl.
Suite 608

LOcaL

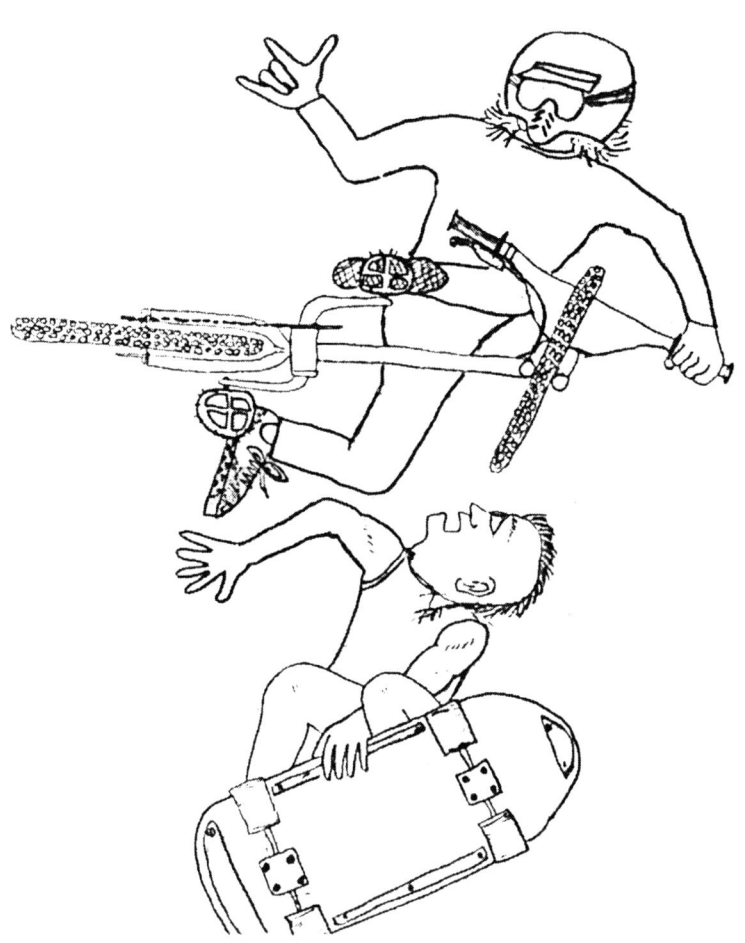

FOcal POinT

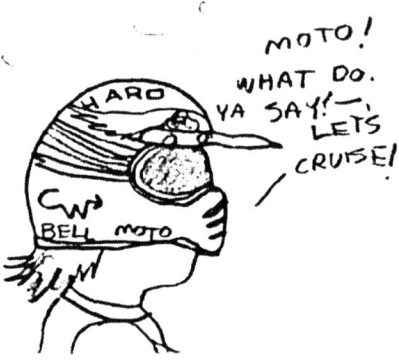

BOSS PULLS AWAY, PUMPING FURIOUSLY. DON'T FORGET NOW, FRIENDS, HE STILL HAS POSSESION OF THE BMX RACING SECRETS. WHAT WILL HAPPEN? CAN MOTO CATCH HIM?

LET'S FIND OUT....

BOSS MEETS UP WITH HIS BAD GUY STUDENTS...

TOTALLY NASTY!! THEY, UH, LOOK AWFULY HUNGRY UNFORTUNATLY...

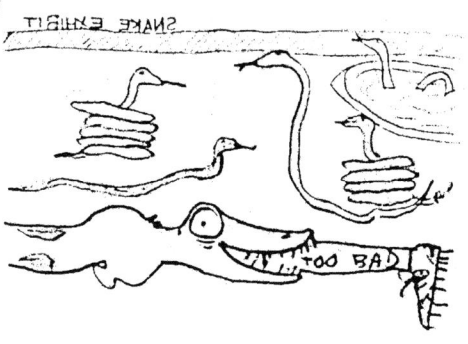

WHAT will happen to the good guys' freestle secrets??? Is Moto going to become a one course meal????Well don't miss next month's rag FOR SURE!!!

AGGRO RAG (1984)
Red Lion, PA
8" x 10½"

2nd ISSUE

B rian Peters doesn't think the name of our freestyle team was inspired by The Cardboard Lords. He explains: "It was purely because of the fact that the ramp was plywood, we stole the plywood from construction sites, and 'Hoods' rhymes with 'wood'. That was the genesis of it. It was just a coincidence."

Brett Downs and Brian Peters, Summer '85, in Litiz, PA, before R.L. Osborn and Ron Wilton performed as the BMX Action Trick Team.

What did it take to become a Plywood Hood? "We had a checklist and it had maybe 30 different tricks on it. You had to do the majority of the tricks on that list: bunnyhop a certain height, do a rolling 360 bunnyhop, get a certain number of feet over the vert, do a tailwhip…"

We let Brett join anyway.[1]

[1] Yoops, Brett's great.[2] Brett "Maverick" Downs could pull most of the tricks, including a battery of Robert Peterson-style balance tricks and kickturn variations. Mav became the Team Driver/Ramps Transporter, Mix Tape DJ and Show Announcer in addition to performing Hood.

[2] Yoops.

Jamie McKulik owned bar rides, multiple hang glider boomerangs and whiplashes in the first three *Dorkin'* videos. "I kick myself all the time that I didn't stay more into it," Jamie says. "If the AFA wouldn't have gone out of business…" Before joining the Plywood Hoods, Jamie was a member of the Cardboard Lords.

Mike Daily: Did you meet Kev and those guys through breakdancing, or ridin' bikes?

Jamie McKulik: Through ridin' bikes. I was the little kid down at Queensgate Shopping Center playin' video games—*Donkey Kong*—and ridin' The Pit, tryin' to jump my little red junker bike, and it was fallin' apart. I went down there with my bike and played video games and they just started messin' with me. I was friends with Tommy [Wales] and we'd go up to Kev's and break. Me and Kev just clicked really well and I became his, like…*pet*. [Laughs.] I don't know if you wanna call it "pet," but we became really good friends. I was a lot younger and my parents got divorced, and he became like my dad, basically.

What effect did that have on you with both breakin' and bike ridin'?

Oh, it was crazy. I mean, as far as like I'm sittin' here right now and I get chills when I think about it. He changed my whole entire life, as far as being able to look at what you do, and how to do it. We'd sit there and just talk about how to get good without actually doing something—just by using your mind. Seeing yourself do it, dreaming about it: Go to sleep and try to see yourself doin' whatever trick you're tryin' to learn, or whatever it is. We'd spend so much time figurin' out stuff. I'd be holdin' ropes and he'd be tyin' ropes up in the garage. Breakdancin', the same thing: We'd see somebody do something, and we'd sit there and just go over it and watch the video and practice.

With Kev, it wasn't how to get good at something—it was "great." You had to get *great*: "Tons great."

"Tons great!" [Laughs.] Yeah. I got some rows—all the old stuff we used to say. I still remember some of it. It's funny as can be. We would say just the nuts-est stuff that all kind of had a meaning—that made some kind of sense, you know?

Oh, yeah. It was a way to kind of disarm people that you didn't want hangin' around or askin' stupid questions. I remember Kev would just go into "row mode".

Oh, totally. This isn't to put Kev down or nothin', but that's one thing—you know, after you get older and you look back and you see stuff—he was a little anti-social. You know what I mean? His thing was: He wanted to be so good at everything, but he didn't really care if people saw him do it. He wanted people to see him do it, but he didn't like the limelight of somebody just sittin' there and bein' like, "Come on! Do it again!" Or—you know—showin' off. He did inside, but as far as outside, it didn't really ever seem to be like that. If somebody came over and said, "Kev, come on! Do that awesome trick!" he'd just do somethin' else that wasn't as awesome. He was like, "They don't *know*. They don't care. They don't know that it's that much harder with your foot crossed, and this over here," or whatever.

FIFTY CENTS CHEAP

BIG NEW ISSUE

AGGRO

RAG!

TRICK RIDING:
EXCLUSIVE HOW-TO!

HOT PRODUCTS

THRASHER'S LIFE
MOVIN' TO THE STREETS

no brag just rag!

EDITORIAL

Whew! Things are really jammin' around here <u>NOW</u>!! You guys totally skarfed on our first issue, so.........
...(Drum roll, please)...We'll be goin' bi-monthly!!!!!
Yup'er, you'll be able to catch our words of wisdom, gnarly stories, exclusive trick how-tos, local freestylin' scene, and scribbled down art work every TWO months!!!
So far, to the best of our knowledge, we are currently one of only TWO freestyle rags in existence today, the other one being Illinois-based. Right now, we're in the process of mass producin' these pups, for a higher circulation rate and to spread the good word of freestyle throughout Pennsylvania.

Trick teams are sproutin' up everywhere in PA, and so are the ramps. Kids are finally realizin' that they have potential.

This rag's purpose is to inform all fellow thrashers of local happenings in the freestyle world, rad places to cut loose with all yer trickin' abilities, and to keep everyone jazzed on this wild new sport.

Zounds!! Next month we start with the <u>REAL</u> editorials, beginning with the controversial topic, Society <u>VS.</u> Freestylers.

LONG LIVE FREESTYLE!!

FREESTYLERS EDGE

This month I'm gonna talk about somethin' most bike berserkos take for granted.....their scoots.

Now think about it,buds.Yer moto machine has **MANY** uses,uses which are valuable to **ALL** freestyle fanatics.

The gnarliest use by far is of course trick riding. Flatland freestyle,small ramp trickin',and quarter-pipe insanity,each one thoroughly gnarly to session to,usually pushin' you an' yer scoot to the limits.

And how about when a total moon babe moves in down the street.Your bike sure does come in handy when you're tryin' to win her heart by cruising your scoot past her house standin' on the seat and givin' her the peace sign with a rose clenched in your teeth!!

Or how about when you call the local bully a "valley."It's nice to know that you could get away without any unnecessary bodily harm.

And then theres the times when you're **SO** mad,**SO** infuriated,that you hop on your scoot just to blow off steam.A little ride alone,away from all others,always tends to mellow you out.

And the ONLY thing that makes all of these activities possible is your bike.Your ped sled is always waiting for you,always seeming to say"Thrash me!"or "Come on,take a ride."

So there you have it,fellow tricksters,our scoots **ARE** very valuable to us thrashers,giving us something worthwhile to do.So zoot on out to your garage and acknowledge your friend with a nice polishing and readjustment.And your bike WILL thank you.

WHAT'S HOT

KUWAHARA FREESTYLE FS
This frame and fork set-up is state of the art. The frame has twin top tubes, twin elliptical down tubes, cable guides, and THICK dropouts. The forks boast THICK dropouts and a unique new feature: FOOT PLATFORMS! This guy can be had in chrome plating or awesome freestylin' white. Dangerous Dave Gianunzio's #1 choice for his gnarly antics. Check it out today at your local hot shop. It's HOT!!!!

DYNO D-2 BRAKE GUARDS 
Ever thrash your ankle on your rear caliper brake arm? It sure does smart awhile. Well, Bob Morales of BME scoped out the problem and invented....DYNO brake guards! No more gimped ankles, pant cuff hang ups, and no more people starin' at your ankles when you go to the beach. Your choice of blue, red, and black. A must for every trickster!!!!!

A unique tread design allows smooth and comfortable riding with ultra handling.

COMPETITION STADIUM TIRES
These tires were originally designed for indoor concrete BMX races, but since that went out about 4 years ago, the freestylers just skarfed 'em up. Tioga now offers these in two sizes: 1.75, and 2.125, and two colors: black and white. These skins are #1 choices of HUTCH trick-stars Woody Itson and Mike Buff. Slap a set on yer scoot today!!

GT PERFORMER HANDLEBARS
New lower design cross bar allows tricks like Woody's incredible quick change and bar hops to be done IN STYLE. Available in white, yellow, and chrome.

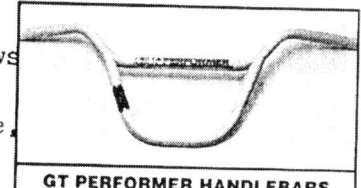

GT PERFORMER HANDLEBARS

A THRASHERS' LIFE

Freestylers have gnarly adventures,but rarely as gnarly as this one!!!Read on,crimestoppers!!!!

"Dad,are you out of your mind?",our teenage bike trickster yelled.

"It's only for two days,son,"his old man argued, "and you'll be back in plenty of time for your bicycle contest.Besides,it will be good experience for you when you become a fine archeologist like your father."

"Ugh, I'd rather become a great freestyler like Mike Dominguez",the thrasher groaned.

What's going on here folks,is our main freestyler's dad is trekin' on over to a location near the Amazon jungle for an extensive search for artifacts possibly left by an ancient indian tribe.The only problem here is that his dad wants HIM to come along and watch to learn the skills of archeology.(Ho,hum....yawn)

"I'll tell you what,son,you can also bring along your bike",his father offered,"and you can even ride while we set everything up on the grounds."

"Allright,Dad,"the biker thoughtfully exclaimed, "but if I ride through ANY elephant dookie,I'm goin' home!!!"

On the chartered flight,the thrasher's dad is calmly reading his newspaper while our rad rider is going through his ground tricks routine which he'll be using in the upcoming contest.

The cabin door opens and out walks a shapely blond stewardess.She sees our two-wheeled terror in the aisle with his scoot and she clears her throat.

TRIX ARE FOR KIDZ
SURFING

Each month THE AGGRO RAG will feature an exclusive trick how-to. This month we're throwin' a hot number on ya called surfin'. Now you can shred all day with no waves o'tay?? Do not even try this unless you're already a radical ripper. Also, wear your safety gear-AT LEAST a helmet, elbow pads, and gloves. This is no easy trick.
NOTE: REMOVE CROSSBAR PAD FOR EASIER STEERING. A LIL' GRIP TAPE HELPS TONS.

1) Coast at a slow pace(a little faster than for a curb endo). Place your right foot on the seat and step up placing your left foot parallel on the crossbar. NOTE: BEFORE YOU TRY ANYTHING GET USED TO RIDING IN THAT POSITION.

2) Try taking one hand off at first. When you can ride with one off then try taking both off, but only a few inches from the grips at first.

3) NOTE: YOU SHOULD CENTER MOST OF YOUR WEIGHT ABOVE THE SEAT, WHILE YOU STEER WITH YOUR FOOT ON THE BAR. After you get your balancing act straight, you can stand up and extend your arms for balance.

4) Assume any outrageous position you like. This is where you get to show off for all the pit tootsies! To gracefully get out of this trick, just reach down, grab on to the bars, an' ride away like it was nuthin'.

C-YA NEXT MONTH!!!

TRiX

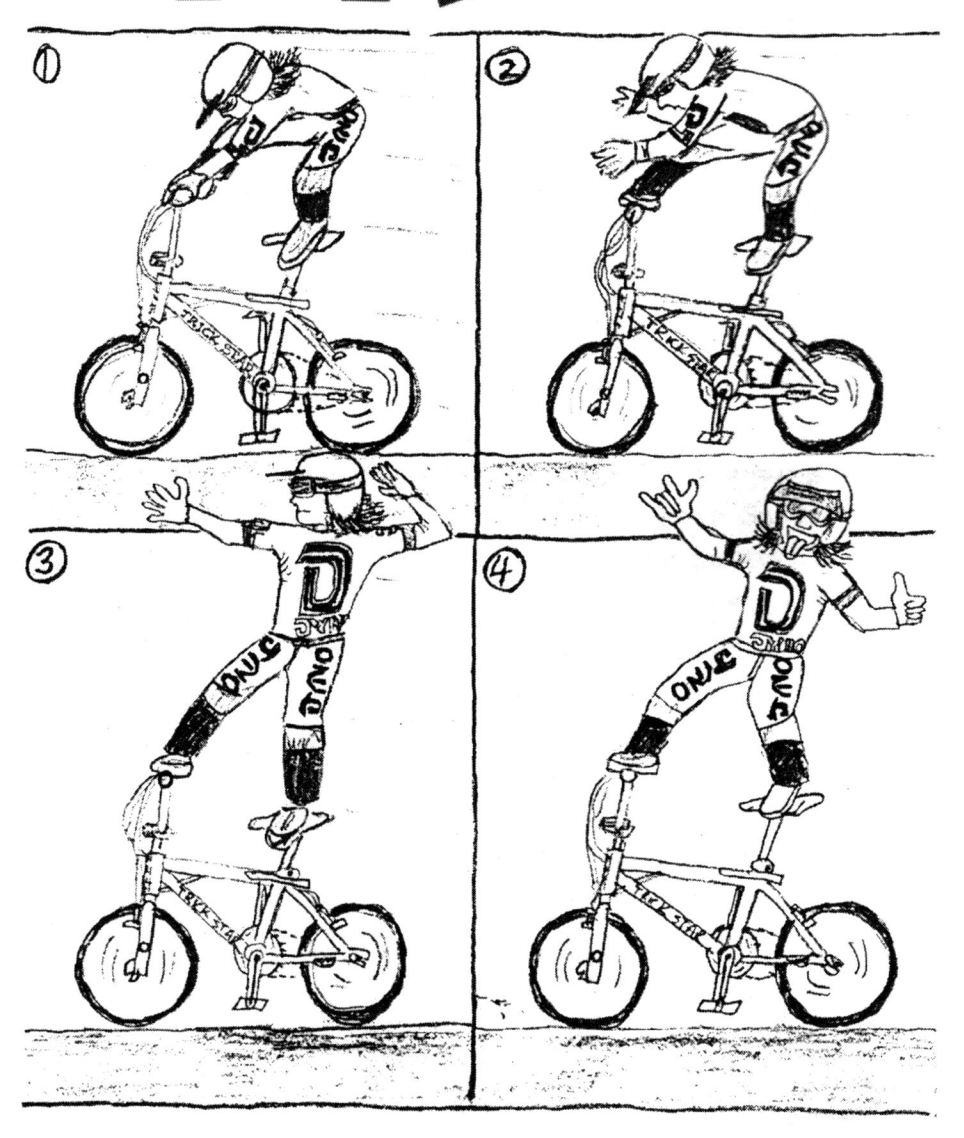

MOVIN' TO THE STREETS

ON THE LOCAL SCENE:

As this is written, there are two trick teams in Pennsylvania: The All About Bikes Trick Team and The Plywood Hoods Trick Team. We're sure that there's TONS more, but that's all we know about so far.

There's a pretty hefty problem around here that a few of the locals are planning to solve REAL soon. It involves us freestylers having nowhere worthwhile to shred. The breakers have someplace to break EVERY friday night-at Show Biz, so why shouldn't we thrashers have some public place like that to freestyle??? We think that it would be a red hot idea if we could write a letter to the head honchos of the York Mall asking if we could have a little room in the mall some Saturday night to have ALL the trick teams locally perform shows. We would all be wearing full protective garb. We actually got the idea from a mall security dude. We could also hand out about fifty of these rags, which could inspire some spectators to become performers. Drop us a line to tell us what you think of the idea and if you would like to be included in the show. Write to:

    AGGRO RAG c/o
    Mike Daily
    RD# 5 BOX 510
    Red Lion, PA 17356

FLASH: Mike Dominguez is the 1985 KING OF THE SKATEPARKS!

WHEN WE LAST SAW OUR HERO, HE WAS LEFT SPRAWLING ON THE GROUND AS A RESULT OF BOSS BAD GUY'S DIRTY ROTTON ICE TRICK.
BUT MOTO IS STILL AFTER BOSS 'CAUSE HE HAS THEIR FREESTYLIN' SECRETS. AND THE SNAKES ARE WAITING..........
..READ ON BUDS!.....
BOSS, HERE HE COMES- WHAT SHOULD WE....
GET UNDER THE RAMP YA NOODLE BRAIN! HURRY!
BAD GUY
BOSS BAD GUY
BOSS
"HERE HE COMES" IS RIGHT! CHECK OUT MOTO!! BUT....
GNARLY!
GT
MOTO MIKE
A HANDY SPEEDOMETER
...THE SNAKES ARE WAITING TO BE FED......
SNAKE TANK
UH OH! THE RAMP LOOKS LIKE A ROAD! HORRORS!
HERE HE COMES! QUICK! UNDER!
MOTO DOESNT REALIZE WHAT TROUBLE AWAITS HIM. BUT HE'S GOIN' SO FAST... MAYBE... HE'LL MAKE IT!
ANOTHER HANDY SPEEDOMETER
WHOOSH!
SIZZLE CRACKLE

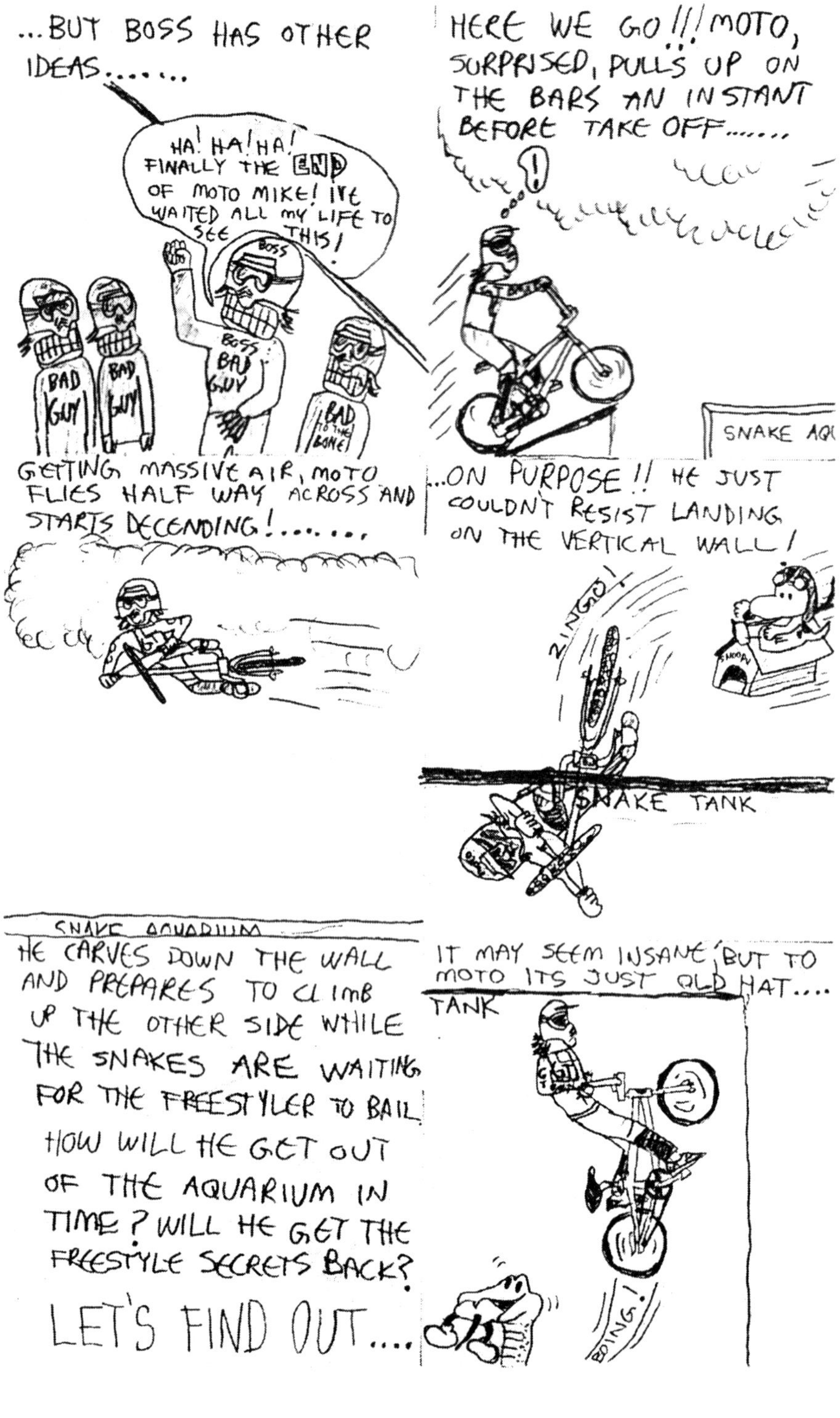
...BUT BOSS HAS OTHER IDEAS.......
HA! HA! HA! FINALLY THE END OF MOTO MIKE! I'VE WAITED ALL MY LIFE TO SEE THIS!
BOSS
BAD GUY
BAD GUY
BOSS BAD GUY
BAD TO THE BONE
HERE WE GO!!! MOTO, SURPRISED, PULLS UP ON THE BARS AN INSTANT BEFORE TAKE OFF.......
!
SNAKE AQU
GETTING MASSIVE AIR, MOTO FLIES HALF WAY ACROSS AND STARTS DECENDING!.......
...ON PURPOSE!! HE JUST COULDN'T RESIST LANDING ON THE VERTICAL WALL!
ZINGG!
SNAKE TANK
SNAKE AQUARIUM
HE CARVES DOWN THE WALL AND PREPARES TO CLIMB UP THE OTHER SIDE WHILE THE SNAKES ARE WAITING FOR THE FREESTYLER TO BAIL.
HOW WILL HE GET OUT OF THE AQUARIUM IN TIME? WILL HE GET THE FREESTYLE SECRETS BACK?
LET'S FIND OUT....
IT MAY SEEM INSANE, BUT TO MOTO ITS JUST OLD HAT....
TANK
BOING!

MOTO CARVES AN AIR OUT OF THE GLASS AQUARIUM AND DOWN THE LANDING RAMP!
SNAKE AQUARIUM
HERE SNOOPY!
...MEANWHILE THE BAD GUYS ARE WORRED......
BOSS! HE MADE IT! WE'VE GOTTA GET OUT OF HERE!
QUIET YOU FOOL! I TOOK EVERY PRE-CAUTION. HE WONT MAKE IT THIS FAR! AT LAST THE SECRETS ARE MINE!
BAD GUY
BADLY SHAKEN
BOSS BAD GUY
WHAT DOES HE MEAN BY.... OH NO! MOTO MIKE IS HEADING FOR THE SIDE OF A TRUCK!
CLOUD NINE
BAD GUYS INC.
NOK NOK
AN OVER-VERTICAL AERIAL CURES THE PROBLEM!
BAD GUYS INC.
WE DELIVER!
HOOS THERE
HAVE YOU KICKED YOUR DOG TODAY?
TACKS
BUT THE BAD GUYS ARE GONNA ESCAPE!!
LET'S GET THE #!@#$! OUT OF HERE!!
BOSS
HEAR NO EVIL
SEE NO EVIL
NO EVIL
BOSS BAD GUY
BUT THE WEAK RAMP BUILT BY THE BAD GUYS WOBBLES..... AND FALLS!!
CRASH!
BOSS! WE'RE TRAPPED!
WHY ME? HUH? WHY ME....
BOSS

MOTO GRABS THE FREE-STYLE SECRETS BACK AND HEADS BACK TO THE TRACK WHERE HIS SIDEKICK RAD LOOSKY IS. HE ALSO BRINGS BOSS AND HIS BAD GUY DISCIPLES. LET'S SEE WHAT HAPPENS........

FOILED AGAIN!!!

"ALLRIGHT MOTO! YOU GOT THE SECRETS BACK! NOW WHAT DO YOU SUPPOSE WE SHOULD DO WITH THESE THUGS?...."

RAD HANDLES THE PUNISHMENT, WHILE....

"AFTER YOU TURKEYS ARE DONE POLISHIN' OUR SCOOTS, YOU CAN WASH THE DISHES, CLEAN MY ROOM...."

"HEH HEH"

"UGH!"

"MOTO MIKE WILL PAY FOR THIS!"

MOTO PRACTICES FOR THE UP-COMING CONTEST ON HIS FREESTYLIN' BIKE.....

THAT'S ALL FOR NOW! HAVE A JAMMIN' GOOD HOLIDAY AN' DON'T FORGET TO RIDE DURING THE WINTER IN YOUR BASEMENT! SURE HOPE YA LIKED OUR NEWEST ISH OF THE AGGRO RAG. JAM ON, FREESTYLE!

"Little did I know that dozens of other writers, mainly poets, scattered around the country had simultaneously chosen to do the same thing for virtually the same reasons. Boldly, I sold the Gretch drums onto which I had been tattooing my demons and purchased a Sears mimeograph."

Douglas Blazek,[3] Green Isle in the Sea: An Informal History of the Alternative Press, 1960-85 (1986)— *printed by a small press at the same time so many[4] of us were making BMX freestyle zines.*

get your name in LIGHTS

get it up there in 8½ x 11 mimeo

Charles Bukowski,[5] The Days Run Away Like Wild Horses Over the Hills (1969)

AGGRO RAG! (January 1985)
Red Lion, PA
8" x 10½"

3rd ISSUE

More than half of the poetry magazines and books made during the "Mimeo Revolution" of the late '50s were not printed on mimeograph printing machines.[6] Cleveland's renegade "poeteditorpublisher" d.a. levy[7]—central figure of the Mimeo Revolution—was one of the few who remained true to mimeo's distinctive look and chemically sweet stank. Pushing the envelopes of writing and design, levy hand-cranked-out his litmag *Marrahwannah Quarterly* and a myriad of cult-classic poetry chapbooks until his suicide in '68, at age 26.

Until the mid- to late-'80s, educators used mimeo machines—a.k.a. "ditto"—to print classroom materials. Amy Anderson,[8] my Red Lion High School English teacher, published the third issue of *AGGRO RAG!* on the school's mimeograph:

> "The inherent problem with the ditto makers was that you could only get about maybe one classroom set, or two if you were lucky. You'd maybe get 50 or 60 copies—if that—and they would get lighter and lighter and lighter. The edge of it went on the mimeo machine and then you had to turn them by hand, and it made a copy one at a time. Dittos were just kind of starting to phase out a little bit when I started teaching. They were moving into a similar-type thing done in black ink, and copiers were starting to show up at that point."

Everyone called copiers "Xerox machines" no matter what company made them.

Mark Lewman[9] said it best in *Generation F*: "The Xerox was our Xbox."

---

[3] Douglas Blazek referred to his magazine *Ole* as "a homegrown rogue variant of *Evergreen Review*."

[4] Zineguys.

[5] Blazek's Mimeo Press published Charles Bukowski's first book of prose, *Confessions of a Man Insane Enough to Live with Beasts* (August 1969; Bensenville, IL).

[6] Allen Ginsberg's long poem *Howl* first appeared as a mimeo-printed edition typed by Martha Rexroth and mimeographed by poet Robert Creeley (prior to City Lights' offset-printed publication in '56).

[7] Darryl Allan Levy, born on October 29, 1942.

[8] Maiden name: Amy Horvatinovic. Everyone called her "Miss H".

[9] Lew.

HARO USA

6065 CORTE DEL CEDRO, CARLSBAD, CA 92008 (619) 438-4812

Jan. 12, 1985

Hello Brett,

   Thanx for the letter. The Haro team is totally hot this year. On tour it's gonna be Rich Sigur, Brian Blyther, and myself and we're gonna blaze. I'm setting up the tours and stuff for Team Haro and I'm also goin' to Europe next month. You heard right, I got married on Jan. 5, you'll see pics in the magazines.

   As for the Haro bikes, they are the best. The geometry is great and we have some new designs that will blow you away. I like the Haro bikes way better than GT's because the GT head angle is to laid back and the wheel base is too long. Well, good luck with your team, the "Plywood Hoods". They sound pretty hot.

                              Thanx,
                              RON WJLKERSON
                              Team Haro

P.S. check us out on tour this summer

JANUARY 1985
Volume 2 No. 1

AGGRO
RAG!

FREESTYLE **TIPS** from
WODDY ITSON!!

MOVIN' TO THE STREETS

Hot
Freestyle Equipment!

THE KID

more
THRASHER'S LIFE

TRICK RIDING:
EXCLUSIVE HOW TO!

CONTENTS

EDITORIAL: SOCIETY VS. FREESTYLERS
We're not gonna take it anymore
.... 2

MOVIN' TO THE STREETS
The latest scoops on the local
scene............................. 3

FREESTYLERS EDGE: TRICK TEAM TIPS
Freestylin' tips from WOODY
ITSON himself................. 4

A THRASHERS' LIFE
Our resident trickster finds
himself in yet another conflict:
Skaters VS. Freestylers!....5-7

WHAT'S HOT
The hippest in sano freestylin'
equipment..................... 8

TRICK HOW-TO: 360 Finger Flip
A fairly easy trick for all of
you aspiring freestylers..... 9

GOOD GUYS AN' BAD GUYS COMIX:
FINALLY!! THE CONTEST!! But
Moto Mike and Rad Locsky will
have something ELSE to conquer
AS WELL!!!!................. 10-12

The AGGRO RAG welcomes art, story,
and black and white photo contributions. Send to:
AGGRO RAG! c/o
Mike Daily

AGGRO RAG! STAFF

EDITOR AND CHIEF WRITER:
Mike Daily

CONTRIBUTING WRITERS:
Brian Peters
Stu Ebersole
Will Bennett

PUBLIC RELATIONS AND PHOTOGRAPHER AT LARGE:
DA-MONE!!

ARTIST:
Mike Daily

LAYOUT/CONTRBUTING ARTIST:
Brian Peters

PUBLISHER:
Miss H!!

DISTRIBUTION:
Greg Baum/FLYING FEET

The AGGRO RAG is published monthly. Cover price is fifty cent and subscriptions are now availabl

If it's good we'll run it an' send

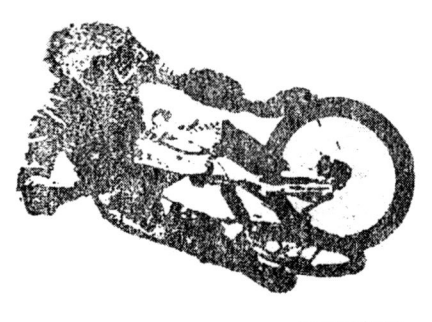

EDITORIAL

This month's editorial deals with a growing problem for today's fearless freestylers. SOCIETY.

When we go down to the mall to freestyle a little, the mall security bud is almost ALWAYS on our tails before we can even get our elbow pads strapped on. We get chased out of vacant parking lots and even dead end streets.

Society forbids us to do all of these activities, activities which enable teenagers to stay out of trouble and blow off steam. I guess society would rather have us breaking windows and engaging in vandalism rather than "getting hurt" on our scoots. I would also venture to say that they'd want us to come home with a serious drug addiction rather than a broken wrist. THIS IS BOGUS!!!! We NEED freestyle. Freestyle gives us a CHANCE to gain self confidence and self discipline, values we'll be using for the rest of our lives.

Maybe someday society will understand that what we're trying to do is NOT as dangerous as it initially seems to them. Someday they'll realize that all along they weren't chasing criminals, but just kids who were TRYING to stay out of trouble. So the next time you are yelled at for doin' what we all do best, stick up for what you feel is right. Tell 'em freestyle's not very dangerous, not nearly as dangerous as dope or vandalism.

We're just not gonna take it anymore. And it's up to us to set 'em straight.

— Mike Daily

Mike Daily

MOVIN' TO THE STREETS

TRICK TEAM UPDATE:

The PLYWOOD HOODS FREESTYLE TEAM is now sponsored by FLYING FEET!!! Greg Baum, the owner of the sport shoes shop, plans on having the team perform shows locally to promote his store and VANS custom footwear, which the shop specializes in. FLYING FEET orders ANY color combination and any style of VANS you can design directly from the California-based corporation. If you're ever around the York area, check this place out. You'll be able to catch Brett, Brian, and Mike all over the place puttin' on shows, so stay tuned to the AGGRO RAG for trick team locations and dates.

SKATEPARK SCENE:

Also in the York area is an abandoned skatepark called THUNDER DOME, and it is an ULTRA cool place to unleash your aerial abilities. It has two large crater-like bowls, a smaller bowl, a gnarly snake run, vertical extensions out of the bowls, some big honkin' moguls, jumps, and tons of smooth concrete to strut yer flatland routines on. You ride at yer own risk, and It don't cost nuthin' to get in and it's open every day of the week. What more could you ask for??!!?

RIDER PROFILE:

Latley there's been alot of talk about a hot freestyler of the Spry area named Ralph Jones. According to a popular rumor, Ralph can attain heights of about SIX FEET atop his backyard quarterpipe ramp. If anyone out there knows Ralph, get in touch with us. Even if the guy ain't Superman, he shore sparked OUR interest!! We want some pictures and an interview for an upcoming issue.

FREESTYLERS EDGE

Recently the intrepid journalists here at the AGGRO RAG were COMPLETLY stoked by a letter from THE flatland freestyle king, Woody Itson of the HUTCH trick team squad. We asked Woody for some exclusive tips on having a successful freestyle team.

According to Itson, consistency is the key. Woody explains, "My best advice for your trick team is to practice on being smooth and consistent."

What about the let-it-all-hang-out hero type of freestyling? "It is better to do a couple of tricks smooth and be able to pull them off all the time," Woody advises, "than to do a bunch of tricks that are rough and you can only do 50% of the time."

"Also, you and your friends should get together a routine and practice it for your shows", Itson adds, "That way you appear more professional to the crowd. OK!"

What Woody is influencing here is hard work. If you're not absolutly positively serious about trick riding, then don't go through the trouble of a freestyle team. But for you freestyle looney tuners, GO FOR IT!!! It pays off in ways of no comparison to money-recognition from your sponsor and from the people who come to see your shows, and an incredible feeling of self-satisfaction. Thanks alot, Woody!!!!

Well, what are ya waitin' for??!?!! START PRACTICING!!!!!!

A THRASHERS' LIFE

What happens when skaters and freestylers meet at the same place at the same time? The same thing that happens when an unstoppable force meets an immovable object. ALMOST ANYTHING!!!! READ ON!!!!......

The scene opens at an abandoned skatepark. A small crowd is gathered around a hot skater. He has long blond hair and is dressed in bold knee-length baggies, a shredded orange shirt, thrashed knee pads, and VANS high top tennies. Amid the small crowd is our resident trickster scopin' out the tricks of the talented skateboarder.

The skater whips off an impressive amount of three sixties, the soft wheels of his skateboard humming on the hot concrete. Finishing the three sixties with a flourish, the skater immediatly goes into some intricate footwork.

The crowd lets out an encouraging series of ooohhhs and aaahhhs. Our fanatic freestyler is even stoked!!!!

The shreddin' skateboarder then strings together a dazzling routine in which the board is flipped completly over numerous times under his skilled feet, the wheels slapping the smooth concrete surface. Grabbing his skateboard on both ends, the skater extends his upper body into a hot handstand! The crowd goes crazy and then even crazier when the young shredder actually does a ROCK WALK HANDSTAND!!!!!! UNBELIEVABLE!!!!!!

Suddenly the attention of the jazzed crowd is diverted away from the skater by a yelp from the far right.

It seems that our trick rider has an audience of his own!!! The unreal gnarliness of the skateboarder was just too much for the thrasher, making him hyperactive to GET RAD on his scoot.

The freestyler whips off a sano boomerang and then a 360 tail spin inside the growing guardrail of eager onlookers. The skater, who a few moments ago was the center of attention, is now wondering who stole _his_ limelight. He angrily makes his way to the front of the crowd and percieves the bike berserko wowing the audience.

The teenage trickster flawlessly pulls off a quick change and the crowd is TOTALLY dyin'. He goes into a full-on cherry picker with complete control and finesse but this time it's the skater doin' the admiring....

The thrasher is SO into getting rad that he doesn't notice the responsive crowd clapping and cheering as he spins a front wheel three sixty directly into a roll out three sixty.

The Kawabonzical Kid ends his performance with a SCURA TUCK and the crowd goes NUTS!!!!! As the onlookers thin out, some of them compliment the young radster on his unbelievable talents.

In awe the skater approaches the thrasher as he begins pedalling away. OH NO.....

"Hey bud, you got some hot moves there!", the skater compliments.

The freestyler shakes the offered hand of the skateboarder. "You're not so bad yourself, pal."

Flipping his board up into his gloved hands, the shreddin' skater exclaims,"Hey, what do you say we session together??!"

"BITCHEN!!!" The trickster pedals his ped sled toward a deep bowl with the sidewalk surfer skating beside him.

They both enter the crater-like pool, the sounds of rubber tires and urethane skateboard wheels combining. Simultaneously climbing the vertical walls, the biker and the skater go for air! The freestyler does a one hander one footer air five feet over the coping while the skateboarder pulls off a four foot ollie.

Climbing the other side of the pool the skater launches an extended invert while the trickster twists a one footed look-back. The two thrashers continue to work the entire pool, pulling off amazing doubles routines that looked as if they were rehearsed runs!!!!

Suddenly a skateboard is deliberatly fired at the biker. A sudden gasp shoots through the crowd as our hero barely dodges the board and screeches to a stop at the bottom of the bowl, suprised. His skatin' buddy hops off his stick and joins the biker.

They look up to the section of the crowd where the board came from. At the top of the bowl stands a flock of skate-gulls looking down upon the two who in their books should be natural enemies. Silence blankets the crowd........

"Hey, what's the big idea sessioning with a PED??!!?", one of the irate skaters bellows into the bowl.

"PEDS??!??", a biker yells from a crowd of his buds. "I oughta wrap that board around yer neck!!"

"Oh yeah, tough guy??", another skater yells to the opposing bikers as he tugs off his gloves revealing clenched fists.

"Yeah!!", a long haired freestyler threatens. "I've been waiting for a skater MESS-SESSION for a LONG time!!!"

"Well we've been waiting just as long as you have, buddy", a tall skater exclaims. "You geeks are always in OUR way!!"

"That does it squids!! Prepare to die, skate-commies!!"

Awe-struck, our fearless freestyler and the hot skater observe from the bottom of the pool the two groups ready to clash as the startled crowd looks on. The two glance at each other, shrug their shoulders, and resume shredding the bowl. They were'nt doin' anything wrong, RIGHT??!?!

At the top of the bowl the two conflicting groups are facing each other, ready to do serious battle. One punch will start it......

Suddenly an amazing thing takes place between the "enemies." Both groups noticed the freestyler and the skater sessioning together just as before.

As they all stopped and stared at the cooperating thrashers, the universal thought between them was something like,"Why are we all fighting??" When they couldn't figure out a prudent reason, the bikers hopped back on their scoots and the skaters stepped back on their boards. Following that tense moment, they ALL combined into ONE, skaters and freestylers. And never again will they be prejudiced to each other. After all, they DO have one thing in common: SHRED 'TILL YOU'RE DEAD!!!!

KEEP RIPPIN'

— Mike Daily

WHAT'S HOT

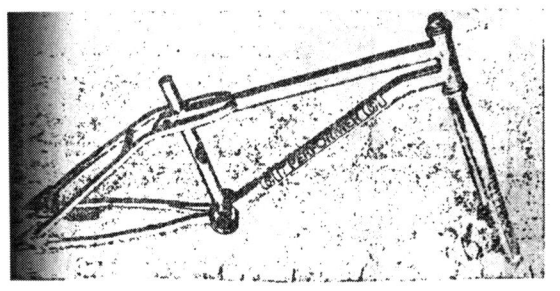

GT PRO PERFORMER FRAME AND FORK

Designed by pro freestylists Eddie Fiola and Bob Morales, this frame and fork set-up is intended for skatepark bashing and flatland thrashing with these trick features: Bent down tube to allow front brake to clear without hang-up, sano standing platform, coaster brake bracket, reinforced head tube, larger chain stays, and a low-profile. These masterpieces are available in chrome, white, and yellow.

VANS CUSTOM TENNIES AND ANKLE GUARDS

What more could we say about VANS that hasn't already been said? Just about every pro and amatuer freestyler wears them. They come in every color comb[o] imaginable and in more hip st[y]les than you ever dreamed of. The ankle guards are a MUST f[or] tricksters everywhere. They ar[e] also available in assorted colors and protect your ankles from the rigors of freestyle.

MOTIVES CASUAL WEAR

Motives surf-inspired casual wear designed by the pioneer of freestyle, Bob Haro, for serious fun and anything else. Bold colors and trendy styling makes Motives the number one choice for freestylers and thrashers alike. Motives offers rider art t-shirts, logo sweatshirts, and surf cut and bermuda shorts. Attack the beach IN STYLE!!!!!

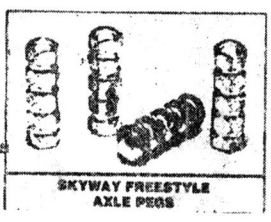

MOTIVES CASUALWEAR

HARO ELBOW GUARDS

These elbow guards offer forearm protection and elbow protection featuring wide elastic straps, velcro closures, and sewn-in plastic elbow cups. Available colors are white, red, blue, and black with zoot new graphics.

SKYWAY FREESTYLE AXLE PEGS

These items are TOO HIP!!!! Simply thread these pegs onto your axles and start riding. They add a new dimension to your routines and they come in chrome and three flavors: day-glow orange, day-glow green, and white. You better believe that these are used on the PLYWOOD HOODS personal scoots!!!!!

360 finger Flip

Make sure right pedal is at lowest position and place left foot behind bottom bracket. Spin bars around 180 degrees and lay bike over onto pedal.

Continue the clock-wise spin and "flip" your fingers around to hold the grip the opposite way. Keep turning the bars smoothly and quickly and.....

....pull the bike back up using your right leg against the seat. Put your left hand

When done quickly and smoothly this is a fairly cosmo lookin' trick.

LAST ISSUE WE SAW MOTO MIKE AND RAD LOOSKY CAPTURE BOSS AND HIS STRAGGLING BAND OF BAD GUYS TO GET THEIR FREESTYLE SECRETS BACK. BOSS VOWED HIS REVENGE THAT MOTO MIKE WILL PAY FOR FOILING HIS PLANS ONCE AGAIN. WHAT DOES BOSS HAVE UP HIS SLEEVE FOR MOTO??
LET'S FIND OUT....
MOTO AND RAD ARE PRACTICIN' HARD FOR THE FREESTYLE CONTEST BUT WHAT ARE THE BAD GUYS DOIN'?
OH NO! HERE THEY GO AGAIN!..
...THIS TIME MY PLAN WON'T FAIL. FINALLY THE END OF MOTO MIKE!!!
BOSS BAD GUY
BOSS, WE'RE STEPPING ON CHEWING GUM.
WHAT EXACTLY IS BOSS' PLAN?
BOSS GOES TO THE STATE PENN TO BAIL OUT HIS OL' ARMY BUDDY, WHO IS IN THE SLAMMER 'CAUSE THE ARMY WANTED TO MOUNT A GUN TURRET ON HIM AND HIS BIKE AND USE 'EM FOR A MINATURE TANK, SO HE TRIED TO JAM FROM THE ARMY!!!!
THE GUY IS AFFECTIONATLY REFERED TO AS.....
.....KILLER!!!
KILLER
HE SHO IS A MEEN
YA OWE ME A HEFTY FAVOR NOW, BIG GUY, SO LISTEN UP...
KILLER
OFFICER
KILLER REMEMBERS WHEN MOTO MIKE HUMILIATED HIM 3½ YEARS AGO AT A SKATEPARK. AND KILLER CAN TASTE REVENGE......
YEA!
HURRAY!
WOW

LATER.... AT THE CONTEST....
RAD LOOSKY CARVES A ONE-HANDER ONE-FOOTER AIR! HE'S REALLY IMPROVED FOLKS!!
WHOA!
AWESOME!
BITCHEN!
20'
THRASHER
LOCALS ONLY!!
...RAD LOOSKY SHREDS!!!
...AND LOOSKY WITH A TABLE TOP FLY OUT! THAT ENDS HIS RUN FOR THE FIRST ROUND!
8½ 8 9
JUDGES
20'
K
J.F.A.
HARD
SKATERS RULE!
NEXT A BAD GUY ENTERS THE FULL PIPE, NOT TO BE OUT-DONE BY RAD......
BAD GUY
ARENT THESE GUYS ROTTON??!
SOON MOTO MIKE WILL BE A MEMORY! HA HA!
BAD
BOSS
BAD GUY
...THE OVER-CONFIDENT BAD GUY MISCALCULATES IN THE AWESOME PIPE AND DOES AN UPSIDE-DOWN PANCAKE LANDING!!!
KER-SLAM!
MEANWHILE... KILLER MAKES HIS WAY TO THE CONTEST.....
KILLER
MOTO

MOTO ENTERS THE POOL.....
... AS KILLER ENTERS THE SKATEPARK AND PROMPTLY DISCARDS THE JUDGES!!!!
20'
ROBIN WAS A HOOD
DYNO
AD KENNEDY'S
MOTO MIKE
20'
KILLER
HE GONE KILL MOTO!
OFF THE W
OTO KEEPS THRASHING THE OOL, UNAWARE OF E IMPENDING OOM.....
WHOOSH
KILLER LEAPS INTO THE POOL AFTER SPOTTING HIS ENEMY...
20'
KILLER
DYNO
DIS AIN'T A CAR POOL
ROLL ON BIG MAN!
HUTCH
H NO!! HERE'S MOTO'S IEW OF THE BURLY ONSTER!!!
KILLER
PLASMATICS
CRUTCH
KILLER
VALLEY GO
WILL MOTO END UP IN INTENSIVE CARE?? WILL KILLER FINALLY GET HIS REVENGE?? IS THIS THE END OF MOTO MIKE?
DON'T MISS THE NEXT ISSUE OF THE AGGRO RAG! WHICH AGAIN WILL BE CRAMMED

From L to R: Brett Downs, Brian Peters, Mike Daily, Unidentified Rider. Standing: Mike Farrington.

"Mike, you were the action guy, the make-it happen guy. I don't know how you did it, when you did it, what avenues you took or what phone calls were made, but you set up shows for us to do. You just made it happen. You were a man of action." —Brian Peters

"Specialists in Professional Freestyle Performances"

Mike Daily
TEAM MANAGER
3320 Spondin Dr.
York, PA 17402
717-757-3096

FREESTYLE FOXWOOD HOODS TEAM

Unidentified Rider (UR) & Brett Downs

AGGRO RAG FREESTYLE MAG!
(March 1985)
Red Lion, PA
5½" x 8¼"

4th
ISSUE

York Rod & Custom Show on May 23, 1985. First performance of the Plywood Hoods Trick Team.

York/Adams News

Sunday News
Section B
May 19, 1985

Sixteen-year-old Brian Peters performs an aerial trick off a quarter-pipe ramp beside his house in Windsor Township.

Sunday News Photos/Glenn Dace

Those daring young men on the 'flying' bicycles

By Mike Snyder
Sunday News Staff Writer

RED LION — Skateboarding, with all its whirls, twirls and topsy-turvies, has given birth to a new form of stunt riding known as bicycle "freestyling."

The fad began in California a few years ago and quickly spread eastward. Now, kids in York County are becoming hooked on the new form of "teen-age expressionism." Bicycle manufacturers have responded by mass-producing the special bikes, which cost between $200 and $400.

The bikes have small wheels and a sturdy frame. They resemble the BMX racing bikes, except they are equipped with a variety of accessories for performing stunts.

Three enterprising Red Lion High School students are hoping to put York County on the "freestyling map" by helping to publish a nationally distributed magazine geared towards the growing fad.

Mike Daily, Brian Peters, both 16, and Dino Petridis, 17, all juniors at Red Lion High School, have banded together with teen-agers from the midwest and California in an effort to put together their dream product, a national freestyling magazine.

It all began about a year and a half ago when Daily and Peters became involved in BMX bicycle racing. "After a while we got tired of racing and decided to try freestyling," Daily said.

After countless hours of practice, Daily and Peters have become professional in the execution of their tricks. Along with friend Kevin Jones, the threesome have formed a trick riding group called "The Plywood Hoods." They recently performed at the York Rod and Custom show.

But performing wasn't enough for Daily. He also wanted to write about his new-found hobby. "I want to get into some form of journalism when I get older," Daily said. "So I decided it would be good practice to start writing about freestyling.

"I think I've read everything ever published on freestyling," he continued. "I think I've even memorized some of the articles. But you can't buy any magazines around here or so we decided to start our own."

With Daily as editor and chief writer, Peters as staff writer, and Petridis as photographer, York County's first freestyle magazine was published in March. It was called "Aggro Rag" and sold for 75 cents in March at a few local bike shops.

While sending for autographs and pictures of some well known California freestylers to use in his magazine, Daily discovered that there were two other teen-agers putting out similar publications in different parts of the country. Kevin Foss, 17, was putting out a freestyle magazine in the midwest while Bill Bachelor, 14, was doing the same thing in California.

Through regular correspondence, Daily became friends with the them and the threesome soon agreed to put out a national freestyle magazine. Daily will be the east coast editor, Foss will be the midwest editor and Bachelor will be in charge of the west coast and editor in chief of the publication.

(Left to right) Mike Daily, Brian Peters and Dino Petridis are currently working with teen-agers in the midwest and California to put together a national magazine on freestyle bike riding. The trio recently published a copy of a local magazine on freestyling which they distributed at local bikeshops.

> *'We will stress the safety factors. Anyone trying these tricks should always wear a helmet, gloves and long pants.'*

Bachelor's father is an attorney and has agreed to help the youngsters with their project. The trio needs to raise $1,200 to have 5,000 copies printed. The magazines will then be distributed by the boys in their three perspective areas of the country. The magazine will be called "Shreddin'," a slang term used to denote bicycle freestyling.

In an effort to get the project rolling, the California teen-ager has invited Daily and Peters to visit him in June. "We aren't really interested in making a profit with this," Daily said. "We just want to get our names known. Maybe someday it will pay off."

The York County teen-agers said the magazine will show other youths how to do the freestyle tricks. But Daily quickly added, "We will stress the safety factors. Anyone trying these tricks should always wear a helmet, gloves and long pants."

The local trio said they also hope to dispel thoughts that freestyling is connected to juvenile delinquency. "We get chased out of a lot of places," Daily said. "Adults really frown upon what we do. But we take the position that we are doing the opposite of what people think."

"We treat this like a sport," Peters said. "We try to try other people's minds with our tricks rather than try our own minds with drugs."

"They put a lot of love into their tricks," Petridis, the teen-age photographer, noted. "People should realize that."

The Red Lion area teens said they hope to do more local performances. "We need a manager," Daily said. "Someone who can get us bookings."

Overall, the three teens hope to gain something from their freestyling adventures.

"I think this will give me some background in journalism," Daily said. "I just want to get my picture in a national magazine," Peters noted. "I would like to direct a film someday," Petridis explained. "Taking pictures of these guys is a start."

Brian Peters goes "surfing" on his freestyle bike, which closely resembles a BMX racing bike. The bikes cost between $200-$400. They contain accessories for performing stunts.

Mike Daily holds a copy of "Aggro Rag", a magazine on freestyle bike riding that he and friends Brian Peters and Dino Petridis put together in March and distributed at local bike shops. The other magazines are part of Daily's personal collection. Also note bicycle art and prints on wall.

Mike Daily up-ends his bike to perform a "cherry-picker" maneuver.

'Catching Up' appears on page B-3

AGGRO RAG

FREESTYLE MAG!

75¢

SKATEPARK ISSUE!

Thunderin' at the DOME

March 1985

VOLUME TWO
NUMBER THREE

Hot Locals!

Killer **PHOTOS!** & TONS MORE!!

MARCH 1985
VOLUME 2 NUMBER 3

CONTENTS

FEATURES
- THUNDERIN' AT THE DOME!!!.........5,6,7
- HOT LOCALS............... 8
- BRINGIN' TOGETHER THE FREESTYLERS-PART TWO....11
- TRIX ARE FOR KIDZ-CHERRY PICKER VARIATION..14

DEPARTMENTS
- EDITORIAL................ 3
- MOVIN' TO THE STREETS... 4
- VERTICAL VIEWPOINT....... 9
- THE RAGGED EDGE..........10
- GOOD GUYS AN' BAD GUYS COMIX...................12,13
- MORE AGGRONESS.......... 15
- RAGGIN'................. 16

ON THE COVER:
Kevin Jones piloting his ped sled high above a vertical extension at THUNDERDOME. INSET PHOTO: Kev doin' a one-handed air over the fiberglass half-pipe in Dallastown.

AGGRO RAG FREESTYLE MAG!

STAFF!

EDITOR AND CHIEF WRITER:
Mike Daily

CONTRIBUTING WRITER:
Brian Peters

ACE PHOTOG AT LARGE:
Dino Petrides

STAFF ARTISTS/LAYOUT:
Mike Daily
Brian Peters

PUBLISHER:
P O S FAST COPY CENTER

TYPIST:
Jackie Daily

AGGRO RAG FREESTYLE MAG!

EDITORIAL

We may be a little slow but we ain't stupid. We estimate that about FORTY PERCENT of our readers are racers, which surfaces an astounding age-old rivalry; RACING VS. FREESTYLING.....

Bicycle motocross is a critical competitive sport pitting BMX'ers of similar age and skill level against each other. Relentless packs of competitors roost around serpentine dirt tracks containing assorted jumps and banked turns. Each BMX racer is striving for one thing: FIRST PLACE. Rewards in BMX are simple: Tall, shiny trophies indicating that THAT individual has succeeded.

FREESTYLE is a unique form of expression, allowing a rider to do whatever he wants to whether it be an aerial on his fave ramp, some 360 bunnyhops in the street, or forming a trick team, originating some choregraphed routines, and puttin' on shows. A freestyler's romping grounds is THE SCOOT ZONE, which spans curbs, banks, walls, streets, and shreddable wooden quarter pipes and half pipes.

Die-hard freestyle purists insist that the reasons they shred are not to compete, but rather to test their individuality by performing tricks that require imagination, strength, and balance.

So, whether you prefer zipping around a bicycle motocross course or jammin' on a hot ramp, don't rag on somebody for choosing their own personal method of biking.

Remember, ALL bikers get the same amount of satisfaction from those chrome-moly, two-wheeled vehicles known as scoots.

Next month we'll delve into some ESSENTIAL subject matter: FREESTYLIN' AND HAVIN' FUN !!!!!!!!!!!!!!!!!!!

LONG LIVE FREESTYLE !!!!!!!!!!!!!!!!!!!

AGGRO RAG FREESTYLE MAG!

—Mike Daily

Mike Daily

MOVIN' TO THE STREETS

TRICKS 'N MORE is definitly the hottest underground freestyle mag published today.

Bill Batchelor produce the sano mini mag for the crazed California freestylin' locals. TRICKS 'N MORE is crammed full of radibolical photos of all the skatepark heavies killer competition coverage, interviews with the stars of freestyle, cool contests, and MUCH, MUCH more!!!! All of you freestyle fanatics will absoiutly want to check out this mag.

If you send Bill one frogskin I'm sure he'll send you his latest issue including back issue ordering info which I'm SURE you'll want to take advantage of!! Tell him we sent ya!!! Send to: TRICKS 'N MORE
8027 Archibald
Rancho Cucamonga, CA 91730

The AGGRO RAG is totally JAMMIN' !! This month's issue is packed with rad photos, hot articles, gnarly cartoonin', and we started advertising!! Also, if you noticed, the AGGRO RAG is now professionally printed!!!

In upcoming issues we'll be scoutin' the hottest tricksters, discoverin' phenomenal freestyle hot spots, and generally promoting the growth of freestyle on the East Coast.

And, (sniff, fightin' a lump in our throat) its ALL because of you guys out there in thrashland. Thanks alot, buds we really appreciate it. But hold onto your HARO leathers, radsters, cuz you ain't seen NUTHIN' yet !!!!!!!

PICTORIAL:
THUNDERDOME!!
STORY BY: MIKE DAILY

For several years bikers have been invading a totally sessionable abandoned local skatepark called THUNDERDOME!! "The Dome" opened around 1977 in the midst of the popular skateboarding craze. Mr. Jim Dohm realized the potential of skating and designed one of the most challenging skateparks on the East Coast. The innovative park offered a winding snake run, a sloped surface used for slalom courses, two deep bowls, assorted peaked moguls and a smaller bowl aptly named "The Toilet Bowl". With the parks growing popularity, Mr. Dohm refined his multi-colored concrete kingdom with gnarly vertical extensions out of the snake run and the red and green bowls, a huge quarterpipe complete with safety railings, and a wooden half pipe.

THUNDERDOME was becoming greater and greater, even sporting a small building which sold skate equipment, skarfing material, and was even air conditioned!

What happened, you ask?? When suddenly dropping skate attendance failed to provide the park with needed money, Jim Dohm decided to call it quits. Jim witnessed the swarming skaters slowly disappear leaving him no alternative but to leave behind his masterful creation.

Since then, water has rendered the Badlands (slalom course) useless and has kept the red bowl from heavy duty thrashing, but everything else is still basically the same! Scattered glass and various objects have deterred many, but THUNDERDOME is still the only worthwhile place to rip. Check out the photos and you'll understand why !! ....

THUNDERIN' AT

THIS PAGE:

LEFT ⟶
Peters rides the DOME the same way he shreds his quarter pipe- With incredible determination and style.

BELOW-Kevin Jones rippin' up the red bowl vert.

BOTTOM RIGHT Peters table-toppin' out of the red bowl.

THE DOME

ABOVE-When Jones is workin' the park you mostly just watch with your mouth open.

TOP RIGHT-Brian hangin' a one-footed air over the green bowl vert.

RIGHT-When the red bowl wasn't flooded, Kev could JAM on it!!!

AGGRO RAG FREESTYLE MAG!

AGGRO RAG FREESTYLE MAG! HOT LOCALS! KEVIN JONES

VERTICAL VIEWPOINT

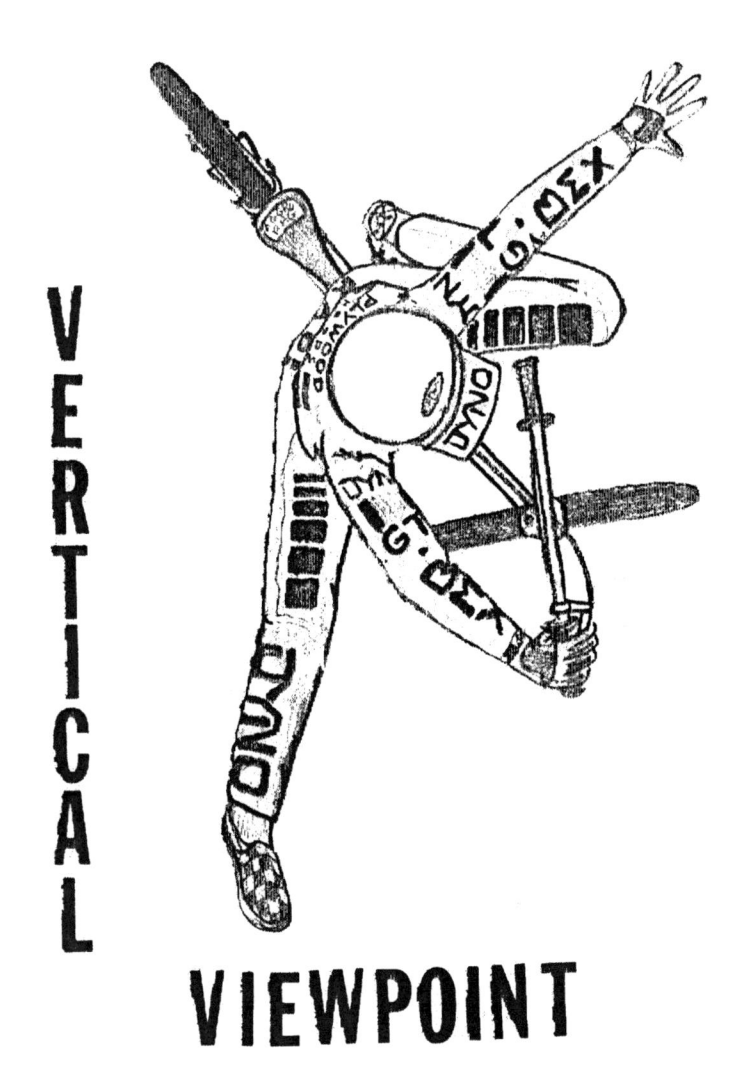

Brian Peters

CRY TUFF AC/DC
GO FOR IT
HEAVY METAL NO BOARD

9

THE RAGGED EDGE

MAIL

Do you know any HOT freestylers you'd like to see in the rag? Do you have any cool story ideas? How about any questions regarding local freestyle happenings?? Sure ya do!!!!

Write us a letter and we'll send YOU a free pair of FLITE donuts !!

Direct all letters to
AGGRO RAG
R.D.# 5 BOX 510
Red Lion, PA 17356

If you guys get hoppin', we're gonna start a letters department. Start scribbling!

The AGGRO RAG welcomes any photo, art, and story contributions. If yer material is truly hot, we'll run it and send complimentry stickers !!! GO FOR IT !!!!!

STICKERS!!!!

Now available in a limited production are NEW WAVE AGGRO RAG logo stickers!!!!!

These trick stickies include trendy green logo with radical purple lettering !!!

Let everyone know that you read the rip-roaringest local freestyle mag printed: AGGRO RAG!!!! Write for more info.....

AGGRO RAG
R.D.#5 BOX 510
RED LION, PA. 17356
ATTN: STICKER INFO

BRINGIN' TOGETHER THE FREESTYLERS

PART TWO

AGGRO RAG
FREESTYLE MAG!

Warm weather's comin' and we stylers here on the East Coast are gonna be shreddin' on the sidewalk, over the vert and in the dirt. If you're a parking lot jammer or a vertical slammer there are plenty of places to rip.

The AGGRO RAG already let you in on my awesome quarter-pipe. Its at my house in York and if your itchin' for some bitchen airs, just send a letter to the rag askin' for directions.

It doesn't matter whether your catchin' seven foot one handed-one footed airs or if you're just learnin' to do a front wheel hop. Its always cool to exchange tricks and styles with other riders.

So don't delay, send a letter to your fave mini-mag today!

WRITE TO: AGGRO RAG
              R.D.# 5 BOX 510
              Red Lion, PA 17356

(We'll send ya the directions and a few stickies just for writin'!!)

— *Brian Peters*

Brian Peters

11

1. LAST ISSUE WE SAW MOTO MIKE AND RAD LOOSKY AT THE MERCY OF KILLER WHO IS SEEKING REVENGE OF OUR DYNAMIC DUO. ARE THEY **DONE** FOR?? THE ADVENTURE CONTINUES!!!......→	**2.** KILLER PREPARES TO SLAUGHTER LOOSKY AND MOTO!!!!
3. KILLER CHARGES RAD FIRST!!!...	**4.** BUT LOOSKY DEFENDS HIMSELF WITH AN ABRUPT 360 TAIL WHIP!!!!
5. STEAMING MAD, KILLER ATTACKS RAD LOOSKY AGAIN BUT MOTO HAS AN IDEA!!......	**6.** ALTHOUGH HIS SCOOT HAS A FLAT TIRE, MOTO SEES AN ALTERNATIVE....

Panel 7: HE BLASTS KILLER WITH AN INTENSE GUSH OF WATER.... WHOOOAA!!! RAD!

Panel 8: ...INTO A FAST MOVIN' TRUCK!!!!! WHAM! KABONG! EAT AT McDONALD, HOME OF THE BIG WHACK AN' McLOOGIES!

Panel 9: MOTO AND RAD RUN TO THE STUNNED MONSTER.... SCRAMBLED. DUH!! UH.. HEY AREN'T YOU MY SECOND GRADE TEACHER?? CAMPBELL'S SOUP IS GOOD FOOD. WHO'S KILLER?

Panel 10: ...AS BOSS AND HIS BAND OF BAD GUYS ARRIVE ON THE SCENE... #!%@#?!/# FOILED AGAIN!! BAD GUY. BOSS BAD GUY. ONE BAD DUDE.

Panel 11: YET ANOTHER FAILED ATTEMPT TO TERMINATE MOTO!!! WHAT'S NEXT??!! DAD! SHUT UP AN KEEP WALKIN' YA BIG GALOOT!! BOSS BAD GUY. KILLER. KELLOGGS. WANTED BAD GUY.

Panel 12: BOSS HASN'T GIVEN UP YET!! HE'LL BE BACK!! WAIT 'TILL NEXT MONTH'S EPISODE!!! BOSS. MOTO MIKE WILL SOON BE A MEMORY TO YOU TURKEYS READIN' THIS MAG!!

13

AGGRO RAG FREESTYLE MAG!

CHERRY PICKER VARIATION

PHOTOS BY: DINO PETRIDES
RIDING BY: MIKE DAILY

1. Picture in your mind exactly what you're gonna do. Holding onto the back brake step up onto the rear axle extender and............

2. ...Quickly swing your left leg over the head tube, landing your left foot on the other axle extender.

3. Now start pogoing to keep your balance. Do about 30-40 hops to show complete control.

4. All in one fluid motion stop hoppin', swing your left leg back over, and smoothly step onto your left pedal. Pedal away and you got it!!!!!!!!

MORE AGGRONESS!!

1) GONZO WAS BUMMED... HE DIDN'T KNOW WHERE ANY OF THE LOCAL HOT SPOTS WERE...

2) AND HE DIDN'T KNOW ANY NEW WAVE TRICKS...

"MAYBE A NEW SCOOT WILL CHANGE THINGS?!?"

3) SUDDENLY... MOTO MIKE AND RAD LOOSKY BURST INTO THE SCENE!!!!

"DON'T FRET IT PAL! HERE! CHECK OUT THIS ZOOT COPY OF THE AGGRO RAG!"

4) "IT'S GOT THE LATEST LOCAL FREESTYLE NEWS, COOL ARTICLES, OUTRAGEOUS PHOTOS, THE FRESHEST TRICK HOW TO'S, AND A HIP COMIC OF OUR ADVENTURES!!!"

"WHOA!! HOW CAN I ORDER EXTRA COPIES??!"

IT'S EASY!!! Just send one dollar (75¢ for each copy plus 25¢ postage) for each reprint of this issue!!! The hippest local freestyle mag delivered right to yer mailbox!! SEND TODAY!!!

AGGRO RAG
FREESTYLE MAG!

Send to:
AGGRO RAG c/o
Mike Daily
R.D.# 5 BOX 510
Red Lion, PA 17356

NAME_____
ADDRESS_____
CITY_____ STATE_____
ZIP CODE_____ AGE_____
PHONE #_____

SEND CASH or CHECK
(Make checks payable to Mike Daily)

MARCH 1985

15

RAGGIN'!!

FREE AD's

Bike shops and local businesses can advertise in the AGGRO RAG for FREE!!! If you distribute the mag at your shop, we'll print YOUR business card at NO additional cost!!

Contact Mike Daily for more information. Call 244-2887.

AGGRO RAG FREESTYLE MAG!

DISTRIBUTORS

The AGGRO RAG is on sale at the following hot shops:
- FLYING FEET
- ED'S BIKE SHOP
- ALL ABOUT BIKES
- YORK CYCLE

NEXT MONTH:

* **SKYIN' AT BRIAN'S**-A totally insane photo session at one of the hottest ramps in Pennsylvania!!! Bonkers photos!!!
* **INTERVIEWS**-We'll be rovin' the streets for the raddest locals!!!
* **TONS** of gnarly articles and stories!!!
* **MORE** cool cartoonin'!!!
    PLUS Much, Much More!!! DON'T MISS IT!!!

*ON SALE MID-APRIL!!

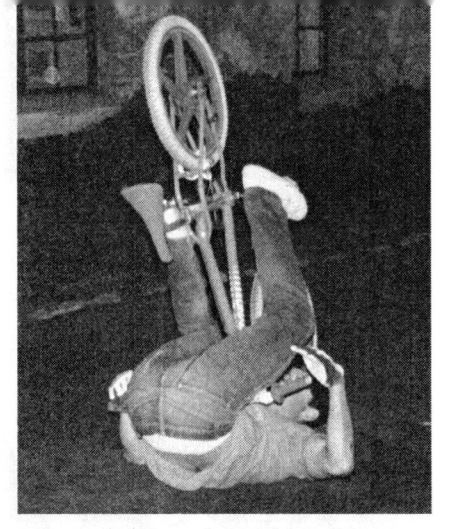

AGGRO RAG FREESTYLE MAG!
(Summer 1986)
York, PA
5½" x 8¼"

5th ISSUE

D ave Vanderspek, **Vander Roll,** Summer '85. Brian took this photo before we embarked on a mini road trip with Vander from Bill Batchelor's house in Rancho Cucamonga to the AFA Venice Beach Championships.

David Lee Roth.
Photo by Mike Dai[...]

"David Lee Roth showed up at the Venice contest that we went to and there was a lot of excitement in the air. I just remember how nice he was. You said, 'Hey Dave! Here, have a *Shreddin'!*' You handed him the magazine and he was like, 'Oh, cool, man,' and started looking at it. He could have ignored it, but he actually looked through everything in the magazine, page by page. Surprisingly—if I remember correctly—he put it in his back pocket and took off with it."[10]—**Brian Peters**

---
[10] Peters remembers correctly. Roth took off with it.

David Lee Roth.
Photo by Brian Peters

Red Lion senior writes Shreddin' for those who rac[e]

LIVING
York Recreation throws itself a party tonight
The York Recreation Commission's summer festival today at Kiwanis Lake celebration of the commission's 65th an[niver]sary. Events include a parachute jump, games and more.
1B

York Daily R[ecord]
York's first newspaper
170th Year, No. 184 • York, Pennsylvania

[Ri]des going to bat once m[ore]

Facing a strike deadline that would begin with tonight's games, there still appeared to be little chance of averting the game's second midseason walkout in four years unless bargainers could break an impasse on salary arbitration.

Today's session was characterized by a spokesman for the owners, Bob Fishel, as "an informal meeting" and not a formal resumption of negotiations.

Fehr, the union's acting executive director, called the impasse "a rerun of 1981" and said the owners were about to get "the strike they obviously wanted."

While saying the owners would not "let this go to a strike if we can help it," ... say that I'm optimistic at thi[s]

Any settlement would hav[e] the day to give players enoug[h] scheduled cities. Fehr said instructing players to return night's games instead of repo[rting]

Then, late Monday night statement saying he had aske[d] the union in an effort to get t[he] "The fans deserve the las[t] energy to resolve the current said.

Brian Peters, who rides his bicycle backwards, is the type of re[...]

Heads up
Kevin Jones flies over Mike Daily to complete a freestyle [...]
Hop. Daily, a senior at [...]

AGGRO RAG

FREESTYLE MAG!

Freestyle Skater
GREG SMITH

A MERE
50¢

SUMMER ISSUE

**Rad Photos
Trick How-To!**

**Ultra Rad talks:
HOT INTERVIEW!**

Contents

1986 Summer Issue

AGGRO RAG FREESTYLE MAG!

```
Editorial..........3
Mumbo Jumbo........4
The Slingshot......5
Ultra Rad Talks....12
Trick Clicks.......
'85 Northeast Comp.15
Skater Greg Smith..18
A Puppet No More...21
Trick Tidbits......22
```

7

15

Official 'Zine of the PLYWOOD HOODS

Staff (?)

Editor and Chief Writer
Mike Daily

Photogs
Darrell Wilt
Chris Daily

Layout/Design
Mike Daily

AGGRO RAG FREESTYLE MAG

" Eat Chrome Moly, C O

An editorial but not really.   By Michael S. Daily

MY TRICK

Something is missing. My session is becoming routine and the tricks I complete fail to satisfy me. Searching for originality, my mind seeks some kind of idea or sparklet of imagination to build upon. Something new...

The bike I own is now looked upon as a kind of safe which holds within it new treasures waiting to be discovered. I begin eagerly testing it for an opportunity. Many ideas are cast aside because they offer no hope. Some are not possible. Suddenly a promising move is conceived and I feel compelled to perfect it.

All efforts are focused on this new venture. It's flawless execution runs through my mind and I try it. I fall. The trick is now an obsession and I choose to challenge it. Nobody else can conquer it. Nobody but I.

Finally, after many attempts, the trick's very own freedom is captured and I've mastered it. I feel a colossal sense of pride that I alone have this trick, though I know this uniqueness will be short-lived. Others will copy it but I don't care. At least for now it is mine. My trick...

MUmBO jUMBO

THUNDERDOHM DEMOLISHED

Our beloved local skatepark here in York was leveled recently because of personal liability rather than urban development. Jim Dohm, the owner of the park which flourished in the late seventies then closed and remained free for the locals to roam, decided to render his concrete haven unrideable for fear that the onslaught of new vertical thrill seekers would end in a lawsuit. Bogus...

BAR EXTENDER MODIFICATION

Last summer at the Northeast Freestyle Championships Billy Rogers had a sano solution for his barend/seat dilemma. He simply attached a Suntour gear shifting device into his handlebar end and with one swift click, balancing moves as depicted above by its inventor are facilitated. Very trick indeed.

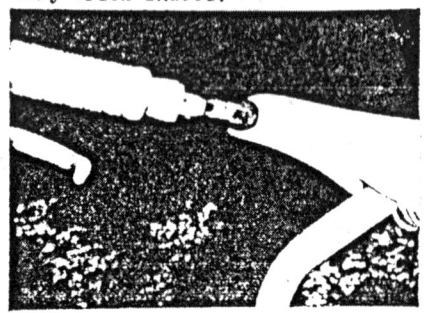

by MIKE DAILY

THE SLING SHOT BY "THE K"

Trick HOW-TO

The Slingshot was invented by Kevin Jones and is an easy to medium-hard trick depending upon how far you glide it. Kev sometimes goes around a few times before stalling these.

<u>Step One</u>- Start at a slow speed with your right foot on the rear peg and your left foot on the front.
<u>Step Two</u>- Swing your right leg by pushing off the rear peg. Roll in a circular pattern while moving your right foot towards the other rear peg for momentum.
<u>Step Three</u>- Come to a stall by resting the bike on the left pedal.
<u>Steps Four to Six</u>- To pull out of the trick push off the rear peg and swing your leg around the bike toward the right pedal and ride away.

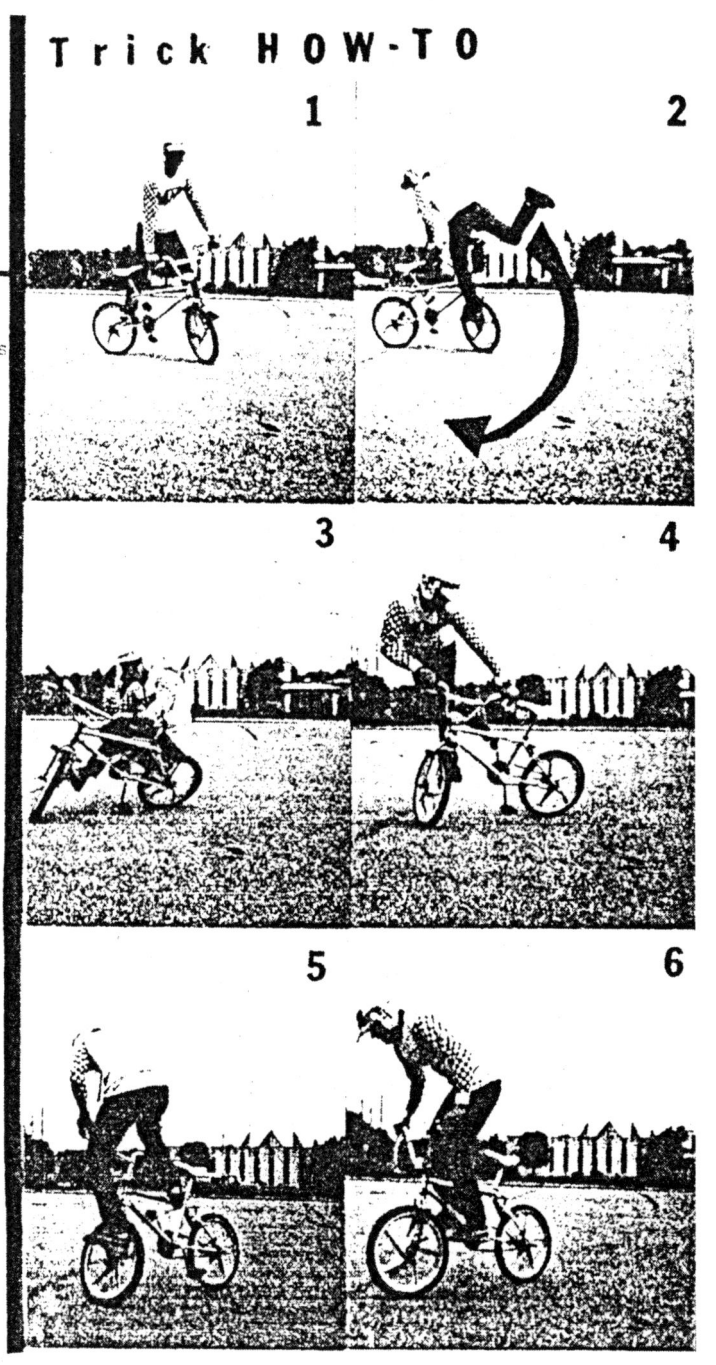

5

AGGRO RAG

FREESTYLE MAG!

SKATEPARK ISSUE!
Thunderin' at the DOME

March 1985
VOLUME TWO
NUMBER THREE

Send stamp for this back issue. A review of it recently ran in Freestylin'.

Send to:
AGGRO RAG
3320 Spondin Dr.
York, PA 17402

Official Stickers!
10 for 1 buck
10¢ ea.

PLYWOOD HOODS
Trick Team

FREESTYLE
PLYWOOD HOODS
TEAM
AGGRO RAG
FREESTYLE MAG!

6

ULTRA RAD

Eighteen year old Kenneth Evans and fifteen year old Denny Howell comprise one of the hottest freestyle teams on the East Coast- ULTRA RAD of North Carolina.

Their innovative tricks are fast and pulled off with precise intent. They've toured Canada with stunt rider Mercury Morgan. Both appeared in the May '86 issue of FREESTYLIN'. Their sponsors include Hutch and SE, two <u>hefty</u> names in the world of freestyle.

It's safe to say ULTRA RAD is on its way... The following candid interview took place in the ULTRA RAD team van at the cancelled Dundalk NFA contest...

YES, THEY

As interviewed by
MIKE DAILY

Kenneth Evans displays his unique version of a Walk Around.

How did ULTRA RAD get together?
Kenneth: "We live next door to each other."
Denny: "We started practicin' together so we just said 'Let's start a trick team.'" After that we built our first quarterpipe and started practicin' then we wanted to compete. There weren't that many contests around. The AFA was the only one holdin' 'em.
What was the team originally formed for, shows or contests?
Kenneth: "We started to do shows. We got asked to do a show so we did one. Then we got asked to do more shows and we said 'Hey, this is fun!'"
Then the contests came...
Kenneth: "Yeah, then contests started happenin' so we started to compete.
Who are your sponsors?
Denny: "I ride for SE Racing and Ultimate PV-1 Power Pedals. I got picked up by SE a couple months ago. Our team sponsors are SKYWAY, VANS, HARO, OAKLEY, COKE..."
Kenneth: "And I'm ridin' for Hutch."
How did ULTRA RAD get hooked up with COKE?
Kenneth: "They saw us at a show. The manager for Mid-Atlantic Coca-Cola saw us do a show and he liked it. He was blown away by it! He came up and asked us if we had sponsors out of the industry and we said 'Not yet!'. So he asked us if we'd be interested in ridin' for COKE.
How far did ULTRA RAD tour?
Denny: "We went to Canada for a couple weeks..."
Kenneth: "Hull...Toronto. We performed at the CNE, it's this great big fair in Canada. I've heard it billed as the biggest fair on the continent. We did shows there for about a week and we had a blast. On tour you dial in all your tricks."
Denny: "We did shows on the East Coast too, like fairgrounds and stuff."

ULTRA

All Photos by Darrell Wilt

A R E......

AGGRO RAG FREESTYLE MAG!

Who lines up the team's shows?
Kenneth: "Merc lined up the Canada tour."
Denny: "Mercury Morgan."
How long did you tour with Mercury Morgan?
Denny: "About a month."
What jumps did he make?
Denny: "He did his ten car jump in Canada and that's the world record. He coulda cleared fifteen!"
Kenneth: "Yeah, he jumped the landing ramp too! It was rad!"
How did ULTRA RAD get together with Mercury Morgan? Did you answer that ad in FREESTYLIN'?
Kenneth: "Yeah, we just answered the ad and he gave us a call and he wanted a videotape of us. So we went out the next day and made a video. We just took our ramps to the high school parking lot and got a guy to film us then we sent it to him. He called us back up and said he wanted us to go with him.
What contests have you guys hit so far?
Denny: "I entered the Rockville contest and got second place in 14-15 Expert Flatland.
Kenneth: "I had a broken wrist from tryin' a backwards drop-in. You remember my cast- that fluorescent one...?"
Yeah...tiger striped?!
Kenneth: "Yeah, neon orange!"
Is ULTRA RAD pursuing NFA or AFA contests?
Kenneth: "Both. I'm not chasin' points or anything."
What does ULTRA RAD think about freestyle competitions?
Denny: "I think it's great for sponsorships. You call 'em up (your sponsors) and say 'Hey, I got first place!' and they say 'allright!' and send more freebies.
Kenneth: "The more you do for them the more they'll do for you."
How much do you guys practice?
Kenneth: "Whenever we can. Several hours at least every day."
How long does an ULTRA RAD show last?
Kenneth: "About a half hour. We have a killer trailor which transports our steel-framed quarterpipe. It's about 8 feet high and 6 feet wide. Four layers of quarter inch plywood. We have a small ramp just like it."
Denny: "It's flat."

R A D : INTERVIEWED

Denny Howell contorts a stomach stand.

What's the main attraction to an ULTRA RAD show?
Kenneth: "We're like all-around. Lately we've been doin' alot of ground tricks for the contests and stuff.

Kenneth with his backwards pedal/ cherry picker sans hands showing the trademark Ultra Rad salute.

Since I broke my wrist I wasn't able to ride the ramp for awhile 'cuz when I'd land from airs it'd hurt really bad. Fallin' down a quarter pipe backwards makes you a little gun shy! The first time I tried it (acid drop) I fell. I layed there for a couple minutes and got up and said 'I might as well try it again before I get scared of it and I tried it again and...'"
Denny: "He broke his wrist!"
Are you guys advocates of safety gear?
Kenneth: "Yeah definitely. In fact we practice in pretty much full gear. Alot of times we'll practice in leathers."
How did you get most of your sponsors?
Denny: "We call 'em up first and talk to them then we send a resume. We send pictures of what we did and we go on tour. That helps out alot."
Do you guys travel alone? No parents?
Kenneth: "Yeah-no parents. Our parents have jobs ya know. They gotta work for a living."
And they don't mind?
Kenneth: "They back us up all the way."
Denny: "We couldn't be where we are today if it weren't for our parents."
Where do you want freestyle to take you?
Kenneth: "All the way. I'd like to turn pro and be one of the best out there."

Denny: "The best all around pros."
Do you guys get harrassed around your house for ridin'?
Kenneth: "No, we never get kicked out of anywhere man. We go to the park and ride. People stop and watch and you attract an audience just out ridin'. It's cool. We were in New York freestylin'. We just started ridin' a little bit and everybody was like 'C'mon do a show! So we went through our ground routines and our announcer is standin' there in the middle of everything yellin' out what we're doin'. Everybody was clappin' and cheerin' for us. It was rad. But I don't like New York City...(Laughter)"
Denny: "Our trailor got broken into there. They didn't get the bikes because they were in Merc's apartment. They tried to pick the front door but we had it locked and all. That's where our tools were at."
Kenneth: "It was pretty cool though..."
Denny: "New York's not! New York sucks! (Laughter)"
Kenneth: "Oh yeah, our announcer's name is Marcus Wooton. He's totally cool. He announced our shows and was like all around handyman. He did alot of drivin' on tour. Denny did some drivin' in Canada. When we were drivin' to Toronto I fell asleep at the wheel and Denny wakes me up; 'You want me to drive some?!'"
How does Ultra Rad pay for motel expenses, food, gas...
Denny: "In Canada everything was complimentary. The bike festival payed for everything."
Donald Sawyer: "Today Denny was doin' footplants off the dresser in the motel! The maid came out the door lookin' at Denny!"

Cont. on page 14

Ultra Rad run their levers on the opposite sides and I never did find out why...

Struttin' some can-can wheel walkin' is Denny Howell. This guy's footwork is dialed!

TRICK CLICKS!

"The K" airing in an inverted fashion out of the Nuclear Pool.

Cont. from page 11

Denny: "She didn't care!
OK, so what was the worst part of the tour?
Denny: "I was practicin' for a show on a dirt track and there was this kid on top of the ramp measurin' my air (Kenneth belches prompting much laughter). OK! Anyways, I got an air about seven feet over and my shoe came off in the air! I landed and my foot hit the sprocket and it split my heel. I got 15 stitches."
Kenneth: "Yeah, in Hull, he had to walk with a cane! He'd walk out to his bike with a cane, get on his bike, and catch about 5 - 6 feet of air! He could not walk, but he could do his freestyle!!!" -*

From L to R: Team Ultra Rad including Denny Howell, Ronald McDonald, Kenneth Evans, and Donald Sawyer.

NORTHEAST FREESTYLE CHAMPIONSHIPS AFA MASTERS SUMMER 85

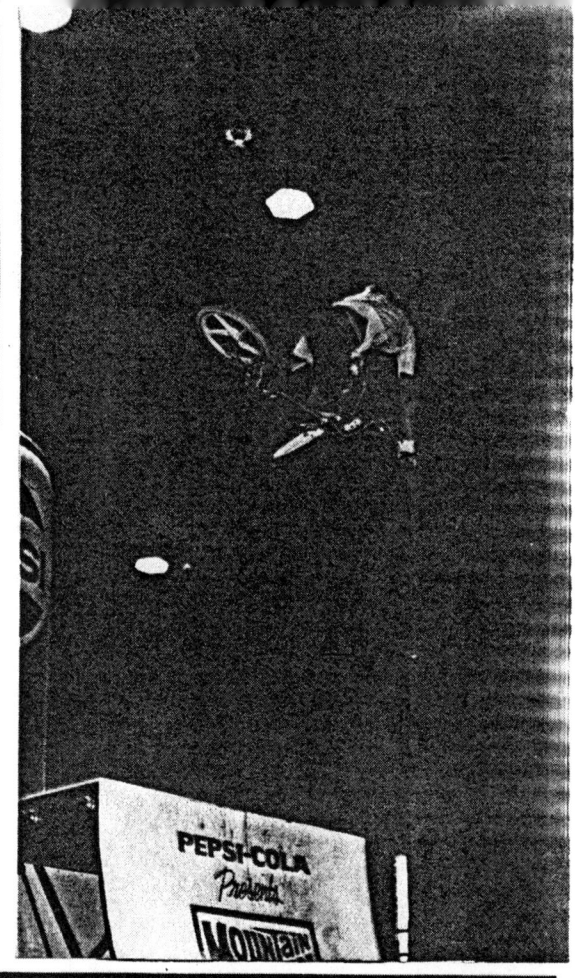

Coverage better late than never... Right- Pro airs were insane and this was just practice. Wilko. Below- The top-name dudes weren't the only ones rippin' it up.

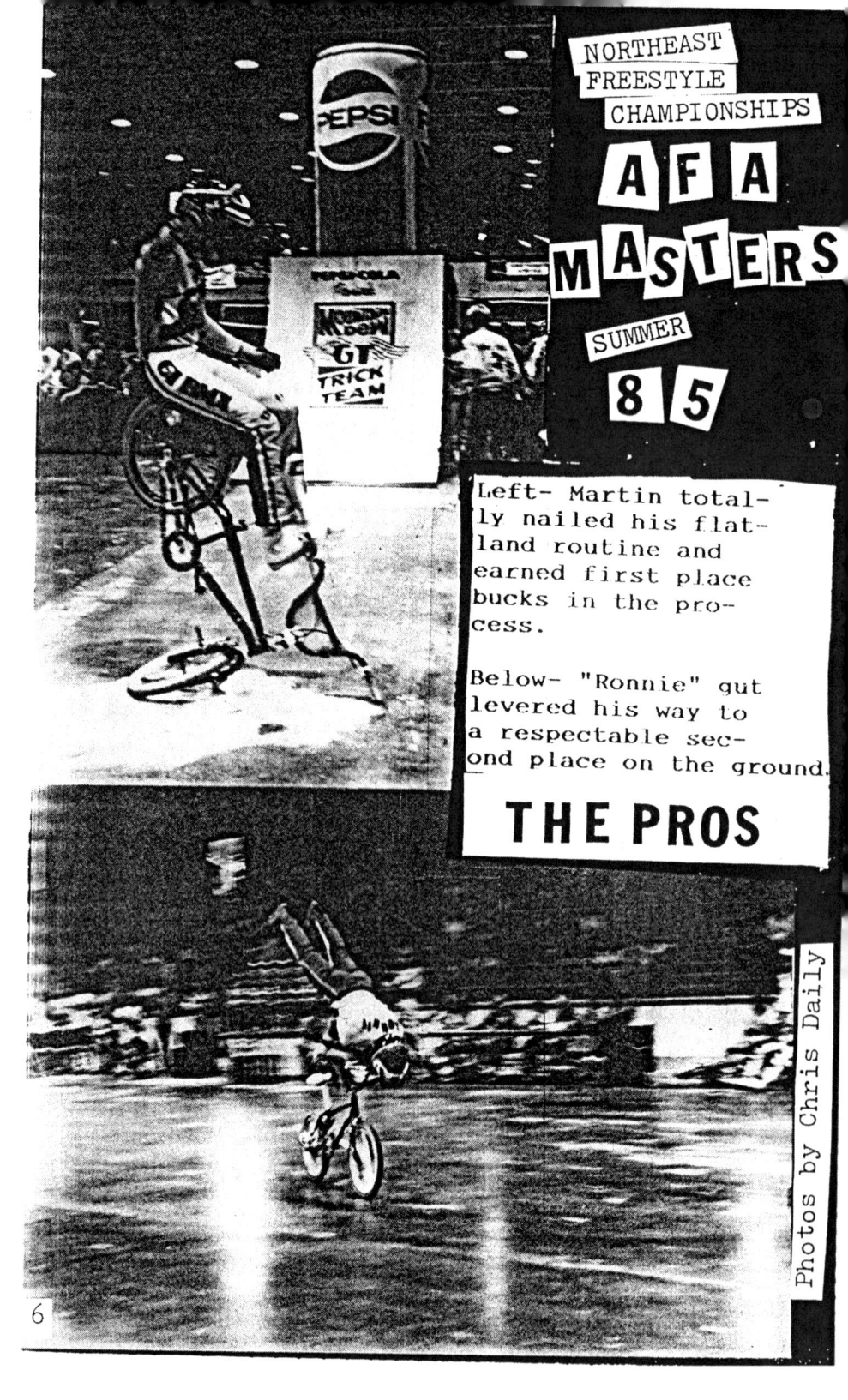

NORTHEAST FREESTYLE CHAMPIONSHIPS

AFA MASTERS

SUMMER 85

Left- Martin totally nailed his flatland routine and earned first place bucks in the process.

Below- "Ronnie" gut levered his way to a respectable second place on the ground.

THE PROS

Photos by Chris Daily

6

NORTHEAST FREESTYLE CHAMPIONSHIPS

AFA MASTERS

PEPSI-COLA Presents

HOT AMATEURS

Left- Gary Pollak came all the way from King of Prussia, PA to compete. Gary now rides for Factory CW and has been seen pulling off Fire Hydrants (a type of rolling tailwhip) into Cherrypickers. We call it "The Gary Cherry" and everybody else calls it RAD! He rips on ramps too.

Upper Left- Brian Wallos of Staten Island, N.Y. skarfed on a well-deserved fifth place in the mega competitive 14& Over Expert class.

Above- T.J. Fallon blazed some BIG airs to take second in 14 &Over Intermediate Ramps.

SUMMER 85

17

AGGRO RAG
FREESTYLE MAG!

Contributed by
BILL BATCHELOR

SMITH
GREG

SHREDDIN': Hi Greg.
GREG: Hi Paul.
SHREDDIN': Nice weather eh?
GREG: Oh yes, it's very fine weather. It's good for all the plants and things.
SHREDDIN': Who are you sponsored by?
GREG: INDEPENDENT Truck Co. and Quicksilver. They both dominate.
SHREDDIN': Yeah, they ARE truly great. Well, what do ya got?
GREG: I got a '68 Mustang Fast Back. It goes fast too. Do you care?

SHREDDIN': Uh, yeah, sure. Do you use coupons?
GREG: No, I don't believe in them.
SHREDDIN': What skaters do you admire?
GREG: Tony (Hawk) shreds hell. Rodney (Mullen) is god. [The editors of this mag do not agree with the reference to God. _Ed.]
SHREDDIN': Why do you skate?
GREG: Because I love it. I have never really been good at anything, and I finally have a chance to be good at skating.

photo by BILL BATCHELOR

SHREDDIN': Do you like heavey metal?
GREG: No dude, bang your head.
SHREDDIN': How many wives do you have?
GREG: Oh, not too many.
SHREDDIN': What do you think about world terrorism?
GREG: I think it sucks. Why can't people just leave others alone?
SHREDDIN': Do you like competing?
GREG: Yes, very much so. I don't ever care if I win or not though. I just skate.

SHREDDIN': Yeah I've heard that you've won two in a row. That's pretty neat.
GREG: Thanks.
SHREDDIN': Do you have any closing comments?
GREG: Yes. If you like free-styling, stick to it. Don't give up because practice does pay. Also, don't be close-minded about stuff like equipment. Just try everything possible and use what works best for you. Create- don't immitate.

"I've got a '68 Mustang Fast Back. It goes fast too. Do you care?"

19

KEVIN JONES IS.....

A HOOD

← Left-
Yet another creative variation of the cherrypicker. Kev hops these.

Right- →
A slight incline serves as an invitation to verticalness. The K.

AGGRO RAG FREESTYLE MAG!

A PUPPET NO MORE

by Mike Daily

A lengthy shock of hair hovered over the right eye of a veteran freestyler as he practiced new tricks for an upcoming contest. A curious crowd had gathered around him and although his maneuvers ranged from simple tricks to complex feats made possible only by specialized equipment, his onlookers applauded in a consistent manner for _all_ of his tricks. The rider could not understand why this occurred and suddenly he felt as though he were some kind of public "puppet" whose only significance to his viewers was as an abnormal attraction. "Do they _expect_ this?", he pondered. Frustrated, he departed from the limelight in search of a more serene setting.

When the trickster arrived at the secluded area the crowds of the past became less important and he began sessioning alone. He neglected to yield to reason and soon his aggression took on a care-free perspective; nobody but himself to impress. The silence was broken only by the wrenching sounds of his scoot and grunts of exertion as he twisted himself into moves never before attempted; moves which utilized his surroundings. The radster bounded onto a lofty ledge, stalled his bike for a moment, then leaped back to the ground, whirling across the pavement in a spinning frenzy.

The thrasher's body harbored heavy perspiration and he prepared to depart from this remote location. He now felt an air of accomplishment and he thought about his future. The freestyler fully intended to continue competing in organized contests but that day he learned why he really rides- For himself, and _not_ for those judges or spectators who perceived his dedicated actions as sheer entertainment. That type of "winning" mattered no longer to him.

The biker shook the bang out of his eye and slowly pedalled away. Perhaps home.

THE END...

—Mike Daily

TRICK TIDBITS

BY MIKE DAILY

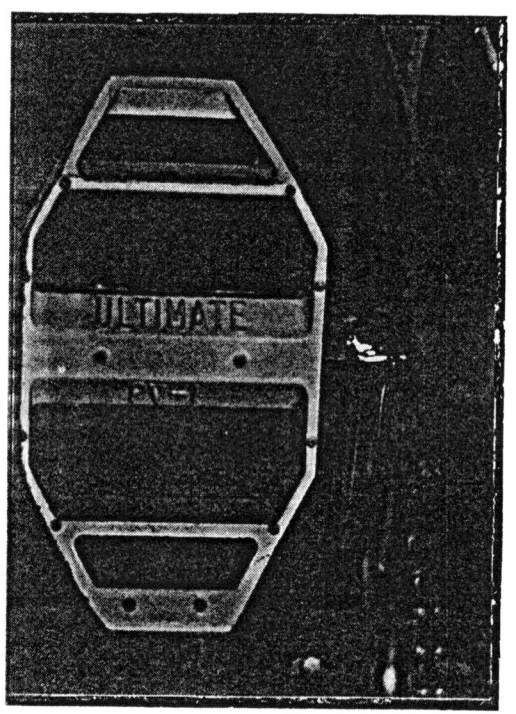

ULTIMATE PV-1 Power Pedals

Need a set of freestyle pedals you KNOW you won't slip off? Try out a pair of ULTIMATE PV-1 Power Pedals. These large platform type pedals offer chrome moly shafts and are made out of aluminum. Denny Howell of the Ultra Rad team uses 'em and says they work great. Here's the address if you are interested: 4013 Nina Drive, Chesapeak, VA 23321

COLOSSAL FOSSILS

The Plywood Hoods encountered these unique frozen treats en route to the New York AFA comp at one of those interstate food places where goop costs a one hander one footer. A Colossal Fossil is a tasty popsicle with lemon and grape water ice but that's not all. Encased within this frozen fortress is a gummy dinosaur! Suprise, suprise! They are good.

SPACE ADVENTURE WORLD
3401 E. PROSPECT RD.
YORK, PA 17402
PHONE NO: 755-8506

-SPECIALS-

SUNDAY SUPER SUNDAY 12:30 - 10:00 P.M.
   8 TOKENS FOR $1.00

TUESDAYS BUDGET BONUS 7:00 - 10:00 P.M.
   50 TOKENS FOR $5.00 (AT DESK ONLY)

FRIDAYS MOONLIGHT VIDEO 9:00 - 12:00 MID.
   8 TOKENS FOR $1.00 (AT DESK ONLY)

SATURDAYS EARLY BIRD SPECIAL 11:00 - 12:00 N
   10 TOKENS FOR $1.00 (AT DESK ONLY)

SATURDAYS COUPLES NIGHT 7:00 - 12:00 MID.
   HE BUYS 5 SHE GETS 5 FREE AT DESK ONLY

```
┌─────────────────COUPON─────────────────┐
│           SPACE ADVENTURE WORLD        │
│             10 TOKENS FOR 1.00         │
│              LIMIT 100 TOKENS          │
│                                        │
│   NAME:----------------------------    │
│           EXPIRES: 08/31/86            │
└─────────────────CUT OUT────────────────┘
```

"Eat Chrome Moly, Coppers!"

AGGRO RAG
FREESTYLE MAG!

c/o Mike Daily
3320 Spondin Dr.
York, PA 17402

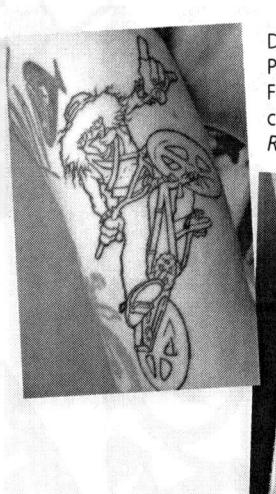

Dizz tattoo on arm of Pat Richardson, a.k.a. Fetus (Kentucky rider, creator of the zine, *ROGUE*, and musician).

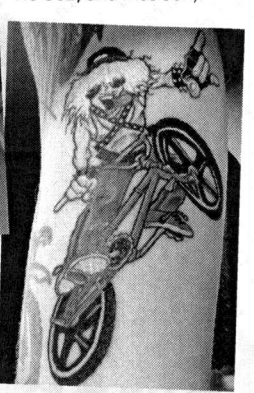

AGGRO RAG FREESTYLE MAG!
(Fall 1986)
York, PA
5½" x 8¼"

6th ISSUE

Ceppie Maes, back tire walk
Alabama AFA Masters, 1986

"The biggest perk [of being a zineguy back in the mid-'80s] for me was being asked to contribute to *Freestylin'*. That was The Shit. As cool as it was to make your own zine, getting something printed in *Freestylin'* was infinitely cooler. Andy requested permission to reprint an editorial I'd published in *Aggro Rag*. It was called 'A Puppet No More' and ran in an 'Off the Deep End' with a photo of my favorite rider, Ceppie Maes. I think it won a design award."
—**Mike Daily**, *Freestylin': Generation F; 1984-1989* (2009)

York group—bicycle stunts

The York Dispatch/Chip Dalton

PLYWOOD HOODS, left to right, Mark Eaton, Dale Mitzel and Kevin Jones perform a stunt on their freestyle bicycles. The three perform for area audiences exhibiting their special bikes. The act is a combination of breakdancing and riding.

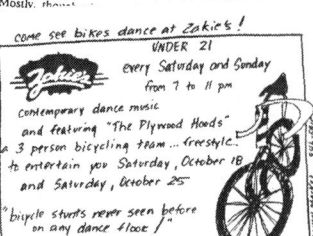

Record photos by Bill Bowden

Kevin Jones does night session work at Dover High School.

Freestylers tackle the night club scene

By BRYAN DENSON
Daily Record staff writer

At about 9 o'clock Saturday night, a rap tune will kick-kick-kick out of the big speakers in Zakies nightclub and four guys on 20-inch freestyle bikes are going to show off in front of about 200 spectators.

One of the riders, a 19-year-old Penn State/York sophomore named Kevin Jones, is going to knock their socks off.

At one point, if he's feeling up to it, Jones, an expert freestyler, is going to ride along the dancefloor and hoist himself into a standing position on his handlebars — and ride that way. He has done it 50 feet without wrecking.

In a word, radical.

"That is intense," said 18-year-old Dale Mitzel, who joins Jones, Mark Eaton, 17, and Mike Daily, 17, as part of the Plywood Hoods freestyle team making the rounds at area entertainment venues.

The Zakies gig is the Hoods third show at the downtown nightspot. They will perform one show at 9 p.m. as part of a special Halloween party for the under-21 set (7 p.m. to 10:30 p.m.)

The Hoods are the only organized freestyle team in the York metro area and have been a hot item since forming two years ago.

The foursome represents the core of only a few serious local freestylers. They are hoping to capitalize on the trend established in California a half-dozen years ago and spreading rapidly along the East Coast.

Please see STYLE on 2E

Hoods entertain in a unique way. 19, Dale Mitzel, 18 17, all of York, are performers. Using tes, the three teens and strength spin-ikes on the dance

ycling, an offshoot nd breakdancing, ac-three, became popu-rs about three years

ride on dirt tracks nd things like that," hen the modifications the new tricks inter-

met while competing ng. "Mike Daily, cap-im, got us together for nes. "He is in college

freestyle competitions around the country. Jones said most of the competitions are in New York, New Jersey and California.

Jones and Mitzel, both freshmen at Penn State/York and Eaton, a senior at York Suburban High School, in addition to their biking experience, got their start in the aerobic-style tricks while break-dancing three years ago. "Breakdancing started dying out and we had gotten enough recognition that we got out of it and into this," Mitzel said.

"How you learn is through constant practice," Mitzel said. "We read the magazines (about freestyl-ing) and then make variations of our own." Mitzel said the magazines teach the tricks through a sequence of photos.

Jones, the most experienced of the group, developed a trick called the "Hang Glider." In this trick, ins out from the seat of his

Style
Continued from 1E

The Hoods all are freestyle competitors, lugging their expensive, highly specialized BMX bikes to American Freestyle Association competitions all over the region.

Mitzel, Jones and Eaton had been part of a six-man breakdancing team called the Cardboard Lords, which performed in the area before breaking up at the demise of the dance form in late 1984.

"It was starting to fade out," Mitzel said. "We couldn't get much better."

Doing bike tricks was a logic step from breakdancing, particularly since the the trio spent muc

the handlebars while the bike is moving. Then he spins back into the seat. The entire trick consists of three spins.

Another trick, the "Lawn Mower Stradle" entails stepping over one side of the bike then back to the other side and then stepping over the bike lengthwise. This trick utilizes balance in that the rider, while stepping over the bike, balances the bike on the special pegs designed for these tricks.

The bikes the three use are equipped with special wheel spokes, pegs on the front and rear tires for standing, and handle bars that spin 360 degrees.

The Plywood Hoods performed Saturday night at Zakie's, 25 W Market St. They will also perform for the under-21 crowd there on Oct 18 and Oct. 25.

Duncan Schmidt, owner of Za kie's said he found the group when he was searching for entertainme the under 21 crowd would like.

of its time jumping dirt ramps at "The Pit" behind the Queensgate Shopping Center.

Davis, who edits a small free-style magazine, *Aggro Rag*, talked the breakdancing trio, all of whom also rode bikes, into forming a team.

Jones was a natural.

"Kevin gets the most air," Mitzel said. He can jump about six feet above a plywood ramp. "He's going to get famous one year."

For now, the Hoods look forward to performing at more Zakies shows and wherever they can get booked.

Mostly, th

come see bikes dance at Zakie's!
UNDER 21
every Saturday and Sunday
from 7 to 11 pm
Contemporary dance music
and featuring "The Plywood Hoods"
a 3 person bicycling team... freestyle
to entertain you Saturday, October 18
and Saturday, October 25
"bicycle stunts never seen before on any dance floor!"
3 dollars Sat. night, 4 dollars Sunday night

AGGRO RAG

FREESTYLE MAG!   BRIAN'

CW FReaK SHOw

75¢

NEW YORK CITY **Assault!!**
BEYOND THUNDERDOHM

Fidge Issue....

NUMBER FIVE

AGGRO RAG

FREESTYLE MAG!

1986 FIDGE ISSUE

CONTENTS

Mumbo Jumbo	3
Air at Brian's	4
CW Freak Show	7
A New Trick	12
Beyond Thunderdohm	13
The Fine Art of Fidging	18
New York City Assault	21
The Crowd	24
Trick Tidbits	26

STAFF

Editor
Mike Daily

Layout/Design
Mike Daily

Publisher
Mack Smith

Photogs
Dale Mitzel
Jamie McCulloch

AGGRO RAG FREESTYLE MAG!

ON THE COVER— From top inset; "the K" flyin' at Brian's last summer, Ceppie Maes rockin' his Antrider at Rockville, and Matt Hoffman rippin' up the General ramp at Madison Square Gardens.

FLASH! - Championship Freestyle Contest-AFA- December-New Jersey; Interested? Call Mario Salas at (215) 265-9173.

MUMBO JUMBO
BY MIKE DAILY

Bar Ride tip
Since Woody introduced the incredible Bar Ride, more and more guys can be seen doing them. The real hotties can quickly be determined just by scopin' on their scoots for this trick mod. Simply affix a lever under the crossbar pointing up, crimp the pivot bolt for added stability, and go Bar Ride your brains out. You'll be utterly _amazed_ at the difference it makes!

Ultra Rad Update
Even though they aren't presently together as a team, Kenneth Evans and Denny Howell of Ultra Rad are still goin' strong.

Kenneth is currently in San Diego doing shows at Sea World and Denny is stylin' up in Hull, Canada again.

Denny, still riding for SE Racing, recently topped the 16 Expert class at Madison Square Gardens with some radical moves such as multiple boomerangs. He is definitely past-due for full factory SE status.

Keep your eye on these guys because they aren't done yet. They're goin' all the way.

Air at Brian's

Engaged in a full-on One Footed Invert air is Kevin Jones.

This much-shredded ramp was owned by this guy: Brian Peters. Did he rip on it? I'll let these photos speak for themselves...

SHREDDIN'
RADNESS MAGAZINE
Mike Daily
WRITER/EAST COAST
(717) 757-3096
3320 Spondin Drive
York, PA 17402

Yours truly was even a Brian's local until my misfortunate bail. I'll stick to land.

6

Words 'n stuff by Daily

Pictures by Jamie

CW FREAK SHOW

It was the show they had waited for since the beginning of their Extended Remix Tour. CW was slated for Rockville BMX on July 7th and they planned to deliver. CW veterans John "Dizz" Hicks and Ceppie Maes were outfitted in distinctive black uniforms and new guys Greg Kove and Gary Rollak were dressed in the standard CW lavender and white. Crowd response was nuts thanks to McGoo. How was the show? It <u>tore</u>...

CEPPI

Ceppie had the crowd hoppin' with his original tricks and wild music. Ol' Creepy even "dorked" an air before the show which amused all. Here's Cep with some fancy wheel dancing, a backwards wheelie in circles, and the T-Stance.

The ever-innovative Ceppie Maes hits his trademark tricks: The Finger Flip and our cover shot; the Antrider. The crowd ate it up.

THEY CALL HIM... Dizz

Dizz draped himself with heavy metal type accessories and proceeded to cause pandemonium with his aggressive performance massively enhanced by (what else?) speed metal. His manuevers on these sloped surfaces were incredible.

Gary Pollak

Pennsylvania's own Gary Pollak put on such a dazzling team debut performance that Dizz shook his head in disbelief!! This kid has a PROMISING future ahead of him. Clockwise it's: Dizz and Gary stoked on the show, a can-can, a hefty aerial, the result of the intense "Gary Cherry", a Pedal Picker, and one tough move- the one-handed peg Squeaker while waving.

Photos by Mike Daily

Kevin Jones came up with this complex manoov with previous knowledge only of Woody Itson's Pedal Picker. As you can see, it ain't no holiday. Wear your gear.

Now check out...

THE K PICKER.

1) Start with the bars turned around with your right foot on a slightly raised pedal.

2) All at once, pull back on the bars, let go with left hand, swing left leg over onto seat post, regrasp grip, and start hopping.

a new TRICK

3) Now the hard (!) part...let go of right grip, swing right leg over onto pedal, and regrab grip resuming hops.

4) Now just put left foot on the pedal and you got it. Now is when you want to flash that no hander...

5) To ride out, let gravity do it's thing and exit with a bar sit.

AGGRO RAG FREESTYLE MAG!

12

BEYOND THUNDERDOHM...

by Mike Daily

AGGRO RAG FREESTYLE MAG!

Thunderdohm was the site of <u>many</u> heated sessions over the years. Abandoned by the park owners, Thunderdohm was thriving with activity.

There were no rules or costly fees in order to participate. Kids payed their respect by becoming adept at handling each portion of the park with much skill.

Practice became progression for these dedicated thrashers. Although this long-standing skatepark was plowed, these same radsters <u>know</u> what they must do- Continue progressing...

"The K" deflecting from the harshly vertical angle of the Green Bowl vert extension in fully tabletopped formation.

13

TRICK CLICKS

This is a vintage photo of Kevin Jones and Mike Strickler doin' some double stylin' into the Green Bowl at Thunderdohm. At the time of this shot, their tricked out bikes were the hot set up for skate parkin'.

BEYOND THUNDERDOHM   BEYOND

Winter sessions ensued at Thunderdohm separating the dedicated from the trendy. Kev.

A tall two-sided wooden structure was shredded by many and awed by all until vandals wrecked it. Rodney Brown.

THUNDERDOHM BEYOND THUNDERDOHM

Kevin Jones, probably the park's most talented biker, utilized the bowl-to-bowl transitions to their full potential.

A local by the name of Jimmy broke all aerial boundries over the Green Bowl vertiaal extension with airs uncharacteristic of that terrain.

The Fine Art of FIDGING!
by Mike Daily

Brian Peters airs by the moonlight.
Summer 1984

Everyone does it. Some individuals <u>live</u> for it. For freestylers it is essential. It's called fidging.

Fidging is fun. The more spontaneous it is, the better. Opportunities arise frequently. Parked cars. Rent-a-Cops. Groups of Betties. Banked walls. Pedestrians. Moving cars. The possibilities are endless.

Take a look at these photos and use your imagination. The rest is up to you.

An unsuspecting motorist was oblivious to this aggro trunk plant by The K.

GQ Pose

Man with assumed authority: "What do you guys think you're doin' here?"
"We're havin' a photo session! Say cheese! Thanks, pal!"

fidging

Wall carve at Hardees before a manager type became annoyed. The editor.

19

"AGGRO RAG FREESTYLE MAG!"

"Upon hearing this his medicine cabinent exploded causing everyone within the building to O.D. On the other hand, the people next door slept through the whole incident."

NEW YORK CITY
assaULT!

Photos by Dale Mitzel

ABOVE-
Take careful note of this photo. This is Matt Hoffman of Oklahoma with a fully cranked Can Can Lookback. This is also (gasp!) the 14-15 Expert Ramps class! Every time Matt went for air the huge crowd went *NUTS*!

RIGHT-
Robert Peterson ended his exciting routine with this Bar Spinner Seat-in-the-Mouth move. Did Bert deserve first place frogskins? You better believe it.

KING FOR A DAY

NEW YORK CITY aSSAuLt!!

Highlights..

Above- Brian Belcher of factory General took high airs and some aggr small ramp moves to a second in 14-15 Expert Ramps right behind Hoff man.

Below- The Master of Balance enlightens the spectators to his "Pete son" during pro practice

You may have read about it in the paper. Well, we were there. Being caught in the middle of a Gay-Lesbian parade in New York City was lame. Being caught in the middle of a Gay-Lesbian arade in New York City n a car with 3 other guys as <u>murder</u>!

NEW YORK CITY Assault!!

Left- R.L. was his usual smooth self with moves like this one hander one footer Fork Wheelie but it wasn't enough to edge out Peterson. **Right-** Does this look like the air of a "retired" ramp rider? Not hardly. R.L. at eight feet.

Before

After

When Todd Anderson went for this Top-Sided Can Can One Hander air... ...he slammed so hard many thought he was a goner. Luckily enough, Todd walked away from the slam with First.

23

The Crowd

A crowd of many gathered to watch us session. Soon coinage and even currency was thrown down to us from the packed boardwalk banisters and we were stoked. Our unscheduled beachfront freestyle performance was completely raging and these strangers loved it. Several Fork Whips in succession earned applause and more coins. Gasps followed a standard no-hander Cherry Picker. Each rider took the floor and strutted his best tricks for his new freestyle friends and the crowd to see and enjoy.

Suddenly our bikes became illuminated by red and blue flashes of light. The yoppies had arrived and they were sore. At first we were inclined to disperse at speed but we opted to stand our ground and hear what these figures of authority had to say.

When the cops told us to find somewhere else to ride the crowd we had been entertaining voiced their disapproval.

"Let 'em ride! Booooo...!" Paper cups bounced off the roof of the squad car from above. The crowd was on our side...

Feeling unusually rebellious I pedalled into the lights of the police car and whipped off a quick Decade to loud cheering from the tourists. My unfamiliar companions took my cue and also cut loose in front of the dismayed authorities causing the crowd to wildly encourage us. By the time the cops leaped out of their vehicle, we were at a safe distance down the street leaving the disgruntled officers to face humiliation. With a wave to our "fans" we left; satisfied.

Afterwards however, as we departed for the night, I felt slightly sorry for those police officers. After all, they were only doing their jobs. But then again, so were we..

— Mike Daily

AGGRO RAG
FREESTYLE MAG!

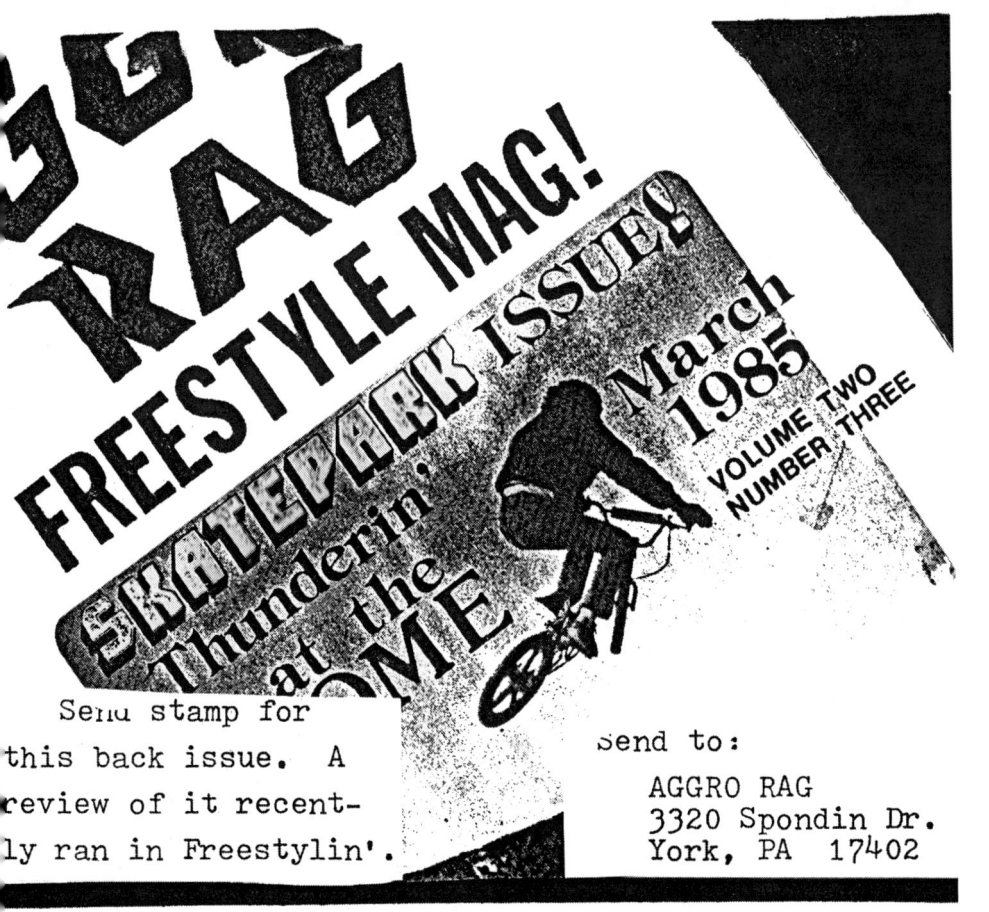

SKATEPARK ISSUE!
Thunderin' at the DOME

March 1985
VOLUME TWO
NUMBER THREE

Send stamp for this back issue. A review of it recently ran in Freestylin'.

Send to:
AGGRO RAG
3320 Spondin Dr.
York, PA 17402

Official Stickers!
10 for 1 buck
10¢ ea.

PLYWOOD HOODS Trick Team

FREESTYLE PLYWOOD HOODS TEAM AGGRO RAG FREESTYLE MAG!

RICK TIDBITS   BY MIKE DAILY

ACIFIC PALMS

Why ride with a handicap, namely leaving your hands unprotected? These new gloves from Pacific Palms will cripple you with delight with features like velcro closures, padded acking, and mellow colors. Check 'em out...

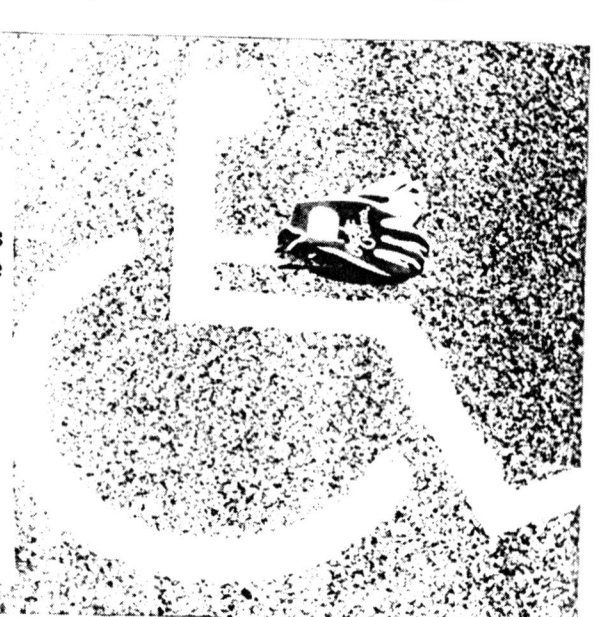

YOO-HOO

When a lengthy session causes atigue and extreme thirst, reach or the beverage that quenches as ell as tastes RAD: Yoo-Hoo! Yooo not only contains rich chocatey flavor but it even supies your run-down bod with vitans and minerals. What more could parched freestyler ask for?

Thief Thwarter Tip

Ever been afraid of leaving your bike outside a convenience store for fear that some spagmump is gonna snag it? If you've got locking levers (and who doesn't nowadays?) you're in luck. Just lock up both levers and maybe flip your bike upside down. If that doesn't discourage the dork at least it will hamper his getaway giving you a primo chance to try out those new karate lessons you've been taking.

SPACE ADVENTURE WORLD
3401 E. Prospect Rd.
YORK, PA 17402

-SPECIALS-

SUNDAY SUPER SUNDAY 12:30 - 10:00 P.M.
  8 TOKENS FOR $1.00

TUESDAYS BUDGET BOWL 6 7:00 - 10:00 P.M.
  10 TOKENS FOR $1.00 AT DESK ONLY

FRIDAYS MOONLIGHT MADNESS 9:00 - 12:00 MID.
  8 TOKENS FOR $1.00 AT DESK ONLY

SATURDAYS EARLY BIRD SPECIAL 10:00 - 12:00
  10 TOKENS FOR $1.00 AT DESK ONLY

SATURDAYS COUPLES NIGHT 7:00 - 12:00 MID.
  HE BUYS 5 SHE GETS 5 FREE AT DESK ONLY

```
*=====================COUPON=====================*
            SPACE ADVENTURE WORLD
              10 TOKENS FOR 1.00
               LIMIT 20 TOKENS


        NAME:--------------------------
           EXPIRES: 09/30/86
*================================================*
```

AGGRO RAG c/o

Mike Daily
3320 Spondin Dr.
York, PA 17402

(717) 757-3096

Mark Wales

"Even the crappy Huffys [Mark Wales and I] were totally dyin' for. We always had the feeling that there was gonna be so much. I remember we talked about it way back then, like: 'When the Japanese guys find out...' We thought: 'Five years, OK...they're gonna be doing all this crazy stuff once they find out.' We had these weird ideas, but a lot of it sort of came true, really."—**Kevin Jones**

AGGRO RAG FREESTYLE MAG!
(January 1987)
York, PA/Lock Haven, PA
5½" x 8¼"

7th ISSUE

The following letter was printed in the April '84 issue of BMX Plus!

Dear *BMX Plus!*

My name is Mark Wales, and my friend Kevin Jones and I are BMX freestylers with professional talent. Kevin and I have millions of the hottest tricks and new and different type freestyle ramps that no one knows about. They are the raddest in freestyle.

We do one-handed, one-footed rollback 360s and 540s. We are just now getting sponsors. On pages 40 and 52 of your November '83 issue you showed maneuvers I was surprised to see, because I was sure I had invented them. I am a graphics designer and a BMX scientist. I know all BMX philosophy. Why don't you consider us for a trick team? We could up your magazine, and you could up our career.

Here are some pictures. Maybe you could print them in your magazine. Yup, East Coasters can freestyle too.

Mark Wales
York, PA

P.S. My friend bet me $1.01 that you wouldn't print this.

Mark Wales
1967-1991

HOODS
PLYWOOD

AGGRO RAG

FREESTYLE MAG!

January 1987
Volume 2 Number 6

LONG ISLAND
COVERAGE

75¢

CONTEST issue!

WIN Gloves!

ZINE ALERT

HOT NEW HOW-TO

HOLDING CONTESTS

& MORE MOD LITERATURE...

January 1987

Volume 2 Number 6

COVER: An unidentified New York local displaying a back side vertical boomerang at the Long Island comp. Photo: Mark Wales.

INSET: Kev takin' the treacherous small to big mogul jump at T-Dohm. Crazy Bits.

Editor and Chief Writer
MIKE DAILY

Layout/Design
MIKE DAILY

Contributors
BRETT DOWNS
MARK EATON
SAMMY LEE

Trick Consultant
KEVIN "THE K" JONES

Photographers
DALE MITZEL
MARK WALES

Aggro Rag is published bi-monthly. Subscriptions are four dollars/six issues. Contributions welcome.

Aggro Rag is the official zine of the Plywood Hoods. The Hoods are sponsored by ODI, Yoo-Hoo, and Flying Feet Sport Shoes.

LONG ISLAND
An AFA Masters event as seen through the eyes of a Hood....10

ZINE ALERT
Rags worth checkin' into....12

KRYS DAUCHY
She's so hot- both on her Haro and off......................17

HOLDING YER OWN FREESTYLE COMPS
16 year old Mario Salas talks about how to set up your own contests....................18

HOOD CONVERSIONS
Hoods who skate............21

A TRICK CONTEST
Do you have originality? You could score some free gloves or grips with it................23

AGGRO RAG
Mike Daily
3320 Spondin Dr.
York, PA   17402

(717) 757-3096

An Editorial?......3
Mumbo Jumbo........4
A New Trick........5
Skank Art..........6
The Dale's Mail....7
Wild Wear.........22

an Editorial?

BY MSD

Eaton-forbidden Spud skate ramp.

AGGRO RAG
FREESTYLE MAG!

    I wasn't concerned with old men or chain link fences as I cranked my bike in a quick manner. Even bright green walls and small dogs were blurred visions. I came to a conservative hot dog stand and stopped to observe it. A pearl-white one.

    A man with a burlap hat peered about nervously and then viciously consumed a salted washcloth. I looked at the other patrons. One swayed and then slumped helplessly over the hard ivory counter, gumballs scattering in every direction. I shoved off and started to leave when the old guy behind the counter hollered.

    "Leave reason but return!," he yelled. "It's just the irritation jackals emit that cause freeze pops to look at drapes of a synthetic material."

    I approached the old vendor with caution. Suddenly he reached under the counter, taking out a small printed booklet to offer me. I accepted it and then looked at the weird elder for some sign of explanation. I wondered if he could do push-ups. He smiled at me revealing a whole section of an old blue snakebelly tire. I reeled away in horror and stuffed the pamphlet into my back pocket. I pedaled away fast, but not fast enough.

    The crazed patrons caught up to me promptly. They were clamoring at my hind region when I realized what they wanted. The damned literature!

    I out-manuevered the attackers and rumbled down a flight of stairs. I looked back to see them sawing tic-tac-toe boards into the soles of their feet with rusty hack-saw blades. They were extremely disturbed.

    I swerved behind a dull grey dumpster and stopped. I saw the carcass of a dead bird but I didn't care. I withdrew the publication from my pocket and looked at the cover: Aggro Rag. I produced a loud sadistic laugh until I heard the doors of the dumpster crash open. The last thing I remembered was a harsh sweeping blow to my cranium and, not blackness, but......

    Aggro Rag is back in a brand new installment after a lengthy delay, spagmumps! And since I've finally adjusted to the advent of my college career, Aggro Rag will from now on be a bimonthly venture. So far, my zine goes out to about 100 freestyle enthusiasts from all over the United States thanks to the ink I received in the Nov. '86 issue of FREESTYLIN' magazine. I'd like to express a BIG thank you to my friend Andy Jenkins, Lew, and the rest of the WIZ PUBS staff for giving me the chance to contribute to FREESTYLIN' and for directly inspiring me, in turn, to continue contributing to this fine sport.

    Readers, feel free to drop me a line about your scene and send any photos, drawings, stories, etc. It's YOU guys out there who I'm doin' this for! Thanks again for your support. Keep the Faith.....

MUMBO JUMBO By Michael Daily

Is **Hutch** going out of business? Probably not, but they had to let pro **Woody Itson** and 16& Over expert **Rick Moliterno** go from the freestyle team. **Woody** went to team **Diamond Back** to join old **Hutch** teammate **Michael Dominguez**. Yeah! With these two together again you can EXPECT to see radical results! **Rick** signed up with **Haro** shortly after the Long Island contest elsewhere in this issue. Rumor has it that **Karl Rothe** is on **Mongoose**. Oh, and could it be true that 2 of the **Plywood Hoods**, who work at a truck unloading company together, had to unload NUMEROUS boxes of **Hutch** parts destined for somewhere in New York? Is **Hutch** selling out its inventory? Hmmmmm...

HOT NEWS FLASH!- Results from the Freestyle Masters Finals just in-McCoy won Pro Ground and Pro Overall (Again!)-Dominguez won Pro Ramps (Also Again!)-You'll see it all in the Aggro one next issue!

1. Start with left pedal forward.

Here's a fast, moderately difficult, contorted, boomerang-type trick which Kevin Jones made up one day. Learning it may just trigger some originality of your own. Don't hot dog it though. Adorn appropriate clothing until you master it.

A NEW TRICK:
the BOOMER dog...

2. Apply front brake and kind of do a can can boomerang landing the right foot on tire.

3. Try to keep your body facing forward. Step on the pedal with left foot and.....

bY tHE "K"

4. Swiftly release brake, push the tire with right foot, and leap off the pedal.

5. Land correctly back on the pedal and ride out of it allowing a little rotation to occur.

Photos by Daily

SOME Skankin' ArtWork...

Submitted by: Sammy Lee, Plainview, NY

The DALE'S MAIL

ACTUAL LETTERS FROM ACTUAL READERS...

WHAT A DECKHEAD
Mike Daily,
  Here's a stamp for the new Aggro Rag. And later I'll send you a copy of my skate rag, Deckhead Zine.
  Rob "Devo" Ayers
  Springfield, IL

WHAT THE.....?
Hey Mike,
  Today I was sick (bummer), so I decided to write you a letter about your mag. It's a good thing that you have skaters in it because I'm a freestyler and I don't want to have them be my enemy. Keep up the great freestyle coverage.
  Matt Bachman
  Minn., MN

SUPER HEROES
Howzit goin' Mike?
  I would have written sooner but I spend all my time doing school work (blah!) or ridin' (yeah!). Your new issue lived up to its name. ALL the articles were good- especially "Air at Brian's" and "Fidging." I'm definitely going to catch the CW show next year.
  Speaking of shows, when we were on vacation this summer I caught a Captain America show (August '86) at Seattle Center in Seattle (duh!), Washington. Todd Schneider, James Stanfield, Brian Hart, and a 15 year old freestyle skater Cameron somebody. These guys were GOOD. Todd was

(CONTINUED)

7

pullin' airs and Cameron's footwork on that board was UNREAL! They were doin' can-can squeakers, seatgrinds, surfers, and gut levers. It was for a kid's fair so the crowd consisted mostly of little kids and their mommies. Some girl next to me said to her mom, "How can he ride with one hand?" It was way rad anyway. Oh! Andrejs Zommers announced. So until we meet again, stay aggro.

   Later on,
   Alex Greenblatt
   Paoli, PA

FISH MAN
Dear Mike,
  Your Aggro Rag TOTALLY shreds! I love it! There is two bucks enclosed. Please send me the next two issues as soon as you can. I was at that very CW show. I have the Slingshot almost down pat. Did you see the GT/Brittania tour? It was sano. My friends think your mag rules too.

   Frank Stark
   Lonaconing, MD

BOY OF A FEW WORDS
Dear Mike,
  Please send me an issue of Aggro Rag. Before it ruled. It still does.

   Thanks,
   Matt Imenheiser
   York, PA

P.S. - I've seen one of your shows-sooo killer. I like Kevin Jones too.

HOT CHILLY
Hey, this is Chilly. You said you were gonna send me a postcard when your next zine is ready.

   Chilly Dray "T"
   Belle Glade, Fla.

*Chill dude! I know it's been awhile since my last issue but Aggro Rag is a one-man operation here. I do the type-set, layout, paste-up, printing, and just about everything. And I try to make every issue count, you know? I really appreciate all the support **Freestylin'** and the underground has given me. Just hang loose, and you won't be disappointed....*
   - Daily

aggro raG
made in U.S.A

Shown Actual Size
Official Stickers!
10 for 1 buck
10¢ ea.
PLYWOOD
Trick Team
HOODS
PH Round
AGGRO RAG
FREESTYLE MAG!
JUNK
AR Pharmacist
AGGRO RAG
FREESTYLE MAG!
AR Yuppy
aggro
raG
made in U.S.A
AR Da Fuzz
FREESTYLE
PLYWOOD
HOODS
TEAM
PH Logo
AGGRO RAG
FREESTYLE MAG!
AR Big
AGGRO RAG
FREESTYLE MAG!
AR Small

AFA Masters Series

LONG ISLAND

Coverage by Mark "Lungmustard" Eaton

Photos by Dale Mitzel

AGGRO RAG FREESTYLE MAG!

Mark Wales-Photo

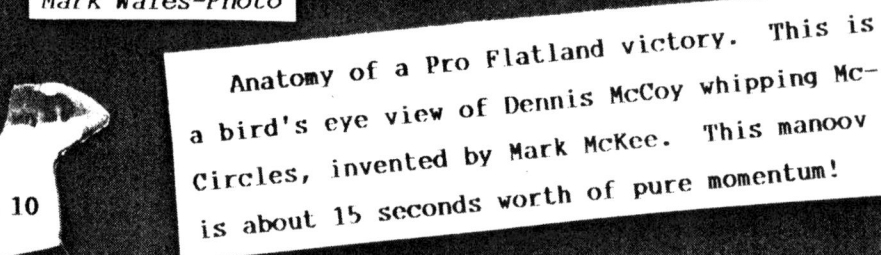

Anatomy of a Pro Flatland victory. This is a bird's eye view of Dennis McCoy whipping Mc-Circles, invented by Mark McKee. This manoov is about 15 seconds worth of pure momentum!

10

HIGHLIGHTS
of a hood

A crazy ramp guy with a foam shark on his helmet was making the crowd scream when Skyway pro Hugo Gonzales took notice. Hugo, with Tuff Wheel in hand, turned to Dizz after the kid's routine and said, *"He's nothin!"*

"When there's a circle of guys ridin', 90% of the riders is him!"- Kevin Jones referring to Dennis McCoy

I saw the Ray Meyer freestyle board and the graphics are great.

All of the Haro boys were runnin' around the hotel. Later, Wilko, Blyther, and Joe Johnson came to our hotel room to try and jump off the balcony to go swimming. It was right over the indoor pool but it was too high.

I also had the chance to see the GTV video. The tricks were totally great but the story of it was lame.

Saturday night we went riding around the hotel. There was a coliseum right next to it which was shredable. Dave Nourie and Jason Parkes were hittin' tricks so we rode with them. Nourie has his Mega Trick stuff dialed. And Jason Parkes can string tricks together like you wouldn't believe.

"Man, you guys talk like, 'Wow! It's like totally tubular dude!'"- N.Y.C. locals to the Plywood Hoods.

The pro class featured twenty of the hardest hitters in the sport today. The count for the experts alone was over sixty riders. Talent in the novice and intermediate classes is surprising today. The numbers are getting higher and the riders keep getting radder.

In the 14-15 expert class, Scott Freeman hit a flawless routine and didn't touch the ground once. Scotty pulls some of the hardest moves in the sport. Special note must go out to General's Brian Belcher-he shredded.

The 16 & Over flatland division was chock full of some of the most exciting amateurs in the world: Rick Moliterno, John "Dizz" Hicks, Ceppie Maes, Jason Parkes, and Gary Pollak.

Lungmustard, the key informant of this article, showboatin' a cherrypicker to a 6th place in 16 & Over Novice.

Continued on page 14

ZINE ALeRT!

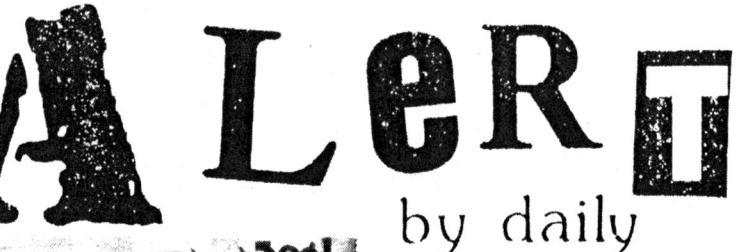

by daily

Rad Zone
865 McAdoo
Blackfoot, Idaho 83221

Freestylers/Skaters Dan, Larry, and Scott Nelson combine outrageous trick how-tos with lots of cool photos to form Rad Zone. In scanning Rad Zone, one quickly gets the idea that these guys are GOOD. No pose shots here, buddy. The best features are by far the depicted new moves the Nelson brothers show how to do. Issue #2 has a how-to page on the Edge Wheelie, a cranking Power Mower type move. Tough stuff. Also in #2 is a detailed account of a Haro show, a skate jam, and more. A must for new trick enthusiasts. 50 cents.

SHRED
70 Gainsborough Rd.
Holbrook, NY 11741

Great half-toned photos and entertaining contents make SHRED one of the best privately-published mags today. The current issue has extensive Long Island AFA Masters coverage, interviews with Dizz and Neil Blender, and more. Very hip to the active New York skate and bike scene. One smacker.

A zine can include <u>anything</u>. Most have action photos, creative literature, and all the latest local info. Zines alert other hardcore freestylers and skaters to your underground scene. This section deals with a few of the best now circulating....

Rip Zine
P.O. Box
Nowhere, USA 00000

A carefully prepared zine heavily influenced by music, skating, and weirdness. Mel, Dewbag, Mo/Scuz, and Dangerman are the beings responsible for its unique contents. Humorous writing is plentiful, especially in "A Big City"- "Soon a colony of bums surrounded us and started sneezing and demanded we do the same." Also included in their first issue are show reviews of the Cure, Black Flag, and more. Rip Zine has a selective mailing list. So how do you request a copy? You don't.

Asphalt Action
2723 Quakerbridge Rd.
Mercerville, NJ 08619

Tom VanGrofski and Brian DeLorenzo are the scoot journalists behind this one. Their latest mini-mag contains an in-depth report of the Madison Square Gardens/General AFA Masters comp, as well as lots of local PA AFA contest info. Product evaluations, a High Voltage Trick Team tour article, and computer graphics round out issue #5 quite nicely. $1.00.

AFA Masters Contest

Photo by Mark Wales

Long Island

The premier Plywood Hood, Kevin Jones, managed to tie CW's Greg Kove in 16 & Over Expert even with a completely blown run. Here, The "K" demonstrates his Hang Glider boomerang.

Continued from page 11

Rick Moliterno produced a flawless run which ended with a remarkable double vertical boomerang. First Place.

Gary Pollak unveiled his ripping new double Fire Hydrant which was good for a second after a tie-breaker with CW teammate Dizz. Gary rides with an almost unmatched intensity and is sure to be a strong contender in the future. He is also extremely versatile, riding both ground and ramps VERY well.

Dizzaster captured the crowd's eye with his spastic flatland follies and even had many of the pros screaming for him! His full bore style at full speed secured him third place.

Other expert notables were former Ultra Rad-sters Kenneth Evans and Denny Howell with some INCREDIBLE routines. When Denny was practicing his seemingly impossible no-handed constant bar-spinning backwards infinity roll, Martin Aparijo was heard to exclaim, *"How's he doing that?!"* Kenneth tied Ceppie after some dazzling moves of his own. They are more dialed than ever before.

Haro's Dennis McCoy topped the pro flatlanders with, not simply tricks, but an amazing series of rapidly executed routines. McCoy's new moves are strung together in an unbelievable fashion, and he has the ability to do decades at will from any position! *"McCoy is The Man."*- Kev

Martin took second with his uncanny smoothness, R.L. snagged a third, and fourth went to Woody Itson. All of the pros' runs were smooth, exciting, and unmistakably professional.

Pro ramps saw a revitalized Michael Dominguez push ten foot aerials with ease and crank an impressive array of variations for 1st. Fiola, Anderson, Blyther, and Wilkerson also gave skilled performances in the air. Wilko hit an impressive no-handed fakie air. McCoy won the overall.

Hugo Gonzales exhibited THE highlight of the Pro Air classification: An insane quarterpipe to trick ramp lookback air covering MUCHO distance! At first, Hugo was met with resistance from AFA officials but that didn't stop him. Does it ever?! *

PRO:AM Stars...

Above— At first, Todd Anderson didn't want to ride ramps but R.L. persuaded him by putting Todd's Redline in the middle of the arena. That was all the persuasion Todd needed in order to get 5th in style. Left— Dino DeLuca hung tough and looked as good as usual with his sick can can variations and hefty airs. 3rd in 16& Over X.

New York

> To air like this is **NOT** human. Dominguez showin' everyone that he still can- and then some. High 540's, aggro lookbacks, and just plain *radness* helped Michael prevail in Pro Ramps.

Pro Air *Pro Air* *Pro Air*

> Brian Blyther rode like a champ. He was awarded second place smackers after daring feats like this fully boned fully whipped lookback aerial.

Pro Air *Pro Air* *Pro Air*

WHO'S AGGRO

A Closer Look at KRYS!

Ohio's Krys Dauchy gettin' flexible. Krys surprised A LOT of people when she pulled out her *dialed* routine. NOT just another Betty!!

Besides being one *hot* lookin' babe, Krys Dauchy is a great freestyler! She was good enough to take second place in 14-15 Novice Flatland beating a LOT of embarrassed guys! Who said freestyle was only a man's sport?! Krys does some way rad Nourie Handstands in addition to pedal to pedal boomerangs, the Dance of Doom, and Miami Hoppers! Way to go, Krys!!

Photos by Mark Wales

HOLDING YER OWN FREESTYLE

AGGRO RAG FREESTYLE MAG!

FEATURE ARTICLE

AFA — AMERICAN FREESTYLE ASSOCIATION

CoNtEsTs...

Mario Salas is a teen from King of Prussia, PA who organizes and holds his own contests. And with much success. A sizable population of great freestylers hail from King of Prussia, and with enterprising guys like Mario around, their scene continues to strengthen. The following interview was conducted by Brett Downs at the home of this interesting young lad.....

Photo by Brett Downs

An interview by Philly correspondant Brett Downs

Mario, how old are you? "Sixteen." **We hear you're doing some work setting up contests...** "Yeah, I just got off the phone with Steve Rulli last night. By the way, for Aggro Rag, there's a Madison Square Gardens Part II comin' up in the summer- he told me about that. He and I are gonna have a contest in December in New Jersey. It's gonna be at a 4-H complex up in Brigantine, NJ." **Why did you start having these comps? Weren't there enough around?** "No, there weren't. Almost a year ago, back in November, we were all getting really excited about contests and the NFA just started back then. We were all getting ready to go to the big NFA contest in January. Then we heard it was cancelled..." **Was that at Timonium?** "Yeah. We heard it was cancelled but it really wasn't." **Yeah, Mike was there...** "So then I just called Ron Stebenne up in Mass. and I asked him about havin' a contest. He was like 'If you're really serious about it you'll do your own, and just call me back and forth for help and all.' So I took it from there and organized one that we had March 8th. And that went pretty good. We worked with Charlie Huber on that one. I got a lot of attention for it. A lot of stuff happened from there. I got a lot of shows goin'. So we just decided to have another one..." **How do they run? Do they generally have a good turn-out?** The first one was a surprise. We were thinkin' maybe 40 riders ya know? But we got up to around 80 riders and a lot of spectators. The place was packed. It was a school gym 'cause we didn't think there would be that many people. And after awhile it was packed." **Do you have trophies and everything?** "Yeah, we had pretty much lame...There's a 1st place trophy (Shows a small trophy). Charlie Huber is in charge of that. That's a 1st place trophy...! **Charlie's the bike shop Mike got first place at. Remember the cruddy trophy you got, Mike?** Yeah, I guess he understands. Well, he knows about Charlie... Right Mike? *(Editor's Note: It should be known that Mario lost a LARGE amount of money at his first contest.)* **Don't you feel stupid talking to Mike like he's a box here?** "Pretty much, yeah. He's probably laughin' right now! But, ummm, it ran smooth. We had a team trophy-that got broken though. We had a ¼-pipe, wedge, everything was fine except for...judging. That was probably the worst thing. **How do you get ramps to the**

Continued next page 19

competitions? We used to use Gary's. Gary (Pollak) had an 8-foot high, 6-foot wide portable one. And then that one got thrashed so he built a permanent one. Right now we're worried about that. We'll probably use General's at the contest in December. **How do you get places to have your comps? You said you did one at the gym at school. How do you go about that?** "Well, the easiest thing to do is tell 'em you're with the Boy Scouts. Did you ever see the BSA emblem on AFA stuff?" Yeah. Well, they have the insurance for the AFA. The school was a little sketchy on lettin' us use it then they heard the Explorers were with it. So they let us in for free. We didn't pay anything. They had lights on, heat on- everything was perfect." **What advice would you have for other people who wanted to start doing competitions?** "Use your head. Don't give up. It's really hard. If you're a kid, it's gonna be almost impossible to have a contest. I was lucky I think. I got a lot of help from a lot of different people. Just keep trying." **Do you have anything else you wanna say?** "Ummm...just, if anybody's gonna freestyle- Stick with it, and have fun. That's all. Get Rad." **That's great...** "Eat green jello." Eat green jello? "Exactly. Mike'll know. On Wednesdays." Yeah, Mike'll do that. **Thanks!** *

KOP Rips

King of Prussian Gary Pollak flingin' an airwalk back in his privateering days before CW. Photo taken at the Northeast Freestyle Championships in the summer of '85 by Chris Daily. Gary's come a long way since then and next issue we'll have a full-on interview and photo spread. King of Prussia is a definite hot spot!

Hood Conversions....

The "K" and Lungmustard showin' how it's done: Skate style.

The "K" directs skate and body in form off the top corner of the Green Bowl vertical extension. Kev did NOT just start skating. Thunderdohm before the bulldozing effect...

Plywood Hood Mark Eaton tears like hell in pools, on ramps, and in the street on a skateboard. Recently, three to four foot airs were reported, and that's not all. Here he touches tile in a local drained oval pool.

21

AGGRO RAG FREESTYLE MAG!

Hey! This is **WILD WEAR!** by Daily

CWCCC SHIRT

Dizz and Ceppie, freestyle's most deranged duo, now have their own official CW shirt complete with cool artwork and a rad 3-color design. These skankers are available from California Condor Collection and served as the tour graphics for the CW Back to School Bash.

TEAM OAK STREET STUFF

Team Oak Street apparel is happenin' with a full line of hot tees, tanks, and sweats. Get into style the Chicago way by adorning these way cool designs at cheap prices- a poultry $15 for a long sleeved sweatshirt (pictured), $8 for a tank, and $9 for a T-Shirt. More info? *Write: TOS, 1522 Rosedale Ln., Hoffman Estates, IL 60195.*

A Trick Contest

A TRICK CONTEST

This contest was designed for those readers who innovate some RAD tricks but never get the recognition they deserve. How would you like to see yourself and your best, _original_ maneuver in the pages of Aggro Rag AND have a chance to win some qual prizes? Read on...!

Rules:

1) Pictures may be color or black and white.

2) Sequencial shots (better) or stills are accepted.

3) No posing! C'mon, guys, be honest! We want to see tricks you can _pull off_.

4) Raddest (not necessarily the hardest) tricks win prizes.

SEND TO: Aggro Rag, A Trick Contest, 3320 Spondin Drive, York, PA 17402

1st Place- Pair of Pacific Palms gloves. Red-Medium. _Donated by CW Racing._

2nd Place- Pair ODI Mushroom II grips. Blue. _Courtesy of Ornate Design, Inc._

Plywood Hoods team members are not eligible.

Deadline: March 1, 1987

AGGRO RAG
FREESTYLE MAG.

HOME
Mike Daily
3320 Spondin Drive
York, PA 17402

SCHOOL
Mike Daily
Box 402 A North Hall
Lock Haven University
Lock Haven, PA 17445

(717) 893-3582

MUSHROOMS

AGGRO RAG FREESTYLE MAG!
(March 1987)
York, PA/Lock Haven, PA
5½" x 8¼"

8th ISSUE

King of Prussia, PA, rider Dave Pak somehow convinced his parents to let him miss Thanksgiving '86 so he could attend the AFA Masters Finals at the Dominguez Hills Velodrome in SoCal with friend and factory CW flatland/ramp star, Gary Pollak. Dave wrote about the experience in the eighth issue of *Aggro Rag Freestyle Mag!*

Mike Daily: In "The Velodrome Finale" article for this issue, you wrote, "Chris Day was incredible. His style is so fast and flowing. He is definitely a force to be reckoned with at any contest he attends. Eleventh in 16 and Over ground."

Dave Pak: Okay.

Somebody that amazing getting eleventh? Man, the competition was pretty fierce.

Yeah, definitely. I remember Karl Rothe's run. That was so fun to watch. I don't think he won. I think he got second or third. The kid who won—I didn't see his run but I saw it on video later—I forget his name[11]—I think he was from Texas—I remember it being a smooth run. He probably didn't touch or anything like that. But you watch Karl's run at that contest, he was such a ham and he was just pulling everything. It was good.

Who could have known that someday **Lungmustard** and **Pinky** would battle? Ohio '87.

Gary [Pollak] was like that—he would always manage to place really high and ride like Dennis [McCoy] and have that kind of…

[Loud fire engine siren.] Hold on, there's a fire truck outside. [Truck passes.] Sorry. What was that last part?

I was saying something about Gary and fire hydrants.[12]

[Laughs.]

---

[11] Reynaldo Santillian.

[12] Gary Pollak invented the fire hydrant (rolling tailwhip into cherrypicker), one of the first combo tricks in flatland freestyle.

Gary always did great in ground and ramps. Did you feel like you kind of had an "in" because you knew Gary and you were part of the King of Prussia crew?

Yeah, I definitely think so. That was pretty much all we did: Get home from school and ride our bikes over to Gary's and usually practice for an hour or two, and then we'd go back down to our high school and ride down there and screw around for another hour or so. It was fun. There were so many different things about it. I don't know if I'm addressing the exact question, but we were always riding together during that time. It was like every day. On Fridays, it would be the same thing except after we were done, we would go home and eat dinner and then come back out and decide what we were gonna do. We'd end up riding our bikes at the mall—usually involving some kind of problem. It would always start out like we were kind of minding our own business, and then inevitably a car would come by with like a couple guys in it and they'd yell something. Gary was always the one who would always yell back. He enjoyed getting into chases with people because he was never gonna get caught. That was like the whole thing: His ability on a bike…if he needed to bunnyhop over something that was higher for most of us, he would be able to do it and the rest of us would have to scatter in the right direction. We never really got caught by anybody. Or mall security would chase us around and we knew they weren't really gonna do much. Years later, we ran into one of those security guards that used to chase us, and he gave us some back-story. He said: "We just used to look out for you guys because it was so much fun chasin' you around!"

That's like the movie *Rad* almost, with the cop on the motorcycle.

[Laughs.] Yeah, it was fun. The contest part of it was cool because Gary was a top Expert in the country, so he was sponsored obviously and went to all the contests. He would come back and he would be doing all these tricks that he'd seen. So instead of waiting two months to see the newest tricks, you could actually see something ahead of time. So that was always really awesome. He would give us the contest run-down, like who won and who didn't win. He would usually get back to school first thing on Monday, so it was always like just waiting for him to be there that Monday to tell you what happened.

I asked Gary about "rogue-ing" and he just put it all off on Dennis.

Sounds like a typical Gary response. That's what was really weird, too: When Gary and Dennis first met, you could tell there was a mutual respect right away for one another. They were both similar-type riders: They both rode ramps, they both rode flatland and they were both very good in their classes. Gary always liked street riding and stuff, too. They were really similar in a lot of ways. Gary was definitely an instigator. I don't really know Dennis that well personally, but I think he did bring the term "rogue-ing" into play.

What do you remember about going to the '86 Velodrome contest?

The big highlight was Dennis McCoy. I remember callin' Ray [Schlechtweg] right after the run-off. Dennis rode to "My Generation" by The Who. At the time, Ray would have been the only one who would've flipped out over that because he was always kind of crazy about The Who. Dennis just clearly annihilated. I think that was the real "test" point for Dennis to be like a huge dude on flatland. Hangin' out with Ceppie and Dizz was a major highlight. And the Nor Cal guys—we had never seen Aaron Dull and he was doin' funky chickens, and that was the first time I'd ever seen that trick. I was just like, "What the hell is that?" It was like a Shingle shuffle with your back wheel off the ground. We went to The Spot and saw Chris Day ride for the first time. That was kind of a mind-fuck at the time. It was like, "Holy shit, this guy is really good!" I missed his actual run at the contest, but I saw him plenty at The Spot and it was nuts.

AGGRO RAG
FREESTYLE MAG!

"Ride First, Read Later."

$1

March 1987
Volume 2 Number 7

NSA BLOW OUT!

Interview with
GARY POLLAK

DICK ISSUE!

Velodrome Finale

NEW HOW-TO:
Tagsanity Hops

AGGRO RAG
FREESTYLE MAG!

"Ride First, Read Later."

Mike Daily
3320 Spondin Drive
York, PA 17402
(717) 757-3096

March 1987
Volume 2 Number 7

Official Raggers

Editor
Mike Daily

Design/Layout
Mike Daily

Contributors
Art Abasolo
Brett Downs
Andy Jenkins
Lew
Lungmustard
Drew Moore
Dave Pak

Trick Consultant
The K

ON THE COVER: Gary Pollak with a fully-twisted lookback. Photo by Brett Downs. Top right: Christian Hosoi blowing minds at the NSA Blow Out contest in Chicago, Illinois. Photo by Art Abasolo. Lower left: Dick Van Patten, straining.....

"It really turns on the betties!!"

GET THE <u>RIGHT</u> SPRAY...

- Denny Howell
16 & Over Expert
Factory SE Racing

SE Racing RIGHT GUARD...
"Our bikes don't stink, but our riders sometimes do!"

Recently SE Racing struck up a deal with RIGHT GUARD to start producing their own deodorant! SE had been testing prototype roll-ons for months and they finally came up with a compound suitable for keeping freestylers smelling good even after the most grueling contest situations. Rumor has it that Fred Blood was kicked off SE because he was caught endorsing Mennen Speed Stick. Other bike companies are jumping on the cosmetics bandwagon as well: GT has been quietly testing a foot powder and Haro will introduce their new aftershave in the coming months. General is supposedly coming out with a new mouthwash also. Look wherever fine toiletries are sold. Tell 'em the AGGRO one sent ya!

Son, I think it's time we had a little talk...

AGGRO RAG FREESTYLE MAG!

AGGRO RAG FREESTYLE MAG! MUMBO

Jim Johnson, our cover rider last issue, scammed a full factory ride from **Schwinn**. Another native New Yorker who has earned a major ride is none other than **Joe Gruttola**, now on **Haro**. Joe does a <u>clean</u> backwards bar ride and has been seen trying BACKWARDS vertical boomerangs! Now, **El Cid** is pulling backwards Rubber Rides, the same basic trick as Joe's, except R.L. stands on his grips. **Pete Augustin**, **Tim Rogers**, and **Marc McGlynn** have been picked up by **CW Racing**. **Dino Deluca** is back on **Dyno** and has signed a two-year contract. Dyno just sent him to London. Insiders say Dino is blazin' better than ever. **Robert Peterson** is now on **Schwinn**, as **Oleg**, **Maurice**, **Hugo**, and **Roman** depart from **Skyway** in search of new sponsors. **Scotty Freeman** and **Matt Hoffman** remain on the traveling team.

Dino's back on DYNO.

Jim Johnson is now bar ridin' for Schwinn.

*special thanks to dewbag for the team scoops!

jUMBO by dailY...

Mario Salas is puttin' together another independent contest slated for April 11, 1987. The location of the event is still being worked out but it <u>will</u> be held somewhere in King of Prussia, PA. **General Bicycles** will sponsor the contest. Give ol' Mar a call at (215) 265-9173 for the latest developments.

CALL NOW... **1·800·CEP·DIGS**

<u>C</u>W....<u>C</u>eppie <u>W</u>orks????

The one and only Ceppie Maes is no longer on CW. Cep reportedly wasn't receiving enough income from CW Racing in order to support himself so he quit and took on a full time job- as a building contractor! Don't worry though, Creepy is still assaulting the environment on bike <u>and</u> skate, and maybe even back hoes. Watch for him to start testing for FREESTYLIN'...

WHO'S AGGRO!

KENNETH EVANS

Step One- Throw on a wool sweater. Or maybe just 50/50 polyester blend. Oh yeah do some rocket hops.

Step Two- Lock lever and swing bike in a forward motion after removing left foot and hands (or something like that).

Step Three- Try to end up in this position, preferably hopping and smiling. Outstretched arm is optional.

He's aggro. Originality can be expected from his riding. He's from Elizabeth City, NC and doesn't think twice about driving the whole way to Howard County, MD for simply a local contest. He hard core. Kenneth Evans. I saw him this past December again at an AFA event at Howard County. It was only a year earlier at this same place that I had interviewed a very promising-looking trick team called Ultra Rad.

Kenneth is still riding for Hutch and Ultra Rad.

ROCKET HOPS TO MEGA TRICK TRANSFER

AGGRO RAG FREESTYLE MAG!

← the dale

Stupid Letter of the Month

INFESTED
Dear Mike,
    I was wondering if you could tell me which way I should turn when I do an aerial. I ride with my left foot forward and right foot back. If I would turn to the left I would do airs like Robert Peterson, but if I would turn to the right I would do airs like Dave Nourie. But if I would go to the left I could do can can airs like Tony Murray but then I would need a coaster brake and then I couldn't do track stands and posers as easy. What should I do? Should I start racing? Or should I learn how to build a quarter pipe?
                Sore and Confused,
                Fester
                No given address

Fester-
    Get a skateboard.
                -The Dale

This issue of Aggro Rag is completely dedicated to actor Dick Van Patten. Dick was a regular on the hit TV series "Eight is Enough," and has appeared sporadically on such critically acclaimed programs as "Love Boat" and "Hollywood Squares." Congratulations dick.

THANK LEW...

Mark Lewman, in his continuous quest to reach for a new perspective, glides back in order to advance. Backwards Rocket Wheelie. LA, California.

The sheer challenge of a ramp-to-ramp fakie stall intrigues one industrious individual in the form of Shinglehead. Kalamazoo, Michigan. Summer of '85

Silhouette of a double can can air at height.

PINKY SPEAKS

A closer look at CW's Gary Pollak...

GARY POLLAK
Interview

Gary-Rockville BMX

Some kind of wild glide

Most photos by Brett Downs

Gary on his toes.

MAVERICK: So what's your full name?
GARY: Gary RL Pollak.
MAVERICK: And how old are you?
GARY: Sixteen.
MAVERICK: Why did you start freestyling?
GARY: I used to race. I started racing when I was seven. I got bored with it when I was thirteen and Scott Guarna and Mike Cutillo got me into it. So I just started freestyling.
MAVERICK: Past sponsors?
GARY: Just Suburban Cyclery.
MAVERICK: How did you get picked up by CW?
GARY: Well, they (CW) had a show in Scranton, PA and we followed 'em for about a week. McGoo, Mike Buff, Ceppie, and Dizz were all lookin' at me, like, 'Yeah, maybe we should pick this guy up.' I wasn't too sure at the time 'cause Haro was lookin' at me too. But then, at Huntington Beach, two months later, I did really good and they said to give 'em a call. So I called and I talked to McGoo and they just started sending me stuff. And now I'm fully sponsored.

Backwards rolling handstands are cake for this guy. Gary was holdin' these babies for some lengthy distances...

Gary juices his way to a third in 14-15 Expert Ramps. Picture taken at Madison Square Garden by Dale Mitzel.

MAVERICK: Who are your co-sponsors?
GARY: A'ME, Odyssey, Echo, DK, Condor, and Vans.
MAVERICK: What is your favorite trick?
GARY: Pinky Squeaks.
MAVERICK: What do you like better- ground or ramps?
GARY: Both (Laughter).
MAVERICK: Who are your favorite riders?
GARY: Dennis McCoy, Ron Wilkerson, Martin Aparijo, and Billy.
MAVERICK: What was your best contest placing?
GARY: Probably Ohio. That was my best 'cause I did my routine pretty much flawlessly.
MAVERICK: Did you tour last year?
GARY: Yeah, all summer with CW. About two and a half months. All over the United States.
MAVERICK: How long have you been riding with CW?
GARY: About a year now.
MAVERICK: Do you plan on

One footed invert high atop "The Wall."

staying with them?

GARY: Yeah.

MAVERICK: Do you get a salary?

GARY: No, they're just starting to work that out now. It'll be worked out in a couple of months.

MAVERICK: What is your favorite food?

GARY: Cheese steaks with extra cheese-NO lettuce or onions.

MAVERICK: Out of all the places you've been, where have been the best and worst girls?

GARY: The best were in Madison, Wisconsin and the worst were in...Colorado.

MAVERICK: What advice do you have for others?

GARY: Practice all the time and don't just practice seriously before a contest- practice ALL the time seriously. And try to be smooth on your tricks.

MAVERICK: One last question- Are there any people around who think you're like, God?

GARY: Not really. Oh yeah, except for one- this kid in school. We call him boner (Laughter). *

"Cheese steaks with extra cheese- NO lettuce or onions."

Can you tell Gary has toured with Dizz? Naaaa... Spinning Wheels bank sesh.

CLUB HOMEBOY

club homeboy

Club Homeboy...Members Only?

I get a fair amount of zines in the mail nowadays which is cool. Checkin' out different scenes via zeroxed literature is a total hype-factor. I love it. Occasionally, I'll get a rag which really stands out- perhaps due to its hip undergroundish flavoring or just because you KNOW that whoever makes it ain't playin' games. The kind of rag not concerned with commercialism or censorship. If you're serious, <u>that's</u> the type zine you'll want to obtain.

Homeboy is one of these such efforts. It comes from the Hermosa Beach area and includes mostly hardcore biking material (<u>Cool.</u>) judging from the premier issue I was sent. Homeboy is written in a very humorous fashion which is immediately evident in the editorial- "Okay, enough bullshit. Go steal some wood for a ramp or something." Lots of action photos also, with a cool report on the Spot.

If you ever, by chance, encounter a copy of Homeboy, scam on it pronto. I'm not going to print the address. If you're not a dick and if you want it badly enough, you should be able to find it...

— M. Daily

CAN YOU HANDLE IT?

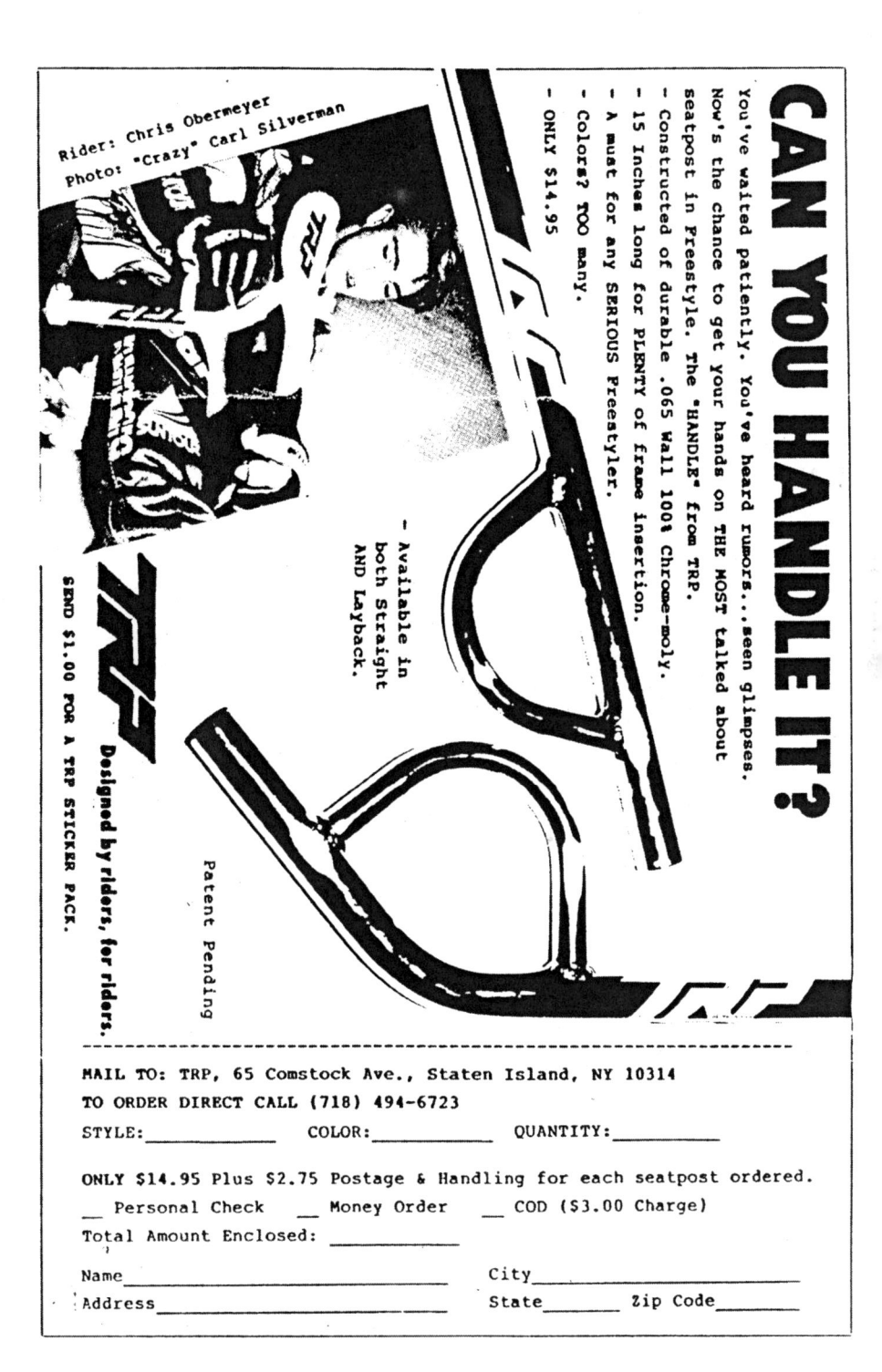

You've waited patiently. You've heard rumors...seen glimpses. Now's the chance to get your hands on THE MOST talked about seatpost in Freestyle. The "HANDLE" from TRP.
- Constructed of durable .065 Wall 100% Chrome-moly.
- 15 Inches long for PLENTY of frame insertion.
- A must for any SERIOUS Freestyler.
- Colors? TOO many.
- ONLY $14.95

Rider: Chris Obermeyer
Photo: "Crazy" Carl Silverman

- Available in both Straight AND Layback.

Patent Pending

Designed by riders, for riders.

SEND $1.00 FOR A TRP STICKER PACK.

MAIL TO: TRP, 65 Comstock Ave., Staten Island, NY 10314
TO ORDER DIRECT CALL (718) 494-6723
STYLE:_____ COLOR:_____ QUANTITY:_____

ONLY $14.95 Plus $2.75 Postage & Handling for each seatpost ordered.
__ Personal Check __ Money Order __ COD ($3.00 Charge)
Total Amount Enclosed: _____

Name_____ City_____
Address_____ State_____ Zip Code_____

BY DAVE PAK...
the VELODROME
finale

Dennis McCoy, Haro's Kansas City sensation, can hang with the best of 'em when it comes to air. Can can at eight feet.

This was it. Gary Pollak and I were finally on our way to California after many days of waiting. We were stationed over at McGoo's place for a week of adventure that was highlighted, at the end, by the AFA Masters Series Finals at the Velodrome in Dominguez Hills, California.

Saturday's action was hot. The novices and intermediates are getting better at each contest. However, more eyes seemed to be focused on the shred circles formed by the experts and pros.

Sunday's festivities were no doubt what everyone had been looking forward to and there were many surprises in store. Here are some of the highlights from Sunday's event....

* Robbie Van Patten was blasting six feet of air in the 13 and Under Expert class which gave him the win.
* There were some David Lee Roth look-alikes who entered. I think one was Colorado's Chuck Johnson.
* Joe Gruttola from New York totally rips. He won 14-15 Expert ground with the help of a perfect backwards bar ride. It was insane to say the least.

* Aaron Dull took second in 14-15 Expert ground. Besides having plenty of originality, he also has the most bizarre haircut.
* Skyway's Scotty Freeman adopted the Martin Aparijo style of riding for the contest but he had to settle for fourth this time.
* Kuwahara's Tim Rogers took the win in the 14-15 X ramp class beating the incredible Matt Hoffman of team Skyway.
* Brian Belcher of General took the 14-15 Expert Overall title for the contest and the year. Good job, Brian!
* Adam Jung of Hawaii and Kevin Jones of Pennsylvania are probably the most original amateurs in freestyle. Adam took eighth (Have you ever seen I-Hop handstands?!) and Kevin tied Chris Day of Dyno for eleventh in a class of about 60 riders.
* Renaldo Santillian, from Texas, surprised a lot of people by winning the 16 & Over Expert ground class which is NOT an easy task.
* Karl Rothe blazed to a second in 16 and Over Expert ground. He is incredible and fun to watch.
* Larry Manayan's routine was well choreographed and was well rewarded with a third in 16 and Over ground.
* Chris Day was incredible. His style is so fast and flowing. He is definitely a force to be reckoned with at any contest he attends. Eleventh in 16 and Over ground.
* I saw freestyle veterans Mike Buff and Donovan Ritter in the stands.
* Joe Johnson (Haro) aborted an aerial at around eight feet high but luckily he wasn't injured.
*Josh White shredded ramps and took the win- Again! Josh also took the 16 and Over Expert Overall title for the year.
* Dizz got his bike stolen after his ground run which forced him to miss ramps.
* Dino Deluca rode without a sponsor in the contest but it didn't affect his ramp riding at all. Second in 16 & Over X Ramps.
* And then there were the pros. Haro's Dennis McCoy and General's R.L. Osborn both pulled off phenomenal routines and in the process tied for first place. In the one minute run-off, "The Real McCoy" prevailed and El Cid had to settle for second.
* Woody Itson, in his new black and grey DB duds, turned in a fine routine and grabbed third. Mongoose's Rick Allison and GT's Martin Aparijo clinched the fourth and fifth places respectively.
* The Pro Ramps class saw Dennis McCoy execute one of his finest ramp routines ever which was good for third. Flyin' Brian Blyther (Haro) pulled off a clean second with his usual controlled lunacy.
* Mike Dominguez was unbelievable. He did some insane variations which had the crowd ROARING. And then he ended his run with a high 540 OVER THE CANYON! Yeah, he won...
* Dennis McCoy took the overall for the finals and the year. Congrats, Dennis!

...and now the version of Lungmustard.

"Well guys, it's time for me to go home and watch 'Shred with Fred.' Maybe I can learn the 'Chocolate Swirl.'" **Eddie Fiola to Brian Belcher.**

Eaton: Hang Glider at Redondo Beach.

Kev: Bar strandin'

Reactions from Kev's Uptight "K" Wheelie and just general Kev-comments...

"What do you do-sit around and think of tricks all day?"- Dave Nourie

"Wow! Way rad!"- El Cid

"Hey, I saw you on the New York video."- Chris Day

"The man don't joke about bodmerangs."- Rick Moliterno

"That dude is bad ass."- Pete Kearny

"Hey, how'd you do that again?"- Dennis McCoy

NOTES OF A LUNGMUSTARD

The ever-stylish L. Mustard thrusts a tabletopped air as an eager row of skaters looks on.

HAPPENINGS...

R.L.'s riding a special General which is half chrome and half black.

Chris Day is fast.

Fred is getting better, but touched 15 times in his route.

Club Homeboy were the hot stickers of the contest.

Vision Street Wear shoes were seen on the feet of Pete, Craig Grasso, Kove, Cepple.

Various bouncer-types were showing authority at the comp.

After Dennis' run, he went up on top of the Velodrome to practice more. He knew he'd have a tie coming, so he practiced his minute run-off and won. He was so fast and smooth, he had to win. He pulled off his footwork routine without touching, and ended with an around.

Pictures taken by Lungmustard generally:
A) look like those of a 93 year old invalid.
B) are off-center and blurry.
C) show guys like Joe Gruttola trying backwards decades.
D) Just B

PROJECT: FIDGECYCLE
PROJECT: FIDGECYCLE
PROJECT: FIDGECYCLE

Head tube ride.

AGGRO RAG
FREESTYLE MAG!
JUNK

Tricks by Kev

Pics by Daily

Backwards infinity roll while pedaling.

PROJECT: FIDGECYCLE

Fixed gears; the capability of pedaling forward and backward. Pat Romano has had fixed gearing forever. Some Swedish guy on a segment of PM Magazine was pullin' stuff like head tube rides, head tube twirls, continuous roll-back spins, and bar spinning backwards circles on his specially made bicycle, complete with fixed gearing. It was sick. Well, after seeing what fixed hubs were capable of, Kevin Jones HAD to have one. He rode unicycles before, but nothing quite like these chickens...

Kev had been collecting parts for his rendition of a fixed-hub wonder bike for months. It wasn't easy since specialty stock parts for these bikes are virtually non-existent. He purchased a mini sprocket and five-inch cranks from a junkyard for five bucks. Then one day, while browsing through a local sports shop, he found a complete tire and wheel set-up with a fixed hub. It was probably made for a unicycle. After shellin' out thirty greeners, The K was home in his garage installing the new wheel on his Haro Master.

After a short period of adjustment, Kev was lookin' killer on the bike and havin' some major fun in the process. Roll back spins (I saw him do eight), head tube rides, and backwards infinity rolls WHILE PEDALING were just a few of the manuevers Kevin was whipping up. It takes tons of balance, coordination, and patience. Don't expect to just hop on and instantly be the hit of your neighborhood. It takes time.

I tried out the bike and it was fun. LOTS of fun. It also seemed to be a very feasible outlook for the future of freestyle. A word of advice: If you can get your hands on one of these set-ups, experiment with it a little. Don't wait 'til Woody and Martin get 'em. By then it might be too late...!

-DAILY

The drive train.

Fidge

Left- Kev in the midst of some roll-back spins. These are tough.

Right- Take a look at the picture of the complete bike again. No front brakes, right? Well, that didn't stop The K from boomeranging. Hang Glider at full swing.

ART by ANDY

JEFF PHILLIPS INVERT A.J. DISTORTION

A NEW TRICK

photos by mike Daily

the "rubber hand" variation?

TAGSANITY HOPS

Oh wow. It's time for a new trick by Kevin "The K" Jones. This one is called "Tagsanity Hops" and is guaranteed to have the tags downtown screamin' for more. It is not overly complicated, especially if you're good at pogos.

BY THE K

ONE: Kev stalls the bike on the left pedal and locks his lever. He stands on the right peg with his left foot also.

TWO: He ever so swiftly steps over the bars, landing on the left peg with his right foot, and hops sittin' on the bars.

THREE (not shown): the cool part. He grabs the grip with his left hand and swings out of it to his left, allowing his left leg to lead the way. Then he rides away. ILL.

NSA BLOW OUT

With six dollars clenched in my hand, I paid the spectator's fee to get into the odeum. I walked into the place not expecting any kind of rush with that kind of tag. Picking out a righteous seat in the front row, I was set for the Pro Finals on Sunday. Saturday, Jeff "Ffej" Hedges won hands down for the amateurs.

Practice was in session as I moved about in my metal chair, waiting impatiently for the contest to begin. The competition rolled right in and I was blown away by the talent. Christian Hosoi was jammin' eight foot rocket airs over the channel. Monty Nolder aced his rad trick, a no-footed air walk five feet out, while Steve Caballero looked hot with his judo airs.

But the trick of the day had to be Hawk's back to back McTwists. I was truly stoked. It was DEFINITELY worth my green!

- ART ABASOLO

A Rocket Air as portrayed by Christ.

Photo by Art Abasolo

Stevie Cab blasts a Judo Air.

Photo by Art Abasolo

Flailing an air walk; Monty Nolder.

Photo by Art

Hosoi levitating.

Photo by Art

NSA BLOW OUT!

PRO RESULTS
1) Hawk
2) Caballero
3) Hosoi
4) Mountain
5) McGill
6) Nolder
7) Gator
8) Park
9) Alba
10) Staab

AGGRO RAG
FREESTYLE MAG!

Tuned In

by Drew Moore

D.I.- Horse Bites Dog Cries

This album is one of my favorites. I'm in love with it. Totally innovative and exciting to listen to. "Pervert Nurse" is an immediate turn-on, and songs like "Youth in Asia" and "Johnny's Got a Problem" are gripping and habit-forming. Definitely an impressive album from D.I.

- Drew

SUBHUMANS- First 4 EP's Compilation

Wow, having "Demolition War," "Reason for Existance," "Religious Wars," and "Evolution"- all on one album! Buy it.

- Drew

Dead Kennedy's- Bedtime for Democracy

The last inspired work by the masters before their tragic demise. Characteristic social criticism with the hardcore prowess only they can produce. The lyrics are intellectual on songs like "Macho Insecurity" and "Chickenshit Conformist." The sounds are a bit lacking compared to their earlier stuff, but still captivating.

- Drew

Flipper- Blow 'N' Chunks

The baleful tremor released by these guys is totally uninvigorating. Kinda all used-up. I was bored. I have to admit, though, "Shed No Tears" was interesting but it was so fucking drawn out.

- Drew

...and one by the dale...

Dead or Alive- Mad, Bad and Dangerous to Know

If you're into a consistently upbeat, synthesized sound with more than a hint of pop, acquire this album. Dead or Alive's lively mixes of dance-intended tunes were well-liked by myself. Some cuts which explode with energy happen to be "I Want You," "Come Inside," and "Son of a Gun." High octane sessioning music for sure.

- MSD

FACTORY

651 Loma Dr #2, Hermosa, CA 90254

Andy J. on bass, Dave on drums, TV on right

The front door of the bi-level Tudor style house opens and a tired executive-type with 5 o'clock shadow saunters in.

It had been another exhausting day at the office. He hangs up his coat, loosens his tie, and casually walks over to his well-structured stereo system. He ponders briefly on his vinyl choices but inwardly knows exactly what record he plans on listening to.

The man puts the record on the turntable and then sinks into his favorite easy chair. He stretches luxuriously and gently pats his dog's head; which has just lain down at his feet.

Sound suddenly permeates the room and several thoughts shoot through his head. "Churning, varying tones with a strong Butthole Surfers style" thinks he. "Electric Buffalo' and 'Rat Inside My Head' - interesting names", thinks he again.

"Great to sit back and mellow to with a hot mug of Maxwell House and a good dog at your feet-especially after a hard day at the.....FACTORY!?!

—Drew

"Tom considered television a poor alternative to a challenging jigsaw puzzle or sit-ups on a cold cement floor."

NOT TOM

TOM'S WORLD

AGGRO RAG
FREESTYLE MAG!

Kev (not tom)

Tom was mostly pleased that his family's carpets were thicker than usual. Riding his bike without wearing sweat bands was Tom's perfect way to spend a sunny Sunday afternoon. Every time Tom returned to his house, however, he was met by not much more than a tan breadbasket and a dark green wooden stool. The aroma of a good home-cooked meal rarely entertained Tom's nose and when it did, Tom usually found himself reading old comic books in his closet. Tom considered television a poor alternative to a challenging jigsaw puzzle or sit-ups on a cold cement floor. Although Tom was viewed as an active fellow, he disliked falling so hard that he could taste his sinuses. As a result, Tom remains isolated in a peculiar way. Tom still will not go near picnic tables for fear of bothersome questions or just dry red beets on plates of white cardboard. Whatever the case, avoid asking Tom about his uncle's goiter......

- MSD

I'd like to thank Dick Van Patten for personally endorsing this issue of Aggro Rag. Dick can currently be seen doing replacement window commercials for a company in York, PA (No lie!) if you stay up late enough. Anything for a buck, huh Dick? And he STILL found the time, despite his grueling work schedule, to promote Aggro Rag! What a guy Dick is!

Said Dick, "Aggro Rag looks to be a good, wholesome, family-styled zine. I wouldn't miss an issue."

DICK SAYS:

"Read Aggro Rag!"

*- Dick appears courtesy of ThermalGard.

Stickers- Send $1 for assortment...

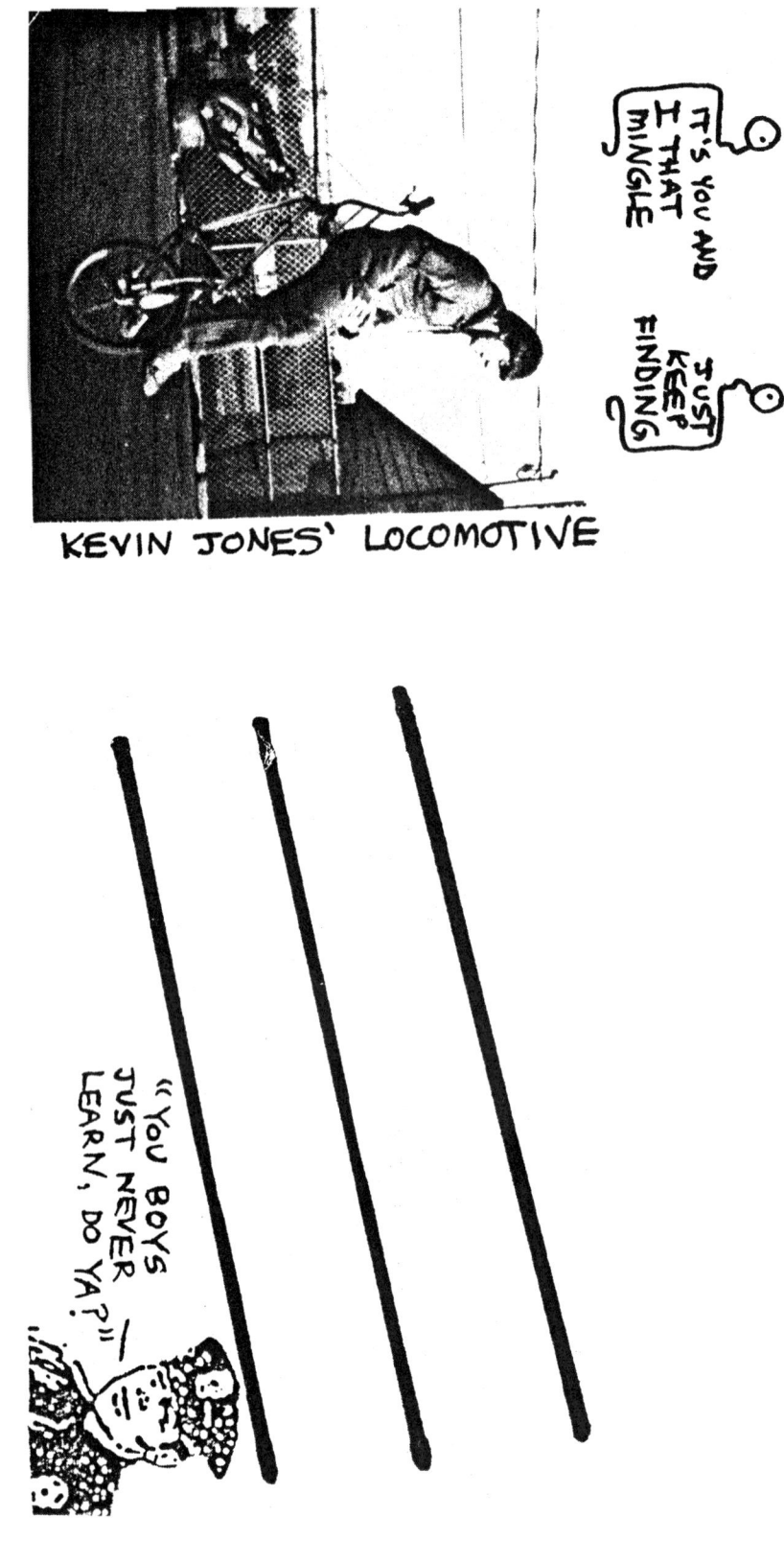

AGGRO RAG
FREESTYLE MAG!

TO MIKE DAILY
3320 SPONDIN DRIVE
YORK, PA 17402
(717) 757-3096

"IT'S YOU AND I THAT MINGLE"

"JUST KEEP FINDING"

KEVIN JONES' LOCOMOTIVE

"YOU BOYS JUST NEVER LEARN, DO YA?"

AGGRO RAG FREESTYLE MAG!
(October 1987)
York, PA/Lock Haven, PA
5½" x 8¼"

Yellow card stock cover, pink interior pages (some printed with brown toner ink) and outspoken interviews with Craig Grasso, Ceppie Maes, Dizz Hicks and Jason Parkes made the ninth issue of *Aggro Rag* my favorite. I interviewed John Swarr, Ross Bicycles/Team Toxic rider (and later partner with Mark Eaton for Eaton Film) about it…

9th ISSUE

Mike Daily: I took the cover photo of you at Spinning Wheels, for this issue.

John Swarr: I remember that day, totally.

This photo is so iconic to me: the trick you're doing, you're wearing Converse hi-tops and you can see part of the full-on Mohawk that you had.

[Laughs.] Yeah, '87; '88's when I cut it off because I was goin' to Bermuda that year.

You were riding a Ross. Was it the Piranha?

Yeah, it was the custom one that we had made because the Piranhas were just crappy bikes. We basically handed them a CW and said, "Make this." And then they put their loops and stuff on there to make it look a little bit more like their Piranha, I guess. That's really all it was. They did a really good job, but it was just a CW with extra tubing on it.

What CW was that? The Stunt Vessel?

Uh…gosh, I don't remember. It was probably that year—'87—the one Gary [Pollak] was ridin'. I couldn't tell ya. I don't remember.

It probably was not the California Freestyle, because that was so tall with the kicked-back seat tube angle and the super steep head angle.

I liked that head angle, actually.

Me too.

It might have been that one.

It was an all-black bike that you had set up. What is this trick that you're doing? Inside, it says that it was called the backsimple.

Yeah.

What do you remember about the trick?

I thought I called it "the left ear of a dead dog". I don't know why, but I remember calling it that for some reason. Somehow it ended up being backsimple.

Is the seat on the ground? I can't tell from the Xerox.

Yeah. It was just an inverted decade of some sort—an upside-down decade. I had it on the seat upside-down then came up on the pegs, went over the head tube and made it back on the pegs. I held the pegs on the forks.

Nobody did this. This is your trick.

Yep.

I think one of the reasons I also like it is because I did the upside-down lawnmower—that was one of my little variations. This is the exact same position: holding onto the fork pegs with the bike upside-down. You had the lever locked, right?

Yeah, I did have the brake lever locked.

That is rad. Were you influenced by Ceppie [Maes]?

Uh…I don't know. I'm tryin' to remember. No, it kind of seemed like I didn't really have an influence. It didn't feel like I had an influence in '87, although [Bob] Haro, R. L. [Osborn], [Mike] Buff, [Eddie] Fiola and the early California riders influenced all of us back in the beginning of freestyle. Everybody was kind of new at it, you know what I mean? I think R.L. did that trick later, though.

Really?

I'm pretty sure, because we would do tricks and we used to say R.L. had a satellite watching us. [Laughs.] Because he'd be doin' 'em a couple months later. It was just a running joke we had. It seemed like he'd find these tricks somehow on a video or something and he'd learn 'em real quick. I'm kidding. R. L. was an amazing rider.

You had your own style. What music were you listening to around that time?

Probably like Minor Threat and DRI, Dirty Rotten Imbeciles. We were into DRI. They'd come to City Gardens all the time. Any of the harder punk bands, we'd listen to. I was really into it. We'd see Circle Jerks and 7 Seconds and all that stuff.

Who went with you?

It was the King of Prussia gang. Gary didn't go—it was more like Scott Guarna, Wally [Mike Cutillo], Marvel [Warren Marchese] and me. We'd go all the time.

How long did you guys ride for Ross?

I want to say that was probably a year at the most. We were all gung-ho at first and then I think it just sort of fizzled out. They didn't do much with their marketing. Ross is a big company. Like any of those companies, they just lose interest real quick. Whenever they feel a trend comin' on, they try to jump on it and then they just jump right off of it, and that's what that was. And it was us, you know? We weren't necessarily like all-American sweethearts for Ross Bicycles.

Wasn't Gary kind of an influence?

Gary was always way better than all of us. He was younger, too—a couple years younger—so I didn't feel like he influenced me, necessarily. He just picked everything up in two seconds and learned it and did way better than us. That's kind of how it worked. He was just a natural, you know? He practiced way more than us. He picked it up fast and he was just really good. I think we all just influenced each other. Everything was just different back then. There were so many tricks you could still create on your own—it felt like you could just make tricks up. I couldn't imagine tryin' to make up a trick now. How do you do that? If it's even possible. It still *is* possible, but back then it was easy: flip your bike a different way, put your feet in a different spot and just come up with something.

AGGRO RAG

FREESTYLE MAG!

"Ride First, Read Later."

WALL RIDES

Blockbuster
ISSUE!

October 1987
Volume 2 Number 8

60 pages!

**BIG INTERVIEWS
SOME CONTESTS
AND OTHER GOOP**

AGGRO RAG
FREESTYLE MAG!

Volume 2 Number 8
October 1987

ON THE COVER: Hardcore straight-edge styler John Swarr of Team Piranha flailing through his trick- the backsimple. Photo by Mike Daily. Top right; Kevin Jones bounding up the bank/wall configur- ation we came across in California. Photo by Mike Daily. Bottom left; Craig "Bone-Rock" Grasso takin' a hand and foot off over a quarter-pipe somewhere. Photo by somebody.

Features

Las Vegas.....................5
Ross Piranha team............7
Grassroots..................10
Texas.......................14
Travel Fun..................21
Dan-Up......................24
Trick Contest results.......26
Genuine Riding..............28
Ceppie Maes.................30
Name LungM's Car............34
Velodrome...................35
Spinning Wheels.............41
Are You a Contest Zombie?...42
Dizz Uncensored.............44
The Cure....................46
Hoods go to Torrance........48
Wall Rides..................50
Jason Parkes................54

Normal Stuff

Mumbo Jumbo.......3
Skankin' Artwork...4
Trick Tidbits.....6
A New Trick.......9
Art from Mel......33
What a Hood!......47
Den Diddle it Den..53
Editorial.........59

staff

Editor/Nerd/In the Hole
  Michael Daily

Contributors
  Mel Bend
  Lungmustard
  Sammy Lee
  Lew
  Warren

ride

QUOTES

"Basically, if you <u>know</u> Vander, you're a Curb Dog." - Aaron Dull explaining the qualifications to becoming a Curb Dog.

"They (the AFA) took the free out of freestyle." - Mike Cutillo.

"This is a fucked up place!" - Joe Gruttola at the Spot as we watched a male stripper entertain drunk women OUTside.

MUMBO JUMBO by Mike Daily

I present to you, the hipster just a-hankerin' for juicy rumors and such-nots, the following underground utterings. Believe accordingly...

Lungmustard just arrived home from a two day Ross Bicycles demo in Buffalo, N.Y. John Swarr, Dave Pak, and the Lung boy were the featured Ross-ers, all riding fully prototyped Pirahnas (watch for a test on this fish). Eaton was pleased-he carted home 200 bucks, the bike, and a co-sponsorship from Vision....Skyway flew The K out to sunny Cal. last weekend to shoot a new ad with Eddie Roman. Should be interesting....Which well-known pro flatlander was spied at the Zeronine offices recently propositioning a young lady with 50 big ones just to go out on a date with him? And isn't he engaged?? What a bloody disgrace....Rick allison and Chris Potts on Hutch? Eddie Fiola talking to General? Perhaps so.... Alex Greenblatt wouldn't mind some coverage....Aaron Dull is reportedly ripping hard. New trick-chicken squeaks (funky chicken tail whips)....Ian Clemmens up to 30+ pinky squeaks? Yowza....Is ODI coming out with Mike Daily signature series buffguards?....Nor Cal legend Tim Treacy is <u>heavily</u> sought after by this zine for an IN-DEPTH interview....Did Raybo really have CW custom design a Stunt Vessel for him? Is he planning on finally getting into freestyle and learning new tricks? Sounds cool.... Word has it that Karl Rothe and friend were in a major fender-bender recently. The car ('75 Camaro) was totaled but both are safe and sound thank God....A one-off Homeboy issue as big as Rolling Stone? Uh oh....Speaking of Homeboy, did Lew actually cut off his purple locks and select a bright orange butch hairstyle?....Is the high salt intake from Dale's fave snack, pretzels, making him crazy bits lately? Only his psycho-analyst knows for sure....Mario Salas is currently negotiating with Jiffy Pop popcorn....And lastly, underground freestyle folklore hero, John Doenut is finally considering organized competition. John, who was a neighbor of Kevin Jones <u>many</u> years ago and now lives in Nebraska, has dozens of the freshest tricks guaranteed to bake your mind. More later....

SOME Skankin ArtWork...

- Sammy Lee
Plainview, N.Y.

Las Vegas Scene Alert

Hey Mike,

I dug your mag, dude! It shreds! Dude, I've got some info on the Vegas scene for ya (Hot riders, hot spots, teams, etc.). Here goes...

*Hot flatlanders: John Guilorry, David Reid, John Stotts, Chad Flint, Keith Henderson, Greg Higgins.

*Hot rampsters: Gary Laurent (factory Free Agent), Kurtis Kunz, Chad Flint, John Stotts, Brent Dalton.

*Hot ridin' spots: Stardust "texaco"(the strip), "OK", Kurtis' ramp, John's ramp, Daryl's ramp.

*Teams: Absolute Madness, Shinz, F. in S. (all teams have done shows and demos)

"insight"- Las Vegas is pretty much a freestyle "hi town"-no local pros, contests, mag coverage... but the riders keep up with what's goin' on by making various trips to San Diego (ground moves) and the Pipeline (air). The local ground riders stay up with the latest moves, rampsters also. It's a very fun and unified scene (lots of group sessions). There is a certain rider (whose name I won't mention) who claims to be "the best"-and no one needs that...know what I mean? But we are all fun-loving guys who _love_ to shred and hope to start getting to contests and building our scene.

I guess you could call that a run-down of our scene here. Until next time, shred hard.

- Greg Higgins
Team Shinz

by the dale
CRC

If you dislike bogus braking, and brakeless tricks just ain't yer bag, you need CRC. CRC Disc Brake Quiet is a red gooey substance used in cars. All you need for drum brake-like stopping is a little dab on each side of the rim. Smear evenly for about 2-3 inches, wait a couple minutes, and ride. Your brakes'll grab (and squeak!) like never before.

This goop makes your brakes work so good you'll think yer uncle's name is Cream 'O Wheat. Lew told me to obtain this revolutionary new cleaner called Simple Green and apply it to my rims and brake shoes for the utmost in braking efficiency. I did, and by golly, it works. Just spray some on a not-too-aggro rag, wipe, and ride. Simple. It lasts about 3-4 hours before its rim-screeching effectiveness diminishes. Works on mags or alloys, and can be found wherever automotive supplies are sold. Try it.

TRICK tIDBITS

REPORT BY STUDENT PROTEST COMMITTEE

Fellow Students of __Aggro Rag__ (FULL NAME OF SCHOOL)! We members of the Students for a/an __Aggro__ (ADJECTIVE) Society are meeting here to decide what action to take about the Dean of __Dale__ (PLURAL NOUN). He has just fired our friend, Professor __Tom__ (NAME OF PERSON IN ROOM), because he wore his __bangs__ (PART OF THE BODY) long, and because he dressed in __loose clothing__ (ARTICLE OF CLOTHING) and wore old __Converse__ (PLURAL NOUN). Next week we are going to protest by taking over the __Aggro Rag__ (NOUN) building and kidnapping the Assistant __Editor__ (NOUN). We also will demand that all students have the right to wear __Trendy__ (ADJECTIVE) hair and __shaved__ (ADJECTIVE) beards. Remember our slogan: "Down with the __Dale__ (PLURAL NOUN)."

- Lung

simple green®
Information

Wally

CORROSIVE

the ROSS PiRAnHa TEAM

Report and photos by Mike Daily

With seat scraping asphalt and emitting sound, John Swarr twirls around and around, bike upside down.

AGGRO RAG FREESTYLE MAG! SCENE ALERT

"Bombing back into the bowl from a curb-inspired abubaca is Mike Cutillo, also known as "Wally.""

Team Toxic, that searing underground bike/skate force from PA, is no more. John Swarr, Mike Cutillo, Scott Guarna, and Brian Hamel were all bona-fide members of Team Toxic before it disbanded. All four are extremely dedicated, <u>hardcore</u> riders, quite capable of melting minds with their innovative styles of riding. All are now cuttin' it up for Ross Bicycles, team-mounted on Ross' new line of freestyle attack vehicles- Piranha.

The former Toxins are currently working with Ross to design new bikes and to set-up more shows and possible tours for the future.

Doing three shows a day, six days a week at a local dining/entertainment establishment was how John, Mike, and Scott spent the summer of '87. Good or bad? Well, the pay was great, but due to the nature of their jobs, travelling to comps and shows was virtually impossible. However, don't let that fool you into thinking they don't have modern manoovs. These guys BLAZE in the originality department. Just wait until next summer when contest appearances and shred-circling can do them the justice they deserve. In the meantime, be aware that the Ross Piranha team is surfacing...quickly.

Simply put, Kevin Jones is an innovator. Take this cool combination manoov for instance. It could be called the "stall lawnmower into reverse peg picker." Just mastering step one of this how-to could take days...weeks... months...or even years. But not really. If you like it, learn it. Then buy The K a Yoo-Hoo the next time you see him. (NOTE: This trick may or may not be easier while wearing a winter coat. If you sweat profusely, don't wear one. But if you slam often, feel free. Its plush cushioning effect may prove to be beneficial.)

A NEW TRICK by the k

Photos: Daily

1) Get into your basic stall lawnmower position. Kev holds the fork with his left hand and uses his right leg to counterbalance the bike. He can stall these FOREVER.

2) Yank the bike back and swing your right leg over the head tube.

3) Hop. From here, The K goes into his incredible trolly. And I do mean INCREDIBLE.

craig

grasso

NICKNAME(S)- Bone-Rock, Grassroots, Boner AGE- 17 Stones
SPONSOR- General, Vision CO-SPONSORS- Rector, ODI, ACS, Zeronine, Echo
HOMETOWN- Redondo Beach, California AFA CLASS- 16-18 Expert
JOB?- Grave Digger HAIR COLOR- Dark

1) How long were you on SE?
   "3 stones."

2) Why did most of the SE factory guys not talk to General?
   "The best deal."

3) What is your basic deal with General?
   "Anything I need."

4) Do you ride ramps? Why?
   "Yes- Why not?"

5) What is your favorite flatland trick?
   "Stall lawnmower."

6) What ground tricks have you invented?
   "Blender, Japanese Swirl."

7) Care to divulge what new tricks you are working on?
   "Naked G-turn, no-foot boner air."

8) Who do you like to session with the most? Where do you session?
   "Ceppie, R.L., Pete Kearney, Mike Tony, The SPC."

9) Do you like contests? More than shows?
   "No- Shows more than contests (yeah)."

10) What is your favorite snack and why?
    "Fortune cookies-so I know my fortune."

11) What has been your best contest placing and where was it?
    "Venice '85. I won ground all over it."

12) What music are you into? What bands get you flyin'?
    "Death, gloom- Old Cure, Factory, Christian Death, Joy Division, Tex and The Horseheads, Jesus and Mary Chain, Siouxsie, The 3 O'Clock, The Jam, Cocteau Twins, Kommunity FK, The Glove, and G.L.J. to name a few!"

13) What riders do you really respect?
    "Too many."

14) What are your future goals?
    "Band success."

15) What do you do for fun?
    "Walk through parks screaming at the moon, talk and not make sense, play guitar, dream."

16) Closing comments?
    "I'm just so sick of seeing all the same people with different faces. It makes me scream..."

(CONTINUED)

Craig Grasso

Betcha didn't know Grasso ripped on ramps, huh? This should enlighten you...

Craig created quite a ruckus with his Texas dork-a-RAMA routine, complete with a fully careening crash at the end.

CAN YOU HANDLE IT?

You've waited patiently. You've heard rumors...seen glimpses. Now's the chance to get your hands on THE MOST talked about seatpost in Freestyle. The "HANDLE" from TRP.

- Constructed of durable .065 Wall 100% Chrome-moly.
- 15 Inches long for PLENTY of frame insertion.
- A must for any SERIOUS Freestyler.
- Colors? TOO many.
- ONLY $14.95

Rider: Chris Obermeyer
Photo: "Crazy" Carl Silverman

- Available in both Straight AND Layback.

Patent Pending

TRP
Designed by riders, for riders.

SEND $1.00 FOR A TRP STICKER PACK.

MAIL TO: TRP, 65 Comstock Ave., Staten Island, NY 10314
TO ORDER DIRECT CALL (718) 494-6723

STYLE:_____   COLOR:_____   QUANTITY:_____

ONLY $14.95 Plus $2.75 Postage & Handling for each seatpost ordered.
__ Personal Check   __ Money Order   __ COD ($3.00 Charge)
Total Amount Enclosed: _____

Name_____   City_____
Address_____   State_____ Zip Code_____

FREESTYLE MASTERS
AUSTIN Texas

The Alamo is somewhere in Texas. I felt like a fool having to ask where Austin was located. I still can't remember the name of that breakfast place, but it was great. Chili on french toast...with syrup. And five large orange juices.

14

Story by LEW

Find Ray (Hint: He's wearing glasses)

Parking lot? Guarded, but not invincible. Dennis McCoy throws a mean rock with his front tire-he and Belcher played "Rock Soccer" out in front for a while. The manager was a black guy who carried pens in his pocket to get our names with.

Joe Gruttola is a security breach? Or was that Dennis McCoy? Kevin Jones, do that again please. FUUUUUUUUUCK. That guy is hot. Who's his buddy? Mark Long? Ohhh, Mark LUNG...Lungmustard. Those guys have the fresh tricks. 120 riders in 16-18? Naaaa, can't be. I'll sleep on the floor tonight. Hey, let's ride 'til three in the morning and rap into a mini-cassette recorder. Get the fun over with on Friday 'cause none of that shit is allowed inside the arena.

No room to practice. No room to breath. JUST enough room to throw stickers. Leave the room if you get caught-leave permanently. Why does he have a gun? To protect us from each other. GOD is it hot in here. How can he practice in a full uniform? Hey dude, check it out...I snuck in here by forging the AFA stamp on my hand with a black marker. Grasso's run is going to be insane. The stands are insane. Dino is trying to pick up Coleen. Practice is not possible. Start this shit. Cokes cost a buck and a half, but one fills you up. Flatland is fun. Do a boomerang with your legs apart over the crossbar. Bar ride. Side squeak. Play heavy metal. Get 40th place no matter what.

DYNO-mounted Brett Hernandez bustin' out some Pinky squeaks in a shred-circle. Is his record really 19?

Many were not particularly in favor of the AFA's new 10 dollar per day video camera rule. Is the AFA getting a bit "out of hand?"

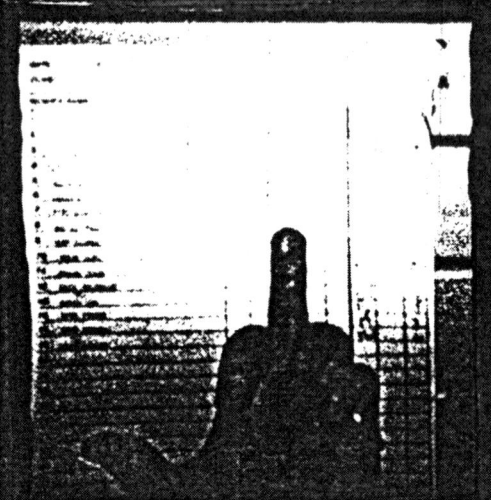

Nor were too many delighted about the results of 19&Over Expert.

This caption is not yet another caption designed to kill Rick. The truth is, Rick had a dazzling run. Kev himself doesn't even care. Said Ricky, "Hey all I did was go out and ride."

16

Lew forward side-gliding at a high rate of speed as one of the contestants in 19 & Over Expert.

Photo by Windy

The center of attention with a stall lawnmower, Kevin Jones. Did the judges dick him over?

A million little kids even. Belcher is no longer
one-he got busted for being 16 and riding in 14-15.
Trouble time. Scotty picked off a win. Finally.
Matt riding ground? Matt winning overall? Matt
stoked.

Pinky jamming. Jason P. jamming but kicked off
Schwinn afterwards. Jim Johnson jamming green beans
and hand plant lawnmowers. Karl Rothe squelched a
bit but still got fourth. I like Karl's style. No
handed backyard? I came.

Some kid from Kansas imaiM poH-poH (backwards hop-
hop). Mitchell Collins tailspin aerial aka medic-
air? 540 tailspin flyout? Still cool but not enough.

Ron and Joe there but injured? Haro must be cool.
Kevin Jones ripped? Yes. Rick wins? Again. Crowd
stoked? Kevin is lord.

Half-wood half-concrete sonic metal disco floor
surface. Brett Hernandez is on the up with squinky
peaks and the jive turkey (funky chicken variations).
Cool chicks on 6th, but no naked hoedown. They smoked
pot instead and we kicked them out of the van for that
noise. Drink, drive, and shoot guns at the same time?
ONLY in Texas. Locals are shit-kickin' jive monkeys.
Burning warehouse is more like a carnival.

Back to the contest. 10 dollar video rule. No
sticker throwing, so let them eat trash. Food fight.
Lyric chant. Dennis McCoy and Anthrax don't fit the
AFA's "clean cut" song rule. DMCELCIDWOODYDAVERICK
was how it went for ground money.

Continued n
page 20

Pinky
catching up
on his
winkies...

All photos by Warren

Clockwise from above: Michael D. sidewinding a lookback for DB; Arcade boredom with Dave Pak, Raybo (stop that!), and Gary; Blyther dorking; Handless hop-hops by a shredding unknown; and Todd Anderson risking it all...for THIRD?!??

Assorted Action

TEXAS

Dave Pak and RAY

Lungbastard said this guy was tearin' it up with fast combo-moves.

Mike D. had the meat with juice in ramps. Brian chicken-butted a second. Todd rode to AC/DC. He did neat tricks. Third once more. Dennis was scared but tried to say he wasn't 'til he hung on that invert. I praise him though, 'cause he turned fear to fury and spun a twist 6.5 to 7 feet out of the coping, then landed it and knee-slid across the flat bottom with his arms raised. That was the raddest spin I haven't seen Michael do ever.

Scooter classes suck. Entertainment was had by chanting, taunting, and illegal tossing. Once that rentable cop gave us the bird, there was no choice left but to start chanting "Fuck YOU...fuck YOU." Karl threw meat patties at 13 year olds. That was the best.

After it got done GT/Dyno hopped on the van roof and started letting loose with adhesive gold and parts. Voelker chased some guy down with a seat post and recovered his shirt from a Texan dirtball. Then at Doobies that night, the nachos were late and Karen told us that she was none of our beeswax. WEELLL!

Brett left. it rained, Dino got fixed (knee and finger), and almost forgot-tabasco sauce quarters got played and McGoo and Dave got sore stomachs. Ha ha on your face.

Dale Mitzel, nervously navigating his Mustang through New York City, waaayyy after midnight, in search of Pete Kearney's house. And yes, the flash did startle him. Photo:Daily

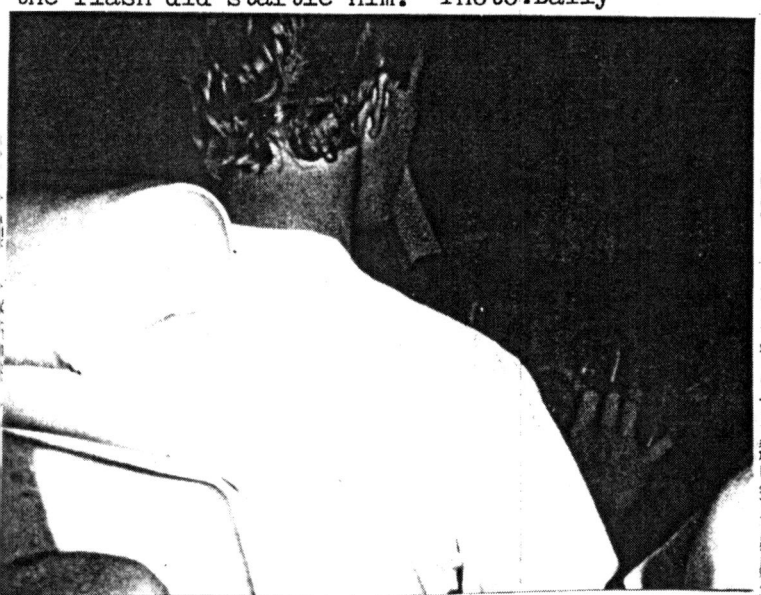

"HURRY UP!!!"

"Will that be all Sir?"

"Uh yeah ('Sir?')."

"Didja bring yer helmet this time?"

"Who has gas money?"

"Hey look they have Yoo-Hoo in cans. And Jolt."

"What a tard."

"Wearin' that Homeboy shirt again huh Dale?"

"Look! Daily's gettin' a sub!"

"C'MON!! Let's <u>cruise</u>!"

"Can you lend me a buck, bud? Pay ya tomorrow."

"Uh...four-fifty of unleaded."

"HEY! Why's <u>my</u> bike have to be on the <u>outside</u>?"

"Ha Ha! Get in! Let's gooooo...!"

Sound Familiar???

PA, THE nuke state.

Trekin' to the big NFA Grandnationals in Kev's old orange Gremlin. The door fit swell-honest.

Brett "MOB" Downes (Shown here in his official "aviator" sunglasses) thinks driving is fun. But then again he also thinks bolt on is better...

travel FUN

Lew (yes Lew) took these motor-driven photos as the '86 CW entourage headed for the next show. Ceppie (posing) and McGoo (picking).

Highway nuttiness on the way home from King of Prussia with Dale Eugene Mitzel, Kevin J., and me, Mikey Daily.

Dennis

Gary

Dennis

rick

Mario's sister.

DAN'UP

The show was at the King of Prussia Plaza and we got there late (as usual) and Jamie's front Tuff Wheel melted from the exhaust pipe and Dennis, Rick, and Gary did a great job and then they told us to just say no.

Gary keepin' it up...

JST SAY NO JUST SAY NO JUST SAY NO JUST SAY
JST SAY NO JUST SAY NO JUST SAY NO JUST SAY
JST SAY NO JUST SAY NO JUST SAY NO JUST SAY

sessions

JUST SAY NO   JUST SAY NO   JUST SAY NO   JUST SAY NO

Clockwise from left: Mark J. Eaton scootin' an elephant glide; Kev's new trick; Joe Schuto sittin' on the shoulders of Unicycle Master, The Dale veering out of the path of Glenn and Dale rocket-gliding, and Dale M. again, rolling.

25

1st Place

Larry Nelson

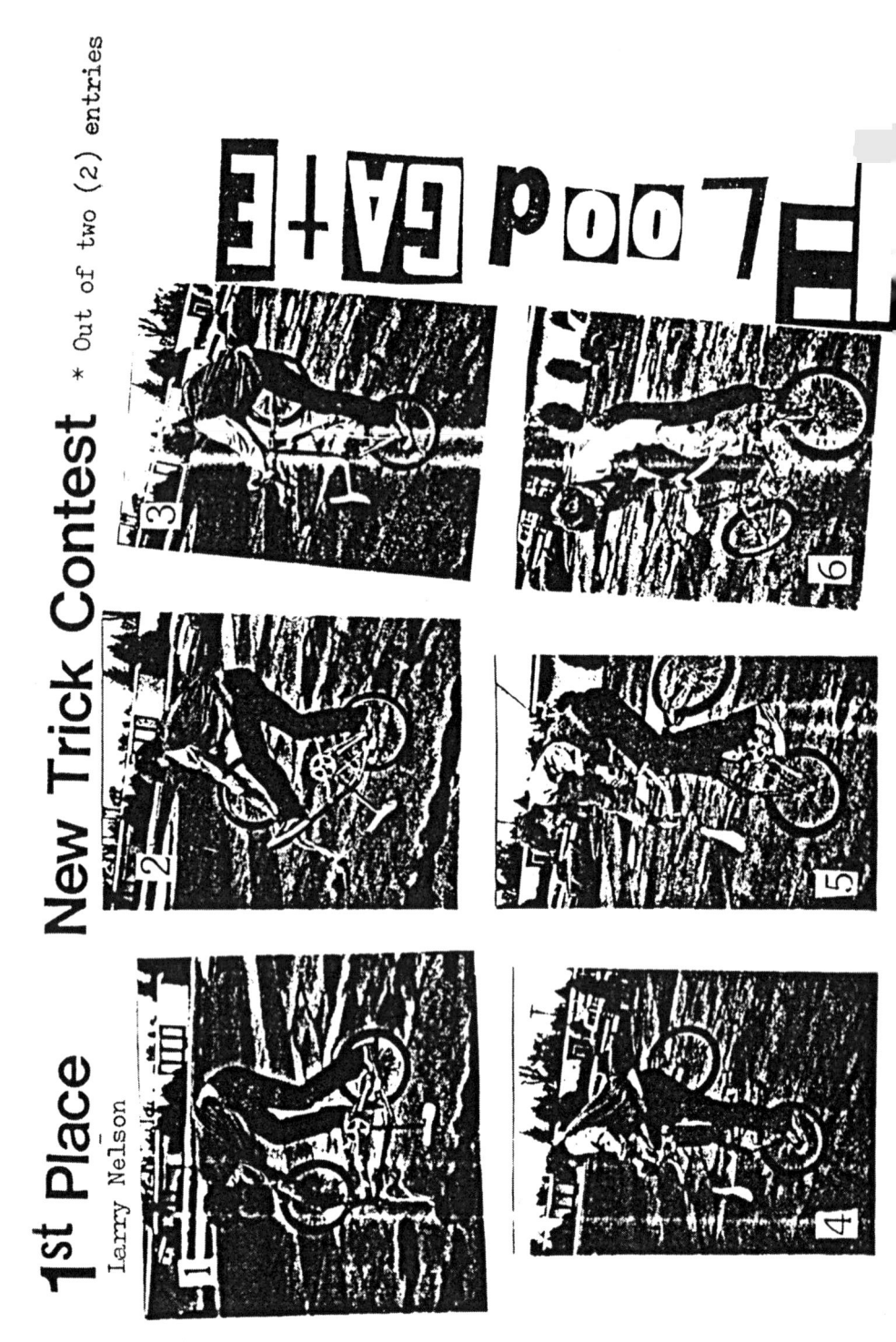

New Trick Contest *Out of two (2) entries

LOOdGATE

Prize: Pacific Palms gloves

2nd P-ace

Larry Nelson   Prize: ODI Mushroom II's

This page: At left; a modern day funky chicken from a fire hydrant. Middle; the hooded Hood of all Hoods coppin' illegal air at Spud. Top; Clearin' the monster mogul at Thunderdohm. Next page: Top; tucked and flatter than a fruit roll-up at Brian's ramp jam. Middle; slashin' a total tabletopper at Spinning Wheels.

Genuine Ridin'

For those of you out there who think Kevin Jones is a newcomer to the sport of freestyle and that he started out by learning how to do a cherrypicker and that nobody jumps anymore and that ramps and pools are gay or too dangerous and that ground tricks are the only way to go....THINK AGAIN. Kevin Jones never limited himself like that. So why should you?

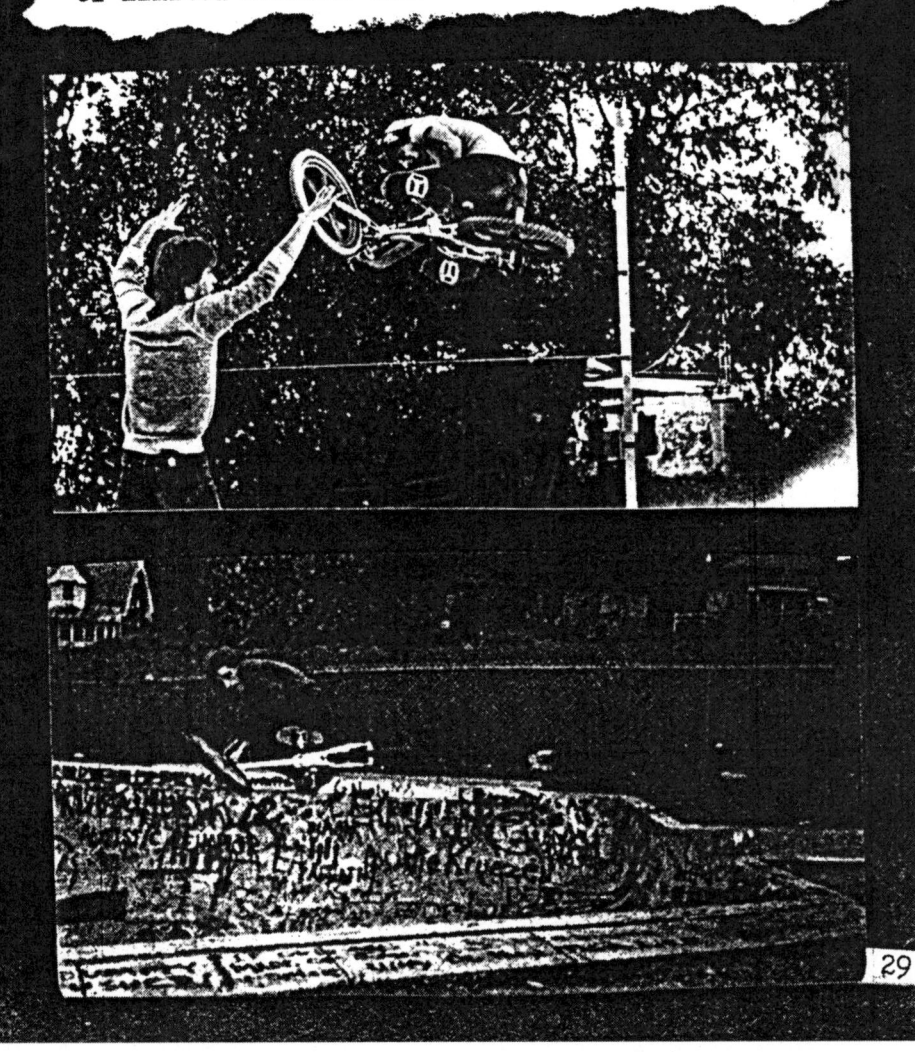

April 8, 1987
   So explain the bike situation.
Cep: "I don't got a bike situation...I got a Dyno."
Bru: "He's got a Dyno that sits in the house."
Cep: "Yeah, I got a Dyno that sits in my girlfriend's bedroom. I rode it like after I put the parts on it so I could see if it was tight."
Bru: "No, you rode it at the spot that one day when those guys were asking you if you were Ceppie Maes."
Cep: "Oh yeah, I was someone else with blond hair then. I was Tom. My name was Tom (Editor's note: "Hey wait a second here..."). I was fuckin' with them. No, I just skate now, a little bit."
   Explain the skate situation.
Cep: "I wake up in the morning, take my girlfriend to school, drive over to Winkle's house, see Bru and Winkle lay there for a while."
Bru: "Hey, I go to work, I don't lay there."

"I want to get a job where I don't have to cut my hair."   -Ceppie Maes

Exclusive interview by Mel Bend

CEP LIVES on

(continued next page)

Cep: "Well, anyways, then I go to the beach or one of the local parks in the Southern California district, and sit there and look at the birds."
   What kind of birds?
Cep: "Pigeons, seagulls, dogs...any kind of bird. Anything with wings. I seen a flying dog. Then about, like, 12 o'clock I go pick up my girl at school and take her to work. Then I go get Bru and me and Bru go skate."
   You're done laying around by then?
Bru: "No, no, I'm through WORKING."
Cep: "Or else we go to the magazine and YOU know what happens there. We bullshit with them."
Bru: "And watch THEM lay around."
Cep: "But most of the time I spend looking for a job. I call all the factorys and stuff like that, but they dog me. For instance, today I called Roger (at CW) and he couldn't do me no good. He wanted me to do sales but he said there was nothing to sell right now, so...'call back in two weeks.' I might die of starvation by then."

C E P P I E

Ceppie Maes
Rockville '86

Bru: "But we're gonna do something though. We're gonna rent Ceppie out. To different people for skate and bike demos."
Cep: "Right now we're trying to work with Visaaaage. Massage my meatus (laughter)."
   So you like working with Tony?
Cep: "TONY! I #&*%$!!*#?)*. I don't wanna ride with HIM. You know how R.L. does it right? We're gonna do like an R.L. thing and rent me out to people. We're gonna try and see if we can make any dinero."
Bru: "I'm his manager."
Cep: "Hey Tony Dwyer's been touring for six years now..."
   OH YEAH!!--everyone in unison.
Bru: "He offered me and Winkle 2,500 bucks if we set up his tour. We're going to go to England, get sponsored by Rebok, and..."
Cep: "Hey you know what? Every sponsor says that, 'We're gonna send you to Europe, we're gonna send you to China...'"
   Explain the food situation.
Cep: "The FOOD situation? Okay. I wake up in the morning and I have a drink of water...after I brush my teeth. Then..."
Bru: "Sometimes he leaves his toothbrush in the car."
Cep: "I always carry one in my car and always one in my jacket-just in case. In case I have to sleep in my car one night. That way I can just go to a McDonalds bathroom and scrub my gums. But ahhh, then I go to Winkle's house so I can get a donut. Bru never has food so I go to Winkle's in the morning. We all meet at Winkle's house every morning. But after that I eat at my girlfriend's house for lunch. She might cook up some macaroni and cheese or a baloney sandwich, or grapes. When dinner comes around, I don't eat. So I eat maybe once or twice a day."
   Why's that?
Cep: "Because I don't have no money to buy food. And Bru's mom don't like to cook."
   And your girlfriends mom doesn't want you hangin' out there?
Cep: "She likes me but she doesn't want me living there no more so I got kicked out. The situation got kinda outta hand over there. My girlfriend was actin' up, treatin' the family wrong."
Bru: "We both got dogged on the same night. He got kicked out and I got dumped."
   Don't you and Bru both have girlfriends with the same name?
Bru: "Yeah, we did. Yvonne. Now both our girlfriends are buddies."
Cep: "They're both the same age. Oh I forgot to tell you, I'm engaged. We'll probably get married next year-as soon as I can make a living."
   So what do you plan on doing?
Cep: "I want to get a job where I don't have to cut my hair."
Bru: "Yeah, it's been a while since he's been trying to get it that way."
Cep: "I don't know who to talk to now. Maybe I can talk to Odyssey. So you got any questions?"
   No, I never have too many questions. I'll just let you guys talk.
Cep: "I'll be back."

AGGRO RAG
FREESTYLE MAG!

Name Lung M.'s Car
and WIN something

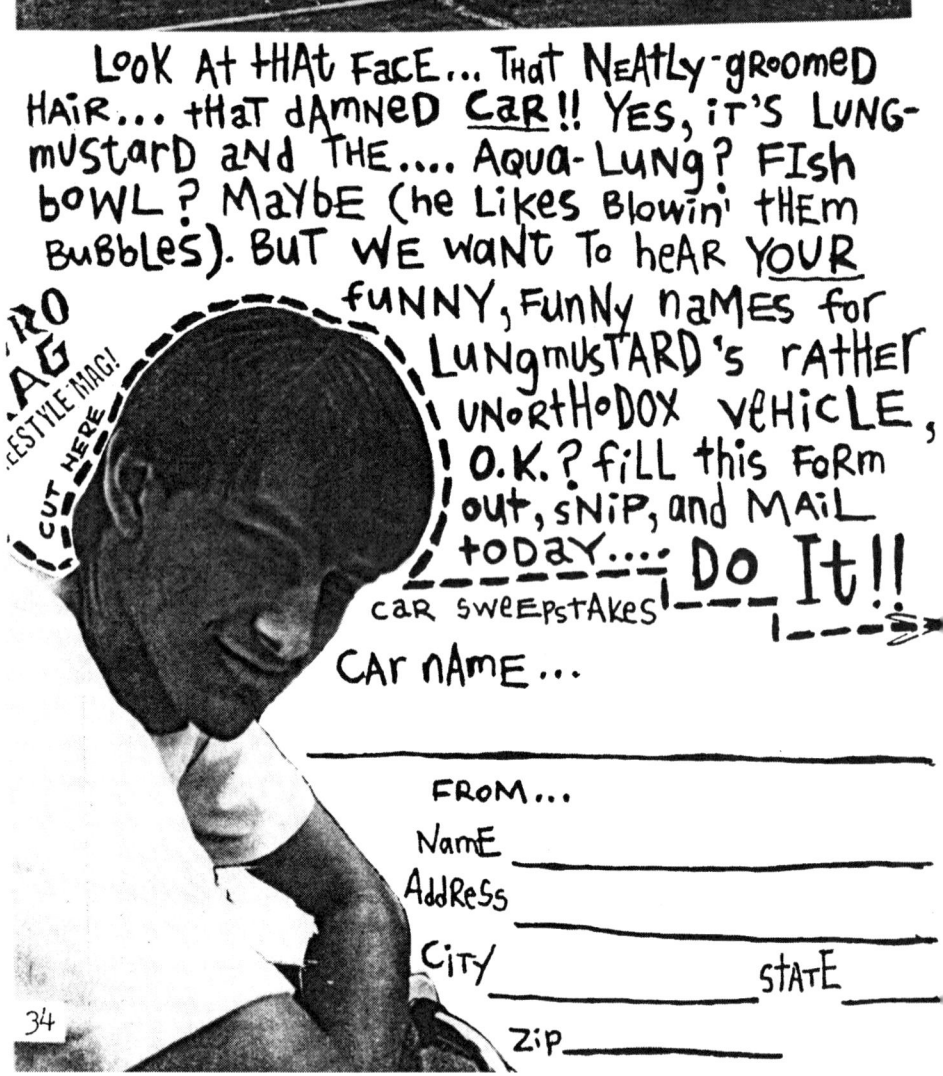

Look at that face... that neatly-groomed hair... that damned **car**!! Yes, it's Lungmustard and the.... Aqua-Lung? Fish bowl? Maybe (he likes blowin' them bubbles). But we want to hear YOUR funny, funny names for Lungmustard's rather unorthodox vehicle, O.K.? Fill this form out, snip, and mail today.... **Do It!!**

CUT HERE!

Car Sweepstakes

Car Name...

From...
Name
Address
City   State
Zip

34

AGGRO RAG FREESTYLE MAG!

No matter what, Martin Aparijo is always on top of the latest tricks. No handed backyard.

another VELODROME contest?

All photos by Mike Daily

AMERICAN FREESTYLE ASSOCIATION

...rode to YAZ. And he did an upside down wheel-kicking thing in a circle.

35

Chris Lashua had two decent runs. Fourth place snaked in style.

Take a look at the guys in the background of this shot. You KNOW they feel lower than whale poo-poo 'cause when Chris Day takes the floor, that's it. You just don't go out after him, it's that simple. Scissors-kicked walkover onto the pedal from a backwards wheelie. Ha ha ha

Robert Castillo scored a second place sneaker with a great ride, Kevin Jones (looking a little dumbfounded here) earned his first first for Skyway, and Pete Kearney (hold that trophy a little higher there Pete) got third.

The judges must have liked R.L.'s llooooonnnnggg rubber ride too.

← dull

THE KING...

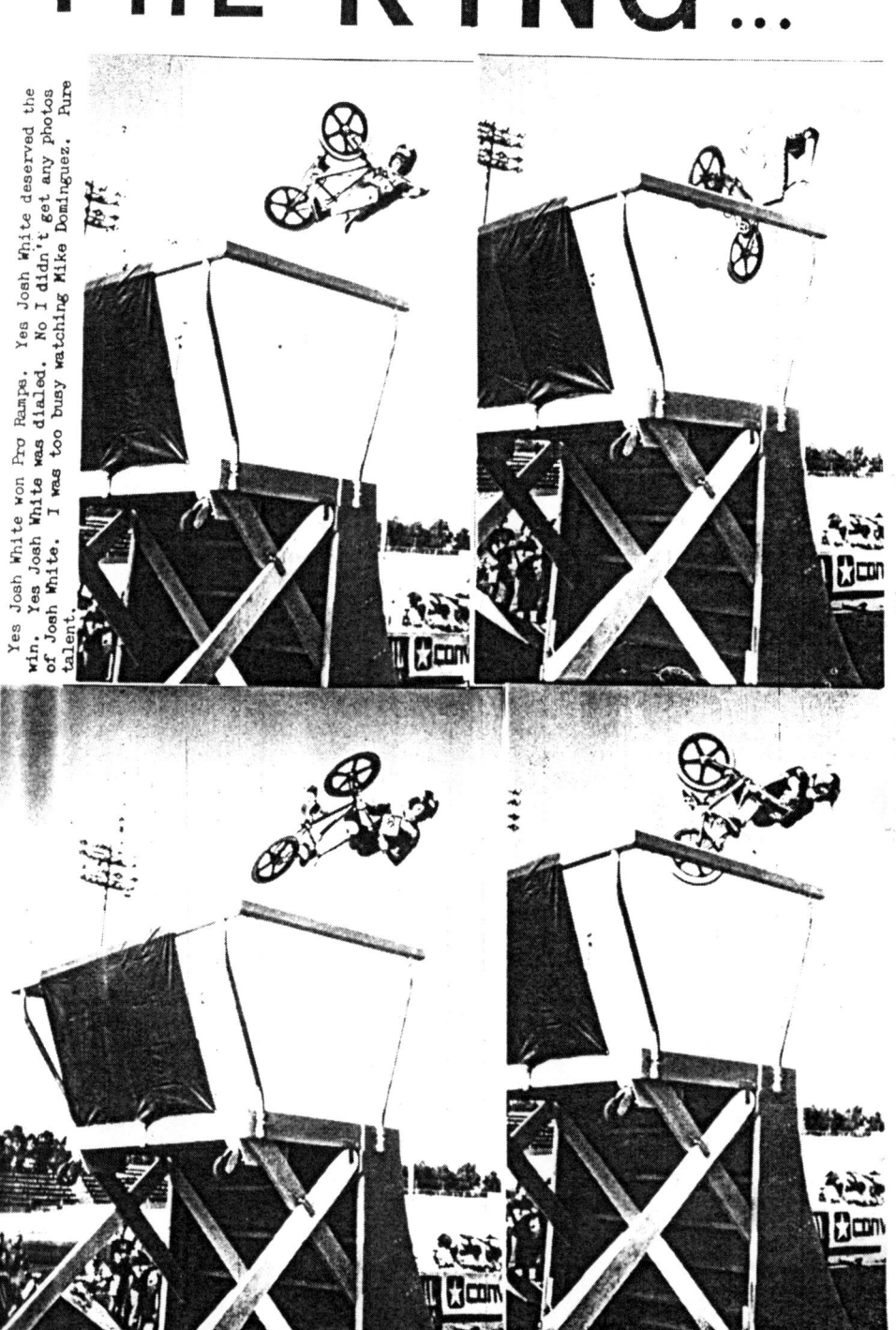

Yes Josh White won Pro Ramps. Yes Josh White deserved the win. Yes Josh White was dialed. No I didn't get any photos of Josh White. I was too busy watching Mike Dominguez. Pure talent.

velodrome

Kev broke his cranks (Odyssey) the night before the Velodrome contest and for awhile harbored the idea of just entering without 'em. Luckily, Dale "Nice Guy" Mitzel stepped onto the scene and offered the usage of his cranks for The K's run. After his routine, Kev returned Dale's cranks and sessioned on...withOUT pedaling implements. Double boom without touching.

Without a water faucet in sight, and without hearing the Beastie Boys, here's some kid kickin' out a backside jumpover. A yellow shirt.

Aaron Dull, sporting co-factory status with Skyway, had a run that was tons great. Backyard in circles, his one-handed funky chicken, the puppet route, backwards rolling boomerang, etc. The judges gave him fourth but they had their heads up their asses because Aaron clearly ruled 14-15 Expert but he had to go first so he got shafted but he didn't seem to care anyways.

38

AFA the Velodrome

Ceppie and McGoo taunted the crowd by tossing them mock stickers made out of toilet paper and hand cream.

Abovegrounder Marc McKee pulled off a large number of double boomerangs without touching over the course of the day. Why's it look so weird? McKee throws 'em the opposite way.

Kevin Jones, Aaron Dull, and Mark Eaton discuss something about something. Here, Aaron uses visual aids to enhance his delivery.

38

Lungbastard and Dale E. scampering through the pits for a better view of the action.

The Vets...

1st

3rd

'40

A graffitied concrete wall provides thrills and spills galore. It's not very suitable for airs, but it rules for fakies.

Spinning Wheels

Reading, PA

This Could Happen

Kev Nuke Pool

The park is miraculously still in operation, owned by some Indians who periodically stop in and collect money from everyone. Still a good deal...go.

41

aRe YOU A cOn

Differing attitudes abound in this activity we all partake in. Every individual rider has a particular attitude concerning each aspect of freestyle, whether it is about tricks, music, clothes, or contests. Influences for the opinionated freestyler include magazines, sponsored riders, and friends. But overactive competitive instincts abound as well in this sport, and simply put, close-minded kids irritate me. The attitudes and riders most irritating to me and the Hoods are the attitudes and riders associated with contests nowadays.

One incident which comes to mind occurred at the Austin, Texas comp covered in this issue. I could not attend this Masters contest because I was in college at the time, but the rest of the Hoods were there in full force. Lung, The K, and Dale E. Mitzel were sitting in a hotel room with a host of rather well-known freestyle personalities watching the day's action on a videotape. Instead of just checkin' the tape out, though, the other guys in the room felt the need to cut down mostly every rider for one reason or another. The Hoods didn't say anything, and it wasn't until later that night that they discovered all three of them had simultaneously thought, "These guys are fake."

That was not all that happened. When L.Mustard exclaimed awe and exasperation at the powerful impromptu style of Jason Parkes, one member of the gawking group turned and said (in disbelief), "You LIKE that stuff?!??!" Jason is mutually admired by our team for numerous reasons, but mainly because when he rides in a contest, that is exactly what he does- He RIDES. No, he doesn't have his routine precisely mapped out down to every single wave to the judges, but so

TesT ZoMbiE??

what? Riding like a pre-programmed robot just isn't his style. Oh, and how did Lungmustard answer the kid? With a very confident "YEAH!"

It seems there are a whole lot of competitive youngsters out there who virtually _live_ for contests. Go to any comp, show or related event and you'll see them. I don't know where the hell they come from, but they are easily identified by their fake images. Picture a kid riding the latest high-tech bike, wearing whatever color-coordinated clothing is "in" at the time, and doing a horde of the trendiest manuevers- all the while worrying more about tapping a foot down than anything else. They hang out in small groups of similar beings. Oh, one of these guys wouldn't want to waste his time meeting other riders. Why should he? To the contest zombie, other riders are not just other riders. They are his competition.

Contests are cool- please don't misinterpret my sarcasm. And no, this isn't another stale piece of literature about the thrills of riding or how you should ride for yourself and not for judges. I wouldn't insult your intelligence with any more bullshit like that. What I'm trying to say is, don't expect every freestyler in the free world to have the same values you have. Not everyone rides simply to show superiority over others. By the same token, not everyone rides solely for personal pleasure either. Just don't look down upon a fellow biker for what he stands for, or what he does in a contest, or how he freestyles. The bottom line is...just ride. There shouldn't be anything else.

DIZZ Uncensored

In this candid interview, the outspoken Dizz Hicks talks about touring, contests, practicing and MUCH much more.

Daily: "Can you describe the origin of mega trick, like when it happened..?"

Dizz: "Oh it happened two years ago. I was definitely the first one to do upside down. Yeah I started it quite awhile ago. Just playin' around you know? Right now I'm workin' on a bunch of new stuff."

Daily: "Like what?"

Dizz: "Just a bunch of new upside down shit. It's gonna be a lot faster and strung together a lot more. You know like McCoy does fast uprock? Well I'm gonna be doin' fast upside down shit. I can pop it from upside down to regular fast. I'm doin' footwork on the frame while it's upside down. It's gonna be cool. It's gonna look good I think. I've been workin' on-Listen! I've got the bike upside down and I'm goin' around the head tube. Boomerangs with the bike upside down. I hold onto the pegs. I know I'm gonna pull that off."

Daily: "Tour plans?"

Dizz: "Kick fuckin' ass! It's plain and simple right there. It started off with me, Gary and Tim Rogers. That'll be cool because I'm kinda weak on my airs right now. I bailed hard a couple times. When you bail you just don't want to get back on the ramp, you know what I mean? So I've been layed off the airs for the last month. When you get on the road it's a whole different attitude. Your attitude changes-you get more back into it. Like right now I'm not really that much into it. I'm not into it that much 'cause if I was I'd be like Ceppie-burned out. Too much ridin' can get to ya. I had my peak in my time. A year ago I was at my peak- I was real good. I had everything-ramps, ground. Right now I'm gettin' kinda down but I know I'm gonna come back strong this year on tour. I've been lookin' forward to that, you know?"

Daily: "How serious do you take contests?"

Dizz: "No, I used to take 'em real serious. Now I just go out there and have a good time. 'Cause I've seen so much bullshit in the judging. I've seen the best rider that should have won and he didn't win. So that doesn't make any sense to me. That kid should've won."

Dave Focks: "Kevin Jones?"

Dizz: "Yeah, Kevin Jones should've won. He got second. He should've got first. And if I was Rick, I would've went up to him and gave him the trophy and said, 'Here, you deserve this buddy.' I would have man, I really would've said that. I wish I would've won, 'cause I would've handed that trophy right to that guy in front of everybody. 'Cause if you do that good, and you got that much fresh stuff, you deserve to win. That guy's been ridin' his ass off to learn that shit you know he has. It's like Gary. Gary rode his ass off for so long and STILL did shitty in contests, remember? And I was thinkin', 'Man, he's gotta have his day.' Now it's comin'. It's all payin' off. If you work hard, and work out hard everyday like he does, it's gonna pay off in the long run. The reason why I don't win contests is 'cause I don't work out hard like they do. If I did, I probably would. But I only get what I deserve ya know?"

Daily: "What do you think about changing the style of contests?"

Dizz: "No, I think the style's fine. It's just that they need to get a system dialed. They need to get some judges that are fair. They shouldn't have anybody judgin' on that panel that has to do with anybody out there ridin'. There's a lot of politics involved. That's the only thing

Dizz INTERVIEW

I don't like about it. Other than that, it's just clean fun and havin' a good time. I don't care about what place I get. Or how I ride. I have a good time out there. That's it. That's all I care about. I have fun goin' out there and ridin'. Lately I haven't been really gettin' into it that much. Just 'cause I've been gettin' kinda bummed out. A lot of shit comin' down lately. I've been gettin' in a lot of trouble...jail."

Daily: "JAIL?!"

Dizz: "I went to jail for drivin' reckless in my car."

Raybo: "When was this?"

Dizz: "Two weeks ago."

Raybo: "What's it like in jail, terrible?"

Dizz: "It's hell (laughter). No one fucked with me though. (Gritting teeth) I got evil in there. Slicked my hair back and sat in the corner waitin' for someone to fuckin' do somethin' (more laughter)."

Daily: "How 'bout the bike?"

Dizz: "This bike's dialed (CW Stunt Vessel). I just switched over to the new one. I always rode my bike real high. Well, I set the bike up for upside down ya know? And no one liked it 'cause it looked uglier than hell. Now I switched over. I realize how stupid I was for ridin' that hunk of shit."

Daily: "How's the girl situation on tour?"

Dizz: "Massive pussy everywhere (laughter)! No-it's O.K. sometimes. Sometimes there's those shows where there's a bunch of chicks out in the audience. I get crazy, point out, get rude. Afterwards I tell 'em where we're gonna be and they come over...I don't want you to-well you can print this, fuck I don't care. My girlfriend don't read nothin' but fuckin' glamour magazines (laughter)!"

Dayve Fox: "Party a lot?"

Dizz: "Yeah as a matter of fact I do. I party all the time. But I don't let it interfere with my biking. Never. I don't ride when I'm drunk. Yeah I party-I'll always party. Just the way I am. I've been that way from the beginning. When I got into freestyle, I had a choice. My parents told me to get a haircut, clean myself up, try to look more professional. And I went into it sayin' 'Fuck it.' If they don't like me the way I am, then they're not gonna like me at all, 'cause this is me. I'm not gonna change for anybody. I'm just gonna stay the way I am and if they like me, that's cool. And it worked out good for me 'cause it started a new image. It's not the same old thing. I still don't ride like anybody else but I used to have a style that no one else had ever seen. Now a lot of people copy some of my tricks. But that's what I'm gonna come back with-another style. In a year. You can't stay at your peak the whole time. I'm not Dennis McCoy. I think Gary's gonna take Dennis' place in a couple of years. I really think so. As hard as he works out and as good as he is now. I just hope that Gary wants to stick with CW-I think he does. They'll treat him right as long as he sticks with 'em. You don't start off at the top. When I started ridin' for 'em, I didn't get paid anything at all. I just rode for 'em for free. But that's how you get started."

Daily: "Who do you ride with."

Dizz: "I ride by myself. 'Cause there ain't nobody where I live that rides at all. There's some posers but that's it. There ain't nobody that's really into it. And I have a better session when I'm by phones on and go."

45

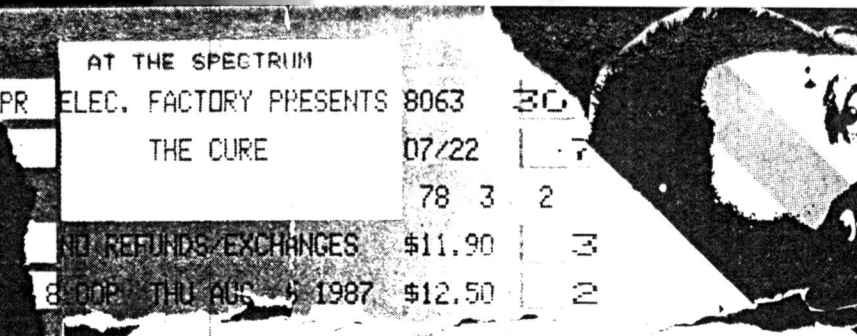

```
AT THE SPECTRUM
ELEC. FACTORY PRESENTS  8063   30
        THE CURE         07/22
                         78  3   2
NO REFUNDS/EXCHANGES  $11.90    3
8:00P  THU AUG 6 1987 $12.50    2
```

Darkness finally swept the Spectrum and the people roared their approval and anticipation to see their heroes- the Cure. Many assembled for the show looked the same, with their Cure shirts and disheveled hairdos. My friend Fred remarked that I looked like a clone, and I had to agree. The unmistakable scent of hair spray loomed in the air and everyone was excited. The large screen in front of the stage suddenly illuminated with the swirling reds and oranges found on the cover of their new album, "Kiss Me, Kiss Me, Kiss Me." It was a bizarre video of sorts, flashing glimpses of Smith's red lips and eyeball to thunderous reactions from the crowd.

Faint music and Smith's faraway, dreamy voice could be detected in the video before the screen fell, revealing the band standing and ready to play. Instantly they introduced themselves with the brash wizardry of "The Kiss," complete with an extra-long instrumental at the beginning. It was loud. Then Robert Smith was spotlighted and revealed to the audience as he nonchalantly wailed out the lyrics, never once raising his hand or drawing attention to himself. Smith's exquisite voice came across beautifully and I thought the band sounded better live.

When Smith introduced "Why Can't I Be You?," he pointed out to the audience and yelled, "This song is for everybody except YOU, because you're a complete dickhead!!" Among the best songs played from the new album were "Torture," "Hot Hot Hot," "Like Cockatoos," "Fight," "Catch," and "Shiver and Shake." Many old favorites were played as well- "Boys Don't Cry,""In Between Days"(particularly good), "The Walk", and "Charlotte Sometimes". They did 3 encores.

If you're looking for wild stage antics at a Cure concert- forget it. They want all the attention to be focused on their incredible music. And when you see them live, you'll agree that's wild enough.

What a Hood!

BEFORE

AFTER BIg dAdDy Gets bUsTeD

Stop Scoot Harrassment

When I saw Andy J.'s desk, squirreliness overwhelmed me.

THE HOODS GO TO
TORRANCE

Mark "Flowmaster" Lewman typin' out some top-notch FREESTYLIN' literature. Lew types FAST.

Spike handling an important business call in his own office.

Me again, this time posing in front of THE street to be.

The K at K-Mart kickin' some tail whips.

Lungmuppet holding A.J.'s now-famous cover deck.

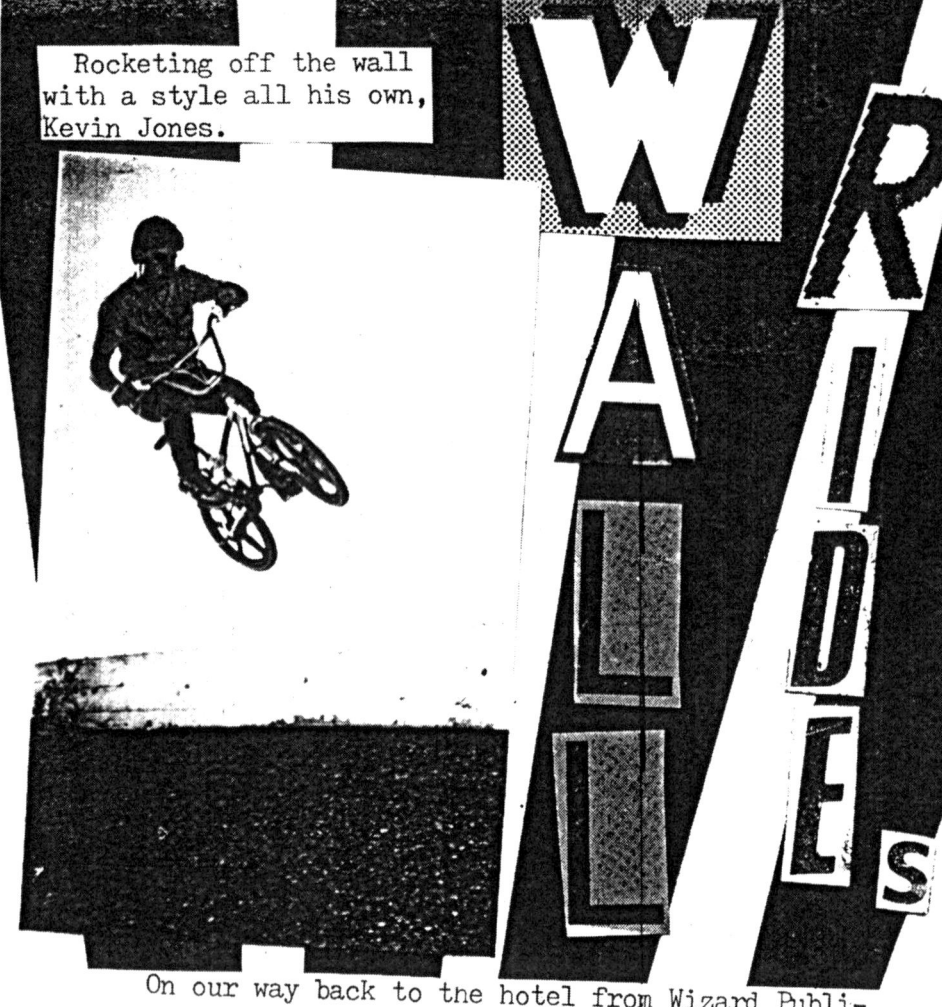

Rocketing off the wall with a style all his own, Kevin Jones.

WALL RIDES

On our way back to the hotel from Wizard Publications one day, we discovered this killer bank/wall set-up. Never having ridden vertical walls before, we Pennsylvanians were mighty stoked. Lungmustard was probably the most jazzed judging from his blatant eagerness in attacking the wall. "This is rad," said Lung as he cranked toward the bank faster than any of us <u>dared</u> go. Kev adapted to the unfamiliar terrain instantly and got equally as aggro as L.M.Tard. Dale went for a few foot plants as did myself. We were having a blast. Then Kev snapped his cranks.

Mr. Mustard planting one off the side of the building. Bzzz zzzzzzzzzz...Slap!

During our impromptu photo session, a Santa Fe train rumbled by. I don't think Dale (far, far left) took notice.

WALL RIDES

Inspect this photo of Lung for the following fine details: BOTH tires are in contact with the wall, the front wheel is nearly five feet off the bank and Eaton's hair is a-flyin'!

Powering off the wall like the Grab On Kid would have (if he was still in syndication), The K.

DEn diDDLe iT DeN...

fig.A
fig.B

Kevin Jones (fig.A) and Dale Mitzel (fig.B) work at Roadway, a truck unloading firm. They work together sometimes. Glenn is a large, black, tough fellow on Dale's shin, who painfully introduced himself one day at work (to Dale's dismay). Let's just say Glenn is not well-liked. He doesn't know when to leave Dale alone, and when bumped by a pedal or similar item, he becomes completely enraged. Kev fidged the following "row" off the top of his head when we were riding the other day...

"One day at work I wrote 'Glen' all over this big box with a magic marker and then I threw it at him. Man, that thing had Glenn's name written all over it. But it missed him... 'cause I spelled it wrong!"

F I D G E page

53

"Anyone wanna buy a Schwinn?"

Jason Parkes

"Anyone Wanna Buy a Schwinn?"

An interview with Jason Parkes by [illegible]

- What's your full name?
  "Jason Parkes."
- How old are you?
  "Eighteen."
- How long have you been freestyling?
  "Uh...four years maybe. Three, four years."
- When were you having the most fun?
  "The most fun? The first three contests I ever entered like San Diego, Venice Beach, Huntington Beach. Those were the best-the way they were set up."
- Was that in '85?
  "Yeah, in '85. They were the funnest for me. I like the environment more than the contest itself."
- Are you entering this weekend (Velodrome)?
  "Yup."
- What kind of music do you like?
  "Exodus, Slayer, S.O.D.-like speed metal groups. The kind the judges don't like."
- Do you skate more now than you ride?
  "No."
- How many hours a day are you riding and skating?
  "Probably about six each."
- Do you get up real early in the morning or...?
  "No, I stay up all night and go to sleep real early in the morning, wake up around three or four."
- What's a basic day for Jason Parkes?
  "Wake up at three, eat, maybe take a shower (much laughter), go ride at the ditch or go ride my bike at the beach."
- Do you try to make money at the beach when you ride?
  "No."
- Who do you like to ride with?
  "Pete I guess. He's not too much into bikes. Just more skating now."
- Tell me something about your sponsors. I heard about Schwinn.
  "Me and Pete and Ronnie said we don't need no more sponsors like that. Gullwing's cool and Life's a Beach is cool 'cause they don't give a fuck what you're like."
- What do you think about Robert Peterson? Do you think he's a dick or do you think he's cool?
  "He's real cool."
- I heard he had something to do with you getting off Schwinn.
  "Yeah sort of. He just seemed to have some authority complex. He liked to give orders but I never took 'em 'cause I don't need to take nothin' from someone I consider lower than myself."
- What did you think about the AFA Austin Texas comp?
  "It was pretty fun. Me and Dizz had fun. We did a good show there."
- What about the competition?
  "It was cool. We got kicked out of all those places we'd go in. I didn't like that."
- Why'd you get kicked out-not wearing a helmet?
  "No...yeah part of that. And for just bein' there without my hand stamped. The security guards-they know what's up. Dizz lost like usual. It was good. I didn't want to go first anyways. I signed up late so they made me go first but they spaced out and forgot me. I went like third or somethin' like that. I lost-so what."
- What place did you get?
  "Sixteenth."

What kind of set-up would you like to see for freestyle contests? Would you want to have like a jam circle-type thing or...?

"Yeah somethin' like that or maybe just head-to-head competition. You know--with elimination and winner/loser brackets. Because when you see one person go right after another you _know_ who won. They used to have skateboarding head-to-head and they'd have like ten people goin' against each other. Then you go to a loser's bracket if you lost or a winner's bracket if you won. With the loser's bracket you could work your way back up to face the winner of the winner's bracket. So you could lose once and still win the whole contest. It's real easy to do."

* Blatantly stolen from the Gullwing ad

- Do you skate ramps?
    "Yeah."
- What pool tricks do you do?
    "Ollies, grinds, handplants, layback airs."

"Anyone wanna buy a Schwinn?"

■ What are your other interests besides skating and biking-if you have any?
"Um...chicks...um...stickers (laughter)...clothes."
■ Weren't you supposed to have a tour this summer?
"Yeah, a real long one-two weeks."
■ Do you drive?
"Nope."
■ Do you have a permit?
"Nope. Just a backseat license."
■ Were you ever arrested?
"I was arrested once."
■ For what?
"Shoplifting."
■ How old were you?
"Fourteen. Made up a good excuse-got away with it."
■ What'd you steal?
"Um...these like little electronic lighters out of Sears."
■ What are your favorite foods?
"Coke. Well, if it doesn't come in a bag or a box I'm not gonna eat it."
*Joe Gruttola: What do you think about Chris Day takin' all the credit for your tricks?
"I don't care. He can have 'em. He's gay. No, he's cool but he doesn't try to take the credit unless you give it to him 'cause you see him pull it off. He might have done something to dick me over but everyone knows who made 'em up."
■ Do you ride with him ever?
"Used to, but not anymore. There's no way-he lives in Redondo. Anyways it used to be like we'd ride with him, me and Pete. Now it's like we <u>try</u> to ride. He rides and takes the whole area and never lets the other people go. We did a show and he just totally hogged the floor and Pete wouldn't even, like, go in. Ya know, Pete just won't go in. It's not even worth it."
■ What are your favorite tricks-bike and skate?
"For skate, favorite trick would be grinding...anything. Like rocks or something. Something harsh. On the bike, I don't know. I just like doing tricks and not even try and think what you're gonna do next, just havin' it all happen."
■ Does that ever happen to you during your routines?
"Yeah, all the time. Just however it ends up and I can stay on the bike, that's how it ends. After I finish one trick up, sometimes I try and do a-nother. But a lot of times it just ends up goin' into one trick and out a-nother."
■ Did you do some of that in Florida?
"I know what you're talkin' about. That one trick into front wheel hops? Yeah. But I can do that all the time."
■ What are you doing in the Gullwing ad?
"Just like ollying onto that rock. Ollie to tail on the rock. They got a bigger rock there now. It's about twice that size."
■ So what do you think you'll be doing in five years?
"Same thing I'm doin' now. Skatin' and ridin' bikes."
■ Do you have a job?
"No."
■ How do you get money?
"Obtain it through various sources."
■ For anybody who wants to ride what do you suggest they start doin'?
"Do about four or five hours every day by yourself. I did it all by myself when I was startin' out. I never watched other people, then I saw others and it changed me. It stopped me from creating so much. I started doing stuff that other people were doing and I didn't even like it. I thought I was better off doing my own thing. When I saw Pete and all those guys at the beach, they kinda like changed what I was doing 'cause I had made up all those tricks and I'd never even seen 'em. After that I started doing tricks like cherrypickers."
■ Where did you ride mainly, in front of your house?
"Yeah, in front of my house-every day, all the time. I'd just come home from school and ride and forget myself."

Jason Parkes

"Anyone wanna buy a Schwinn?"

- Did you ever hook out of school and ride?
  "Oh yeah. A lot. As a matter of fact, I quit school."
- When? This year?
  "Yeah."
- Were you supposed to graduate this year?
  "Yeah, I was supposed to graduate this year."
- Why'd you quit?
  "My mom kicked me out, and I was too far away from the school. Should I go on? No money, flat tire...I just didn't like it. Ya know, she kicked me out and...they were gonna kick me out of my job program. Like my work/education thing. I'd work at this bike shop. Then I had it faked out, the papers. I went to Gullwing and they signed 'em. And the school was gonna take me off the program 'cause I didn't show up for this one class."
- So you quit school.
  "Yeah. I'm gonna go to night school next year. I'm gonna take this test-California State Efficiency Exam. Maybe next year. I don't care."
- When did all of this shit happen?
  "January."
- So you've been riding constantly?
  "Yeah, just riding constantly. I live with my friend's parents. They got four kids now and I just live with him. It's cool-it'll be about 90 bucks a month and I stay in the house and they got a garage out back, too. For all the stuff I own."
- Any reason why your parents kicked you out?
  "Well, I like bailed out of there before 'cause me and my mom didn't get along too good. And then she threatened to go through the contract (with Schwinn) 'cause I was a minor. So I came back and got her to sign a contract. And she got all pissed off at me one day, tried to hit me an' shit and I wasn't gonna let her hit me so she kicked me out. She got all pissed 'cause I was holdin' her wrists."
- Was it a salary contract?
  "They (Schwinn) were paying me around 400 bucks a month. Photo contingency too. But I also had to wear a helmet, leathers, and jersey. They paid me some of it though."
- Is Life's a Beach happy when they see you wearin' their stuff?
  "Oh yeah. A lot of times I've worn their stuff instead of wearin' what Schwinn wanted me to. When I was ridin' for Schwinn, they (Life's a Beach) weren't paying me anything so they should be totally happy. I lost money a couple of times by not wearin' the Schwinn stuff. You know, 'cause they didn't pay me the photo contingency 'cause they didn't have to 'cause it said in the contract I had to wear their shit."
- Did you ever enter a contest and not wear Schwinn stuff?
  "Yeah. At this one contest I just left my leathers at home. I said 'These things are gay' and..."
- Which contest was that?
  "Tulsa. I wore some skull pants instead."
- Oh I never saw that one.
  "You should be glad you didn't. As soon as I went out there they had this nice dust covering all over the floor an' my feet were just slippin' and slidin.' I tried 360 squeakers for the first trick and, I don't know, I was totally doin' it good outside 'cause it was a nice floor-no dust or anything-then I went inside and just fell apart."
- Do you think the expert class is harder than the pro class?
  "Well, it seems like it. Last time there was 75 people in 16-18 Expert. So expert seems a lot harder than pro."
- Any last words?
  "Anyone wanna buy a Schwinn?" ∗

"Read up, Sonny!"

t-shirts are now available. Screened front and back. Quality. A bit risqué. Send ten bucks (postage inc.)

    Freestyle sucks. Now that I've gotten your attention, let me say that we love and live freestyle. You may have determined that from reading this crazy issue. Hey- this is our scene. This is how we see freestyle. I'll always like riding more than anything else- even more than making Aggro Rag. I hope this issue really pumps you up. Now go out and <u>ride</u> for crissakes....

59

AGGRO RAG
FREESTYLE MAG!

c/o Mike Daily
3320 Spondin Drive
York   PA   17402
(717) 757-3096

EMISSION

Aaron Lee

Dorkin' in York came out on May 13, 1988. One of the highlights is Craig Grasso dorkin' for Raybo's video camera. (Ray says on the commentary track for *Dorkin' in York: The Complete DVD Collection*: "If someone coulda followed Grasso around like from the time he left to go to the contest until he went home, there would be some crazy stuff because he was so weird."). Going to major contests wasn't always fun and games—or "fidge" as we liked to call it. We were sometimes chased by police. Aaron Dull (who has since taken his wife's last name and now goes by Aaron Lee) remembers the incident in Columbus, Ohio.

Mike Daily: Do you remember everybody getting chased in Columbus?

Aaron Lee: I do. [Laughs.] It was quite a few contests that we got chased at. You remember Columbus—*everybody* got chased. The police were around the hotel rooms. Were you riding with us when that happened?

Yeah, I was. In fact, the story that I wrote in this issue of *Aggro Rag* describes the chase and mentions that you and I were riding away from the ruckus.

Yeah! I totally remember that, man. The cops were right behind us. The road curved around and we basically ended up on the same road—one level lower. The guard rail that I got off my bike and jumped over, someone in front of me tried to bunnyhop the thing. The whole time, I was just in disbelief. I'm pretty sure it was Kevin Jones. It was unbelievably high. That was pretty wild. And if you think about it, we didn't really do anything. Well, I guess we ran. They didn't know what to make of us, I think. Do you remember them waiting outside the hotel rooms—in the hotel—also?

Yeah.

You had to sneak back into the hotel. The whole thing was pretty crazy.

It was. 🐛

**AGGRO RAG FREESTYLE MAG!
(Spring 1988)**
York, PA./Lock Haven, PA
5½" x 8¼"

10th ISSUE

"There was nothing cooler than going to a contest back then, and the main stuff was the stuff in the parking lot, you know? There was so much crap goin' on out in the parking lot that was better than the actual contest."
—**Raybo**

"I have no idea why there was *Lil Rascals* footage in the video. I literally think that it was on the video and we just didn't edit it out."—**Eaton**

WEDNESDAY
February 17, 1988

LIVING

Comics TV Movies

Expert still learning tricks of trade

Freestyler has his eyes set on pros

By PEGGY SPANGLER
Daily Record staff writer

It seems too much for one person to manage all at once.

The bike spins, flips and rolls on one wheel. Kevin Jones' feet occasionally touch the pedals — one at a time and only long enough to keep the 20-inch bike moving. Most of the time the 20-year-old's legs are either in the air or planted on platforms and pegs jutting from the bike.

You wonder if Jones is double-jointed. Then you find yourself looking suspiciously at the bike for remote controls.

The silver-and-white bike stands on end — one treadless red tire aimed skyward, the other crunching the gravel in the parking lot. Jones has maneuvered himself over the handlebars and draped his muscular frame on what normally is the underside of the bike.

Pedals out of foot's reach, one foot pushes against the tire to keep the bike going. His arms are steady, his face intense, concentrating.

He's doing the Locomotive. Or is it the Caboose? Funky Chicken? To be sure, this trick is not the One-handed Megaspin.

Jones' expression softens as the bike resumes the two-wheels-on-pavement position for which it was designed. The soles of his sneakers bring the bike to a halt. He grins.

In competition, Jones keeps up the pace for two minutes. That's the length of a routine in the expert class of American Freestyle Association contests. One more first place in a national contest will move him into the pro class — then he'll get four minutes to do what, for the time being, is his thing.

"I practice five or six hours every day," the York Suburban graduate says. "If it's raining I practice in the garage — but I can only keep that up for a few hours because of the small space."

When the weather cooperates — and that's just about anything short of tornadoes, thunderstorms and blizzards — Jones and friends are to be found in an empty parking lot. The Plywood Hoods, a pre-freestyle name left-over from their days of jumping and ramping, includes Jones, Mike Daily, Mark Eaton, Dale Mitzel and Jamie McKulik. The group has performed at events in the area.

Jones' interest in riding began about seven years ago with racing and ramping. About three years ago, he veered into the world of trick riding. He devoured magazines — *Freestylin'*, *BMX Plus*, *Freestyle*, *Super BMX*, *American Freestyler* — to learn the tricks being done across the country. And then, he moved on to invent his own tricks.

Freestyle — as trick riding has been dubbed — was new.

"Nobody was into it — and I guess I figured I would have a chance to get in at the beginning and go with it," Jones, son of Brenda and Michael Jones, says.

Flatland trick riding has grown in popularity during the past four years, Jones says. The AFA holds about eight contests each year and the American Bicycle Association holds about seven. Jones will compete in an ABA contest in Arizona in mid-March and an AFA contest in Oregon later in March.

With his recent contract with Skyway Recreation, a bicycle manufacturer in Redding, Calif., Jones' equipment, lodging, meals and travel expenses to contests and exhibitions are paid by his sponsor. A monthly salary and three- to four-week promotional tour in Europe also are part of Skyway team membership.

"We picked Kevin based on his performance in contests and his conduct. We want someone with sportsmanlike conduct representing our product," Ken Coster, Skyway sales and marketing director, said in a telephone interview from California. "The team promotes our product — and they help with R&D (research and development)."

Skyway managers don't ride the bikes, so they don't know what improvements and changes are needed. The team offers suggestions as to what they need in bike design and what would result in the best equipment for the sport.

Hoping to join their ranks, Jones keeps his eye on the pros — a select group of about 20 freestylers. Jones estimates there are about 180 experts, most of whom are striving to become pros.

"Dennis McCoy is my favorite pro," Jones says of the freestyler from Kansas City, Mo. "He can do three tricks in the time it takes most riders to do one. He's really fast."

And Jones hope for the future? Originality. He's one of few freestylers who won't settle for doing someone else's tricks.

Kevin Jones practices his moves as a freestyle biker.

Record photo by Paul Kuehnel

AGGRO RAG

FREESTYLE MAG!

"Ride First, Read Later."

NO. 9

Exclusive Photos!

Kevin Jones Sleeping in a Hotel Room!

TWO BUCKS

Inside:
Contests!
Interviews!
Buddies!
A Star Pin-Up!
No Skating!
One Ad!

PLUS TONS MORE!

60 pages!

OHIO!

Crime on Wheels

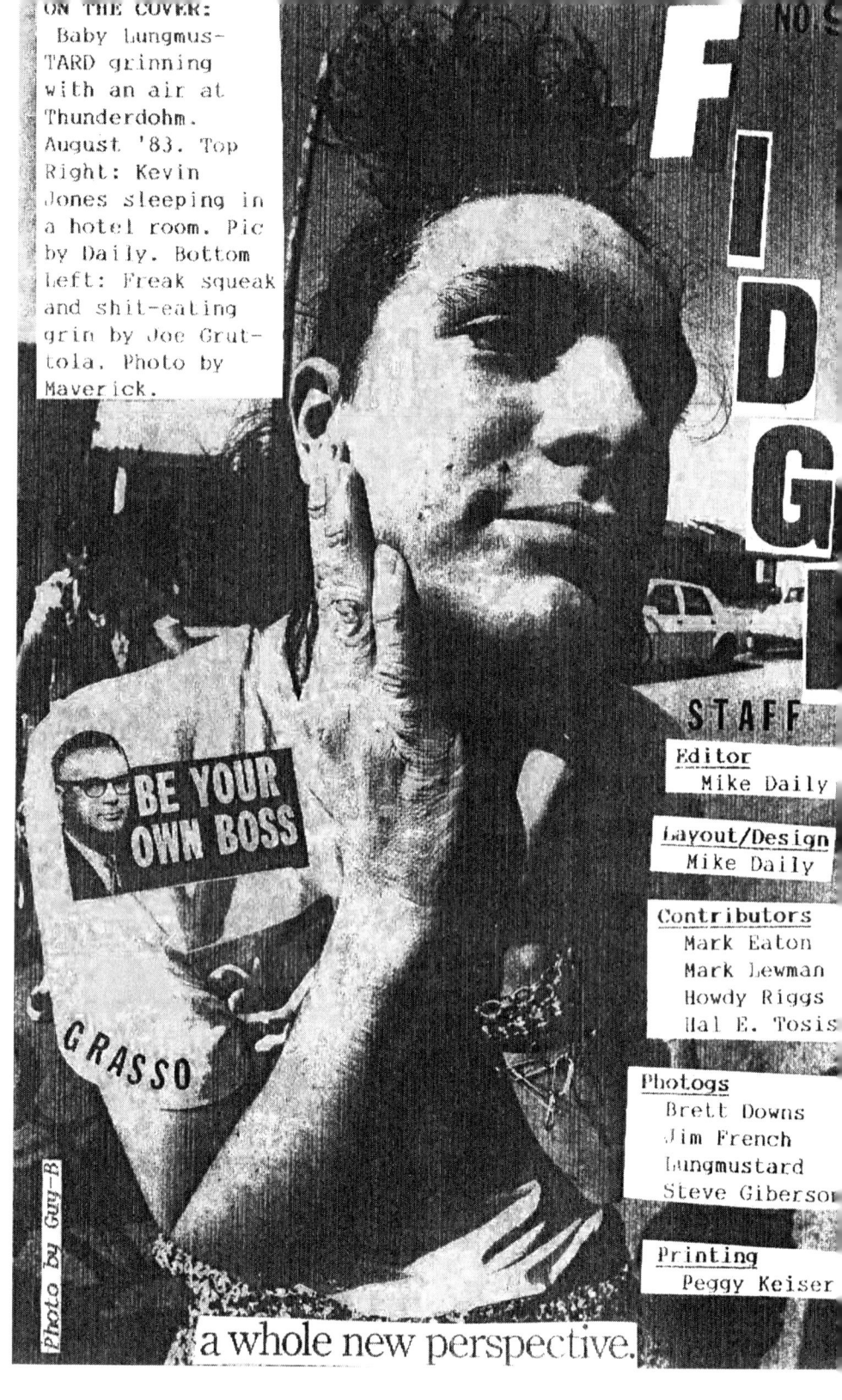

ON THE COVER:
Baby Lungmus-TARD grinning with an air at Thunderdohm. August '83. Top Right: Kevin Jones sleeping in a hotel room. Pic by Daily. Bottom Left: Freak squeak and shit-eating grin by Joe Gruttola. Photo by Maverick.

FIDG

NO:

BE YOUR OWN BOSS

GRASSO

Photo by Guy-B

STAFF

Editor
Mike Daily

Layout/Design
Mike Daily

Contributors
Mark Eaton
Mark Lewman
Howdy Riggs
Hal E. Tosis

Photogs
Brett Downs
Jim French
Lungmustard
Steve Giberson

Printing
Peggy Keiser

a whole new perspective.

AGGRO RAG
FREESTYLE MAG!

Ahoy there! Welcome to issue #9, Jackal. I hope you enjoy reading Aggro Rag as much as we enjoy producing it. This one took over 40 hours and three glue sticks to put together. Aggro Rag is not published monthly. There are no subscriptions. Heavy on Hood pride and personality, Aggro Rag can be thought of as an album. Allow me to introduce the band...

Andy Jenkins and Mark Lewman continually support the Rag with literary contributions, art, photos, and FREESTYLIN' blurbs. I am VERY appreciative of their dedicated efforts. They also ran a Club Homeboy ad in this ish which really helped out. Thanks guys, you're the coolest...

I'd also like to call your attention to GT's T.M. McGoo, who flows mighty hard and really stands behind the team and the fanzine. Steve Giberson issued me some choice glossies which I gladly ran in this issue. Thanks Guy-B (AGGRO shots)!

I'd be the biggest spagmump in the world if I neglected to give thanks to the Plywood Hoods-- Kev, Dale, Eaton, Jamie, and Brett--for being the funnest guys EVER to ride and hang with. You guys are the best!

Now read onward, young soul, and experience some AGGRO-culture...

Keep the Faith,

Mike Daily

Mike Daily
Underworld Character/
Hopeless Curehead

Mumbo Jumbo

By Daily

The Scammer

The Plywood Hoods have been copping copious amounts of ink in a few of the big mags lately, landing predominantly in the "news" sections. However, the items published are often times news to US. Propaganda? Not really, no...The latest card-carrying hoodlum is Jamie "Chief" McKulik, who was on the invincible Cardboard Lords and has ridden with Kevin Jones for quite some time now. James can ride very well, *loves* free products, and has the uncanny ability to completely annoy anyone he comes in contact with. According to recent reports, The Jammer has been riding aimlessly around York scavenging for things to jump. Lung claims the "Dorkin' in York" video will be out soon, hopefully before hell freezes over. Eaton, now riding for Revcore, assures all Hoods fans that some "rad shit" has been filmed for the production. We'll see...Kev's amateur status may soon be coming to an end, and you KNOW what THAT means. The ever-intense John Huddleston has been absolutely RAGING of late, and a factory sponsorship is sure to be a part of his future. A typical line from this young man is as follows: "Oh my God, you could go into locomotive from that." By the way, his locomotives are said to be *hyperspastic*...PA natives John Swarr, Mike Cutillo, and Warren are traveling to Bermuda to do freestyle shows at a resort-type place for 9 months. McGoo flowed Swarr a tricked-out Dyno, while Wally and Warren received complete GT units. Color them stoked. Fidgemaster Craig Grasso and perhaps Pete Augustin will be riding on Diamond Back's new 1988 street style squad. Watch for these nuts at Ron Wilkerson's upcoming 2-Hip street-styled contests.

What a Hood

The K *Circa '85*

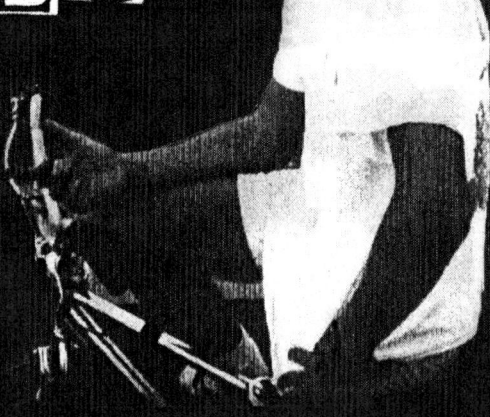

BURNING BRIDGES
In Columbus OHIO

Crazy Gary

Story by Daily
Pics by Maverick

Aaron Dull chopping out stick bitch in the hotel parking lot. Later on he told us funny stories about Jim Treacy.

Boy, did we ever make waves *that* night. We were stationed in Columbus, Ohio for the fourth AFA Masters contest of 1987. This comp was heralded by many as being the best one of the year for a number of reasons, primarily because it was the end of the summer and everyone was DIALED. If you crave info about the actual contest, though, pick up a participating copy of BMX Plus! or something. This story pertains to what occurred *after* the competition one night, when a group of anarchic bikers proceeded to turn the town of Columbus, Ohio upside down.

CONTINUED

Hair by Grasso

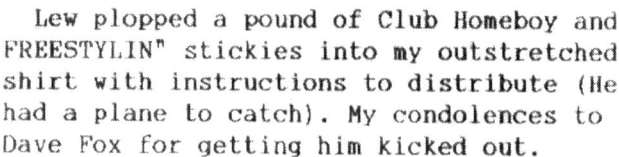

Lew plopped a pound of Club Homeboy and FREESTYLIN" stickies into my outstretched shirt with instructions to distribute (He had a plane to catch). My condolences to Dave Fox for getting him kicked out.

fakie boom

Eaton rode like a champ and I was very proud of him. As you well know, Lung got third place in 16-18 X.

Burning Bridges in Columbus, Ohio

Visions of the legendary L.C. Assassins danced in our heads as we contemplated exploring the town scene. Actually, Columbus was being mentally pillaged and destroyed by each pedaling pirate present for the rogue run. We converged in an old trailor park across the street from the AFA host hotel, the same hotel that forcefully evicted one Dennis McCoy only minutes before.

CONTINUED

OHIO

We waited for Dennis to fix his Haro vessel for the anarchy voyage while everyone chattered excitedly. A lug nut with a built-in rotating washer? We never saw such trickness. Gary was becoming completely restless. We wanted to *thrash*. All three dozen of us.

Finally, Mr. McCoy was ready to roll. A single file scheme was established and we approached the main street. Motorists became alarmed as their headlights revealed a fleet of about forty freestylers riding alongside the road. We felt real proud-like. The first intersection hosted a patrol car and a hollering copper though. He was just plain *sore*.

"HEY!! Get over here! What's goin' on here?! I'll..." Gary sprang into the flee mode and started high-tailin' it through the intersection and onto a bridge. The rest of us followed suit, causing the cop to engage sirens and lights. Bikers were all OVER the bridge at this point, dodging cars in every lane. Most of us just wanted to get to the other side of the bridge so we could get away. Uh...sorry.

The cabatchi proceeded to speed past us on the bridge and screech to a carving halt at the end, thus blocking our intended get-away. We didn't stick around to see what else he learned from watching "Starsky and Hutch." Everyone

Brett Hernandez showing some strong Nor Cal style with a smooth Karl Kruiser.

Lungchicken revealed his temporarily dormant street skills with this fine bunnyhop over a fallen can.

CONTINUED

applied brakeage and promptly turned around. I saw Dale, and his eyes were bulging from his head like golf balls.

    I bunnyhopped the median strip and started cranking for all I was worth. I presume the main goal of the majority of us heathens was to get back to the hotel and hide. A guy in front of me was winding out like crazy on a white Skyway with a tons-low seat pointing up in the air. Yup--it was Aaron! Just before we got to the end of the bridge we noticed about four gumball machines screaming towards us down the interstate, lights and sirens a-wailin.' Aaron and I cruised off the bridge and hung a Louie, which led us down a dark side street. Then *another* back-up patrol car popped out of nowhere at the end of the street. We were instantly spotted like deer by its powerful headlights. "*STOP!! Or go to jail!,*"said the officer over a handy loudspeaker. Young Dave Fox opted for a short cut through some weeds and was forced to deal with a variety of wild thorn bushes VERY quickly. Suddenly Aaron locked up his brakes and I nearly smashed into the back of his bike. He spotted a dirt trail which we took at

CONTINUE

Brian Blyther.
Up there.

Burning Bridges in Columbus, Ohio

Above: Dave Nourie playing in in the parking lot. Top Left: Jim Johnson with a trick of choice in Ohio... the freak squeak. No-handed even. Left: This is Aaron Dull's Nor Cal buddy and he TEARS! Is that a reflector? Below: Joseph Gruttola, RAY, and Mark Lewman.

speed. We ended up on a lower adjacent street... exhausted. Up ahead in the moonlit sky I saw the bridge we tried to cross. We had to keep going. Aaron grabbed his bike and high-stepped a three-foot guardrail like a gazelle. We caught up with Dale and a few others and took a breather. Sirens sounded off in the distance.

"*We gotta get back to the hotel,*" said someone. Dale was mumbling something about Dennis bunnyhopping a guardrail at full-sprint. Holy. The plan was to utilize backroads to sneak back to the hotel. So that's what we did.

Lew and I were talking "politics" in the stands when Brett took this pic.

CONTINUED

SOME PEOPLE

Above: Now THIS is a JAM circle! It's perfectly OK to stand on the outskirts of one with your arms crossed, drooling. Or you can take the floor. Pete Kearney took the floor. Right: Some factory cats.

OHIO OHIO
OHIO
OHIO

RONNIE

Eric Evans

The eight-foot wall surrounding the hotel was scaled after scootage was haphazardly tossed over. We entered the hotel through a back door and jammed to our rooms to stash the incriminating evidence. Swimming attire was adorned and towels were grabbed as all guilty headed for the pool to further elude the heat.

As I strode through the lobby in the D.M. mode, I was amazed at all the commotion. The scene was bustling with irate security personnel, bewildered guests, and of course a large number of sore-looking baton-brandishing coppers. Then the hotel matter-of-factly announced that all freestylers without parents would be evicted *no questions asked*. I overheard a lady say, "It's probably only about ten *jerks* who are just *terrorizing* the place!" Egads. I stifled a smirk and kept walking.

EPILOGUE: A few unlucky souls got busted (Grasso being one of the unlucky), nobody was kicked out (Could you imagine the lawsuits from *that* one?), Jamie was busy playing in the pool the whole time and had no idea what was going on, and everyone had a good laugh or two. Or three. ✶

"B" TEAM BOYS

An abbreviated look at two hot PA undergrounders whom the Hoods like a lot. By Lungmustard...

Huddleston carvin' up a locomotive within the tight confines of Eaton's basement. This guy just DOES NOT stop riding.

JOHN

"B" TEAMERS

Names: Jym Dellavalle and John Huddleston.

They are: Friends, riders, and "B" Team members of the Plywood Hoods.

They both: Own halfpipes, ride flatland, are from PA, break one bike part per week.

John: Tries not to do a decade after every trick, but has been known to do nine (9) in a 2 and 1 half minute run.

Once: Jym did a wall ride, his pedal got caught (somehow), and he stalled it.

Also once: John rode to "Hey, We Want Some Pussy!" and Jerry Holland (Shifty Maryland contest promoter) threw the tape at him.

Jym: Has been seen on many different Dynos and GTs. He used to have a kickstand on his Dyno (he used it, too). He does scruff tricks and forward rolling shit, but what do *you* care? All you need to know is that Jym is NOT a trick sponge, and he just wants to ride with the Hoods. A rolling perverted boomerankle.

John again: He's been known to drop his bike a lot, but when he's on it he RIPS! He usually rides Haro Masters. He had three in one year (1986). *"All I DO is ride. I take a day or two off every week. Just so I can ride MORE!"* John has recently been attempting decades into locomotives. He once did swivels for 15 minutes straight.

J Y M

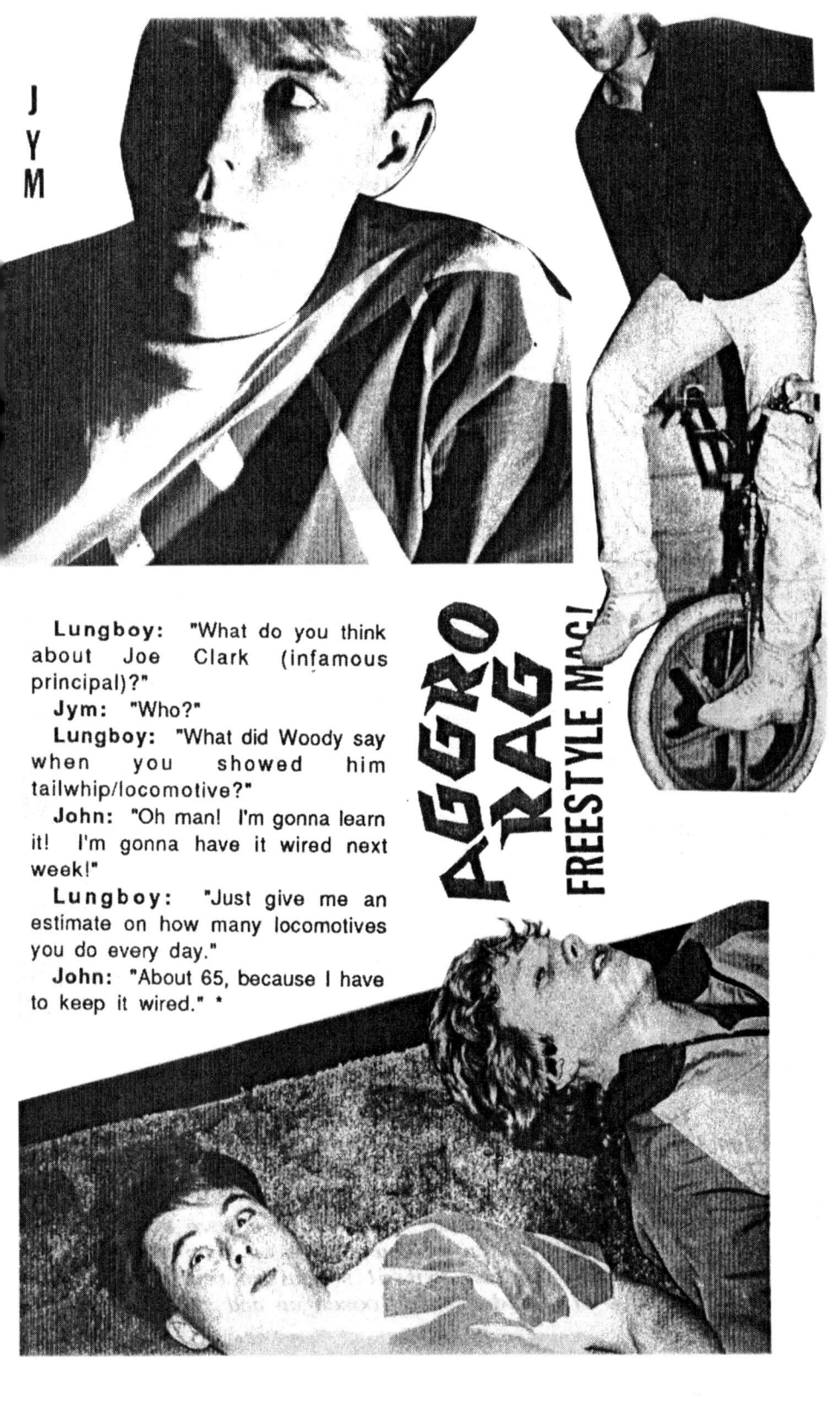

AGGRO RAG FREESTYLE MAG!

Lungboy: "What do you think about Joe Clark (infamous principal)?"
Jym: "Who?"
Lungboy: "What did Woody say when you showed him tailwhip/locomotive?"
John: "Oh man! I'm gonna learn it! I'm gonna have it wired next week!"
Lungboy: "Just give me an estimate on how many locomotives you do every day."
John: "About 65, because I have to keep it wired." *

AGGRO RAG
FREESTYLE MAG!

Being spontaneously stylish is what makes riding ever-so-intriquing to the innovative Aaron Dull. This switch-legged swivel was not designed to make its inventor look cool.

COMPENSATE
By Daily

You don't arch your back this way or dangle your leg that way during a trick to look "cool." Usually, body parts become contorted and stretched to compensate for balance problems or misjudged speed. The mind is saturated with one thought--to make this move WORK. Your stomach muscles tighten as you strain to keep the trick going. Floundering for control sometimes reveals the true talents of a rider. So loosen up and surprise yourself...

Photos Courtesy of Guy-B

It was conceived more as a transitional move for his puppet, a study in genuine style and control.

Right: Aaron Dull receiving congratulations from Frank Garrido after a superb run at the 87 Converse Velodrome comp. Are they "Buddies II?" Photo: Daily

AGGRO RAG

FREESTYLE MAGAZINE!

BUDDIES

August 1987 U.S. $2.00
CAN $3.00 00540 I.C.D.

Maria sighed deeply as Frederick's strong, calloused han[d] stroked her trembling shoulders. Her voice quivering, she kissed Frederick gently and sai[d]

Mike,
Some guy named "Lung mostard P." called, he wants to know if he got the COVER
 BILL

BUDDIES

An ode to some long-time pals by Mike Daily

Photos by Jim "The Weasel" French

"Where's your *buddy*?," asked Karl Rothe.
"What?," said Kevin Jones.
"Your *buddy*. Lungmustard," said Karl Rothe.
"Oh," said Kevin Jones. "I don't know."

After that now-famous exchange, Kev's favorite saying became "Yeah buddy!" He uttered it habitually--while riding, walking through a store, at work, during meals, etc. Karl's term "buddy" was humorous to Kev because he never really thought of Eaton as his "buddy." Riding companion for five years and fun guy to fidge with--yeah. But "buddy?" Come on now...

The truth is, Kevin Jones and Mark Eaton are indeed buddies. Good buddies. In eighth grade, Mark met Kev while jumpin.' "Kev could do a great tabletop," exclaims Mark. Eaton tried to get to know Kev by asking him questions...about anything. "I asked him about his Uni Seat. Like what he thought of 'em and how light they were," recalls Lungmustard. Eaton was answered with the standard KSJ "Don't ask me stupid questions" shoulder shrug and a

BUDDIES

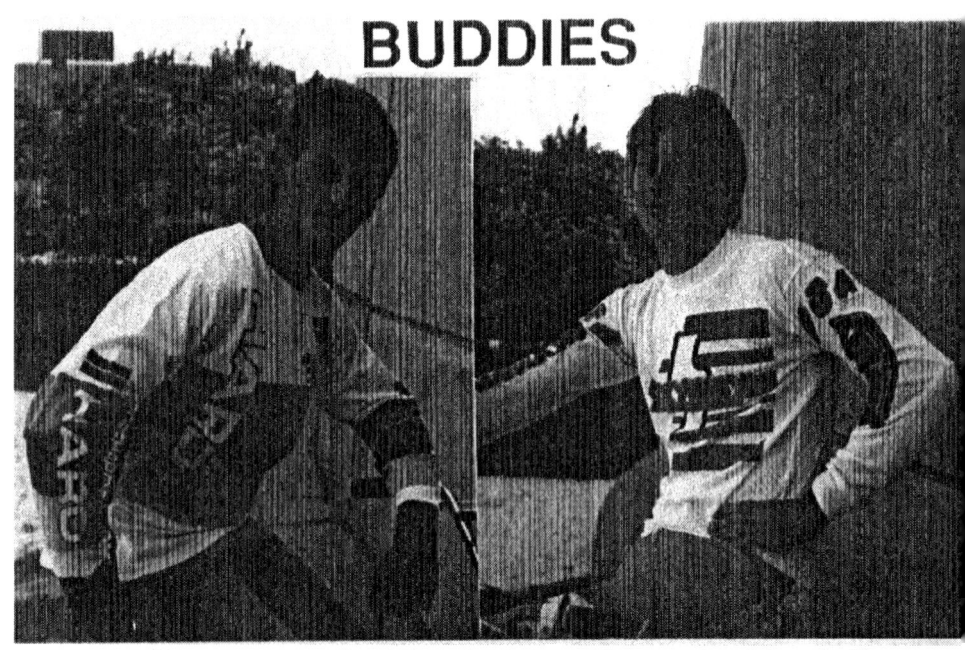

sharp "I dunno." That's when Lung realized Kev was very different...a bit weird if you will. "He didn't care. He just had it, you know?," laughs Lunger. Eaton knew this guy was great. The following week Mark went out and purchased his very own Uni Seat.

Eaton rode with Kev every spare chance he could get. They jumped together at Best Products, The Pit, and Thunderdohm. They skated together occasionally. They rode the street together. They got great together.

Eaton would see Kev in school and they would would plan after-school thrash sessions. They'd anticipate the end of the school day, when they would be totally free to get rad jumping somewhere. Many an evening (or night) they'd return to their houses with sunburned necks and arms, dirty socks, and huge grins of satisfaction. Those were the days, huh guys?

Want to know the craziest thing Kevin and Mark ever did together? There was a good jump located near a parking lot and they went to it one day in hopes of catching some air. But lo and behold, a parked car was blocking the landing area! No problem--after a few moments of surveying the obstacle, Kev blasted up the jump, landed on the hood, rode right over the roof, and jumped off the back. Eaton then mimicked

The K's radical actions and made it safely. They alternated runs on the car, each attempt gaining confidence and aggroness. "Kev was jumpin' the windshield and doin' little tabletops!," said Lung. But that's not even the CRAZY part.

The lady who owned the car came out of the store and got into her "abused" auto (Editor's Note: Eaton said their lunacy left only slight tire marks), suspecting nothing at all. Kev looked at Eaton and said, "Let's do it!" Eaton nodded, and Kev cranked for the jump with buddy Mark right behind him. Meanwhile, the still-unsuspecting lady started up her car. Kev hit the embankment and bounded up and over the auto, making a helluva racket and frightening the woman considerably. As Eatonian was going over the top of the car, the scared lady shifted into reverse and floored it. Luckily for Mark, the car didn't go into gear and it just revved loudly. Eaton dropped off the back of the car and the pair cruised away laughing, leaving a very stunned woman behind the tightly-gripped wheel of her violated vehicle. Crazy kids.

Lungmustard is now 18 years of age and Kev is 20. Eaton was just picked up by CW while Kevano rides for Skyway. Kev has completed two years of college and is now taking a break to concentrate more on his riding. Lung graduated from high school last year and is contemplating going to a trade school in the near future. They both work at Roadway unloading freight and such. They ride together often, but not as much as they used to. That's O.K. though, 'cause Mark Eaton and Kevin Jones are still buddies...

AGGRO RAG FREESTYLE MAG!

Photo by Jim French

The Gingerbread Man

We call it our domain on Friday and Saturday nights during the summer. The Gingerbread Man is located in downtown York. It's a ritzy restaurant with an outdoor cafe. A large grassy hill leads down to a perfect riding area adjacent to a huge creek. Lights on 'til 11PM... plus music. Don't forget the drunken patrons who clap and throw money. Once an intoxicated man offered twenty bucks to the first kid who jumped his bike into the water at speed. I did it, and got a standing ovation and $21. My dad said I could have been impaled on a half-submerged shopping cart. If you ever come to York you'll know where to find us.....

"BUSINESSMAN"

Dale's Rolling Nightmare

FREESTYLIN' Co-Editor Mark Lewman agreed to write about Wayne, New Jersey for the Rag and we thank him. This is also the first Aggro Rag story ever written on an airplane...

Camerawork: Maverick
Writing: Dewbag

THE hardest way into the caboose...a forward-rolling fork-holding peg wheelie transition. Big Daddy.

Sitting in the stands and observing a contest, you're likely to see quite a bit, depending upon how many trips you make to the snack bar. RIDING in a contest is a completely different story.

Wayne, New Jersey was round five of the dreaded AFA Masters Series. I couldn't tell you who won if my life depended on it. Summing up the weekend on the plane ride home...this is what I came up with;

New Jersey is pretty cold in October. And rainy...meaning it did rain, forcing would-be practicers indoors only to be slapped in the face by a practice area roughly the size of a public phone booth. But there were only about 90 guys at a time riding, so it was cool. . Ha.

Getting to the contest was a bit of a mystery. Signs on the William Patterson College grounds were nil. I took a taxi from the airport in Newark and was left with a smoking hole in my wallet where $50 once rested. The gymnasium it was held in conveniently had a giant-assed net put up, thus blocking the practice area from the view of the arena floor and vice-versa. Every time loud cheering rose from the stands, kids in the practice area would crowd around all the small holes in the netting to catch a glimpse of whoever was riding.

Most of the classes were packed--including pro flatland and ramps. I'm pretty sure the usual guys probably won. Karl Rothe got kicked out on Saturday for spiking a volleyball into oblivion. In my eyes, seeing Karl being escorted down the bleachers with his hands raised over

Kevano

Jim Johnson

Denny Howell

Kevin Jones

Goro

Kelby

Kev

N.J. MASTERS #5

his head in disbelief as the stands screamed and booes in unison at security was the highlight of the day. Karl Rothe is just the ultimate dude. If there were ever somebody I considered my hero (aside from "Bert" on Sesame Street), Karl is him.

Dale Mitzel, charter member of the Plywood Hoods and regular "top-tenner" in the 19 and over expert flatland class, owns an '84 Ford Mustang. That Mustang, along with myself and the rest of the Hoods, never did make it into the depths of NYC on Saturday night due to several incidents involving rain, traffic, and bad jokes...all of which had an adverse effect on Dale's stress glands. I think we did see Woody Itson crack up his rental unit on the freeway that night, though. Spooky.

Speaking of spooky, on his way to a win in 16-18 expert flat, Joe Gruttola pulled a double whiplash. Jesus. I noted several riders of prominence used AC/DC for their music during routines. Hmmm. Move over rap music. The floor wasn't bad, but the sound system more than made up for that--in a word, it was SHIT. The radio in Dale's car was louder.

Amidst all the chaos that went down Saturday, I'm pretty sure a few people managed to have fun, regardless of my cynical attitude. The stands were large and packed, and at times, they even cheered. Wow.

Sunday was a day of oversleeping, 7-11 breakfast, and a fashionably late entrance. We completely missed 16-18 expert ramps.

Little did Dale know that six torturous hours of driving awaited him. 19 & Over Expert Flatland.

CONTINUED

Josh

Jones

Dale's Rolling Nightmare

I heard Matt Hoffman did this double-candy bar (like a barhop) air. Figures. Joe Johnson was the God of thunder and rock and roll in 16-18 ramps. But you already knew that too, huh?

Dave Voelker was once again blessed with a win in 19 & over ramps, beating out guys like Dino DeLuca, Steve Broderson, and Marty Schlesinger. The air zone was repeatedly penetrated with violations in excess of nine feet. Voelker slammed on a no-handed fakie WAAAY out, Dino met the floor hard on a pedal picker drop-in, and Steve Broderson went to his doom on a rollback.

Pro ramps were sicker than a cancer ward. Dominguez did this one fakie sooo high...it's no use explaining it unless you saw it, and if you saw it, you know what I'm talking about. On the variation scale he gave us a no-hander, a one-handed no-footed can-can, and what looked like a no-footed helicopter.

Jamie

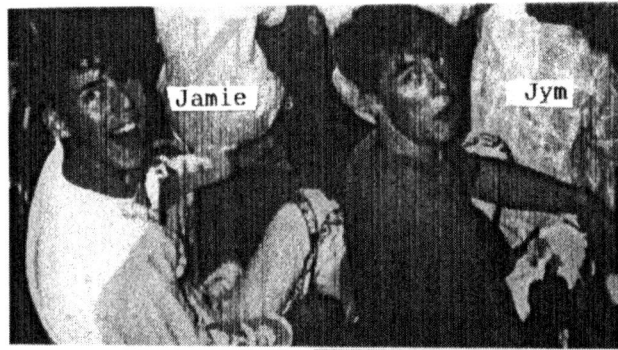

Jym

C. Day

Chris Day

John

The Doc (aka Josh White) performed a little aerial surgery and barged his way into second place...not bad for his first contestsince his shoulder injury. Following Josh was Dennis McCoy in third, Blyther in fourth, Wilkerson (yes, RON) in fifth, and Sigur was sixth. All provided raging entertainment.

About the time the contest ended everybody decided the moment was right to mill around and generally get in the way of everybody else for about an hour, so that's what I did too.

Hours later we were racing time on the way back to Newark airport...Dale was pushing 60 in the 'Stang, biting his nails the whole time. By the time I boarded the plane, I was the last guy on. I pulled out a pen, asked for some extra napkins, and began writing what you are now just finishing up. It was completed somewhere over Colorado.

- Dewbag

Trevorlabagest

Kevin's Rope-R-Roni

STAR PIN-UP!

HOTEL FUN

The Vagabond Inn...Redondo Beach, CA. We Hoods had some trouble signing in because we're all under 21, but they graciously "bent the rules" (i.e.- They needed the money). The guys blamed me for this hellish mess but there's no way.

> Hotels are fun. For one painless fee, you and your friends are entitled to a warm shower, clean beds to jump on, an idiot box, a large swimming pool, vending machines galore, free soap and towels, the lobby microwave (ask Raybo about this one), a free continental breakfast, the opportunity to fidge maids who despise tire marks, spare room keys if you tend to lose them (Dale), and of course a paved parking lot to rip up, complete with ample lighting for those all-night sessions. We don't pull fire alarms but we still have fun...

HOTEL FUN

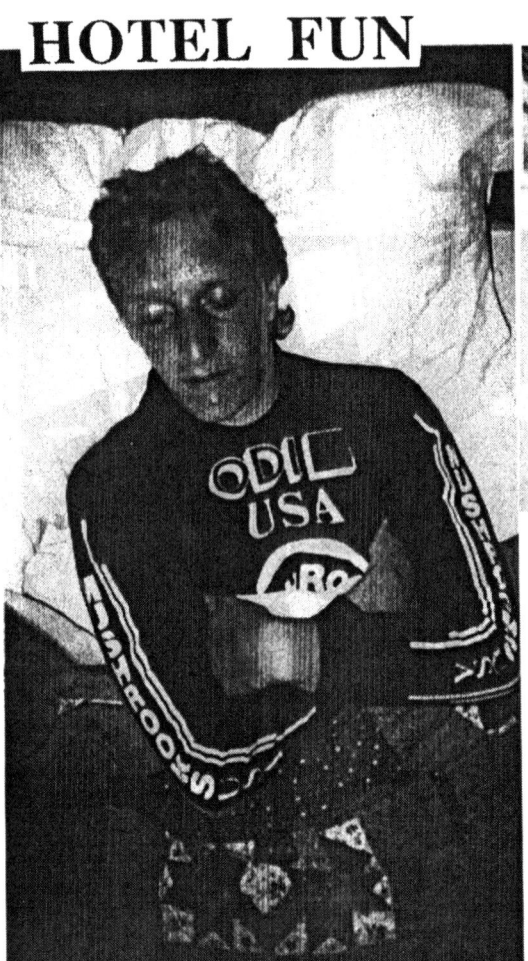

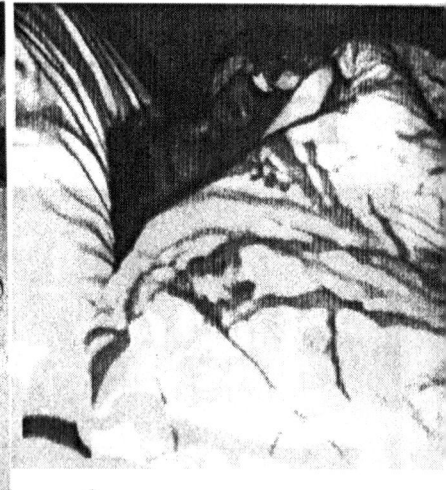

Flamingo HOTE

Above: Kevin Jones sleeping in a hotel room. Photo by The Dale. **Left:** "The Businessman" entering REM stage # 4. Straddle photo by Daily. **Below:** Hoodscoots in New Jersey. Pic by Maverick.

MEMBER THE BEST Western MOTELS B.W.M.

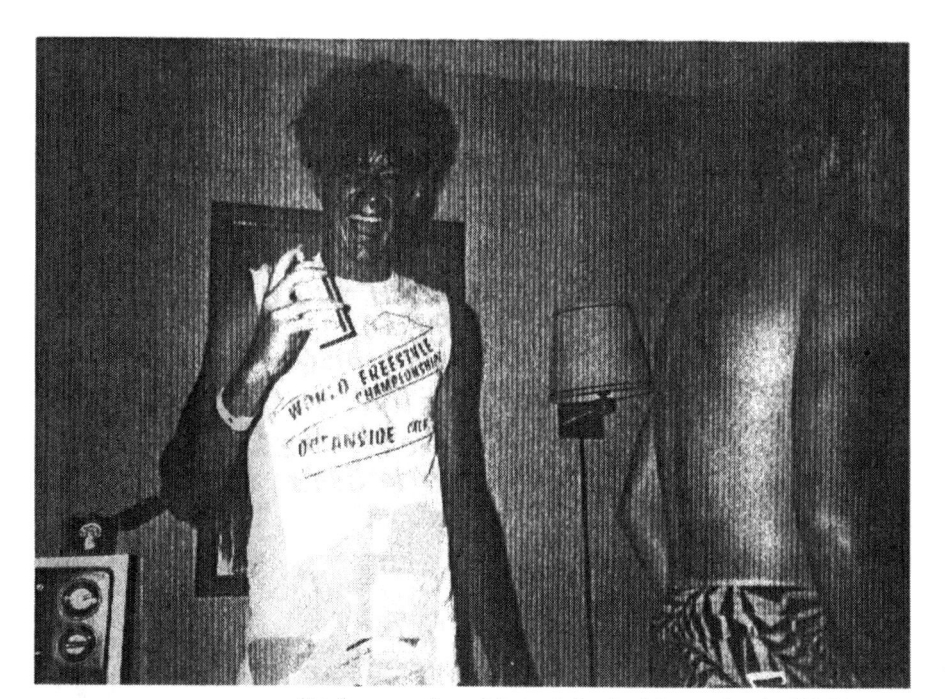

Dale made the mistake of falling asleep on Redondo Beach. He payed for it dearly with a SEVERE sunburn. The next thing Dale payed for was one (1) can of Solarcaine which he requested I apply. Hey ho hey ho ho Dale ho ho...

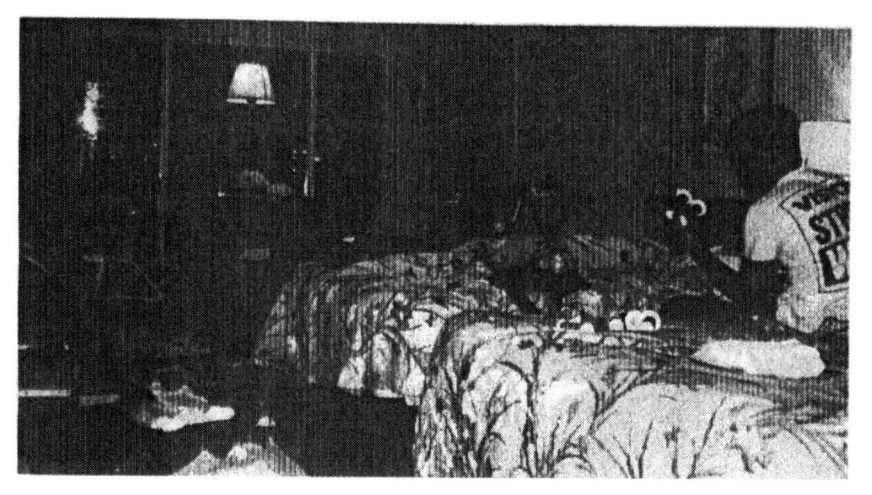

After an exciting day of visiting ODI (Thanks for the tour, Herb!) and dorkin' around Wiz Pubs, we made it back to the Vagabond Inn with our goods. Note Kev gettin' a little squirrely here.

ON THE Ragged Edge

A story about love

Hey, lunch time's over

A six-foot tall Grinning Insect stood on a doorstep holding a box of candy in one of his bristley arms. Poking the doorbell twice, he awaited his girlfriend Jan, grinning. Jan opened the door and the Grinning Insect swiftly presented the box of candy. "Hi!" grinned Jan. "Thank you very much!" The Grinning Insect was welcomed into Jan's home and led to the kitchen. Jan's mother wiped her smooth hands on a dish towel and warmly greeted the Grinning Insect. "We are going to the movies," beamed Jan. But when the father of Jan saw the Grinning Insect, his eyes bugged out of his head. "Bye Dad," snapped Jan.

— Not Tom

BACK ISSUES!

AGGRO RAG FREESTYLE MAG!
"Ride First, Read Later"
$1
March 1987
NSA BLOW OUT!
Interview with GARY POLLAK
DICK ISSUE!
Velodrome Finale
NEW HOW-TO: Tagsanity Hons

AJ

Miss some rags? Have no fear... Back Issues are available. You'll pay out yer ass but they're worth it! Write for back-ordering information

CLUB HOME BOY

PAY ONLY $10.00
ONE ZERO CTS CTS
pob 849, lomita, ca 90717

A section devoted to our beloved announcer/rider...

The BRETT'S GREAT Department
The BRETT'S GREAT Department
The BRETT'S GREAT Department
The BRETT'S GREAT Department

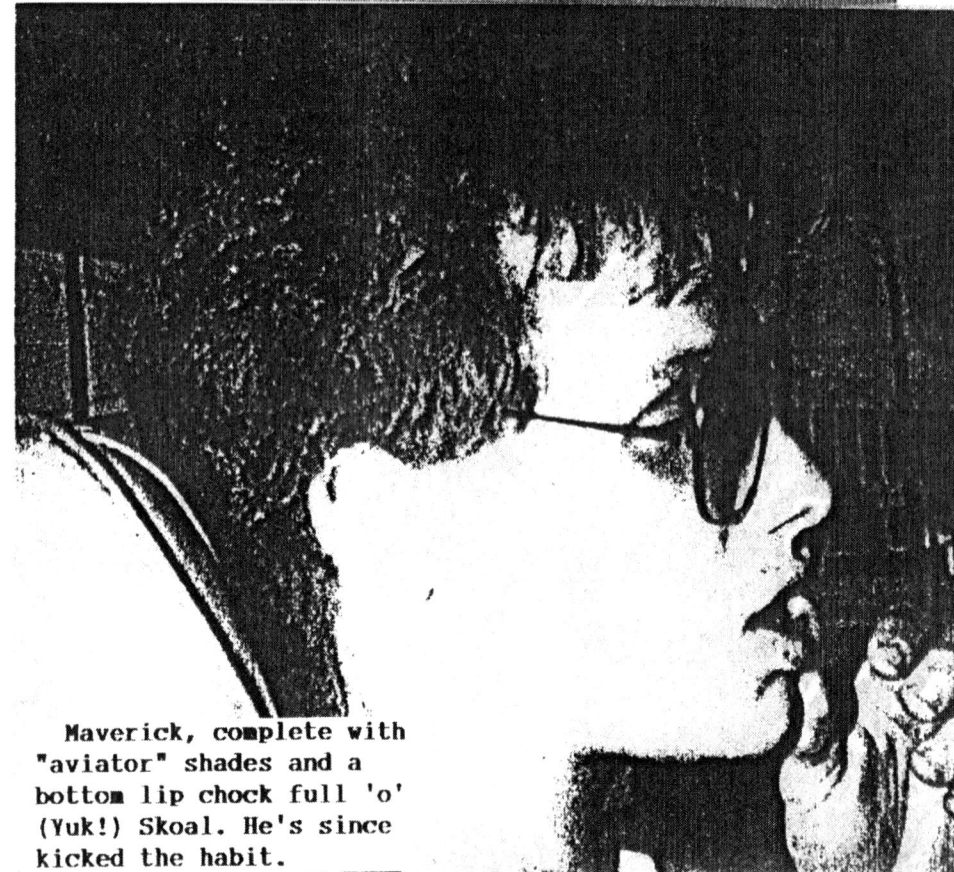

GRAVY MASTER makes gravy rich...brown...tas

STICKLERS

A lousy Sigur imitation...

Maverick, complete with "aviator" shades and a bottom lip chock full 'o' (Yuk!) Skoal. He's since kicked the habit.

An acid drop from a man who once quipped, "I'm glad we're not skaters 'cause then we'd have to dress up to ride."

I might fidge Brett a lot (OK then, *constantly*), but he's *very* street-oriented. 270° picnic table drop-in... with gusto. Hot.

Give Brett *any* kind of transition and you don't know WHAT he'll come up with.

Check out how far into the bowl Brett is landing this 540° air. CRAZY. Interesting tidbit: Brett can chop a mean stack of firewood.

NOT A HOW-TO
NOT A
HOW-TO
NOT A HOW-TO

Try to think of a hard new trick that takes you about 3 weeks to invent/get the feel of. Do something like reverse tail whips into it. Make sure you keep the whipping motion of the tail whip action as you... step over the bars while catching and pulling the seat w/ your left hand. Feather and flail in a fitting manner. Think of a tough way out of your new trick. Yeah... that's right — THINK! This is <u>not</u> a how-to by Kevin Jones....

PART ONE

The scene: It was November of 1987 and a contest situation at the Velodrome in Carson, California had attracted bicycle enthusiasts from all over the United States, including some Plywood Hoods from York, PA. A conservative hotel room contained Lung-bastard (recorder in hand), Jamie "Out in Left Field Without a Glove" McKulik, Dale Mitzel, and TRP bigwig Ken Mann. The following questions and answers were exchanged over the shrill chirping a determined Dale Mitzel produced "custom-fitting" his complimentary TRP seatpost...

Lung: "I'm talkin' with Ken Mann of TRP. OK Ken, tell me how TRP first got started..."

Ken Mann: "Simon made pants from his living room. Not one person bought them so he made seat posts. And they messed up the first order and then R.L. made him pay a lot of money."

Lung: "Whoa! How did R.L. get in on it?"

Ken Mann: "Simon payed him."

Lung: "Oh, Simon payed R.L. to use his products?"

Ken Mann: "Yeah."

Lung: "Can you tell me how much?"

Ken Mann: "He didn't tell me how much."

Lung: "Did the seatposts sell at first?"

Ken Mann: "Yeah, we sold 'em all out."

Lung: "How many did you make at the beginning?"

Ken Mann: "Uh...first batch was only 200. Then it was like 200 every two weeks."

Lung: "Roughly how much did it cost to get this thing going?"

Ken Mann: "I have really no idea. 'Cause Simon has a partner that has a lot of money. So it's like..."

Lung: "Yeah, how DID he get the money to get this thing going? Did he take a loan out or something?"

Ken Mann: "I think he borrowed it from somebody because I know he doesn't have a lot of money himself. His father might. He's always working--never riding. That's where he gets his money from."

Lung: "When did TRP start?"

Ken Mann: "1984. That's when he made pants. Then he dropped it..."

Lung: "How old was he when he made the pants?"

Ken Mann: "Fifteen."

Jamie: "What...is he like a businessman or something?"

Ken Mann: "Yeah."

Jamie: "Why doesn't he make handlebars and stuff?

Ken Mann: "It's way expensive. And if they don't sell he's out so much money. He's a little company. Real little."

Lung: "Does he have some kind of office?"

Ken Mann: "My room."

Lung: "Do you handle all the stuff or what?"

Ken Mann: "Yeah. He does designs in his room. There's no main office though."

Jamie: "Do you guys live together or something?"

Ken Mann: "No."

To be continued...

LEW'S SCOOTER SLAMFEST!

Lew (baseball cap on backwards and up to no good) repeatedly dropped the warehouse scooter off the roof of Wizard Publications just for the hell of it. It was *thrashed*. Here, Lew demonstrates his patented "Dizz Hicks Mega Trick Torture Test."

Step One: Lew holds the scooter aloft to see what potential energy feels like.

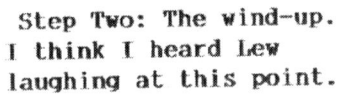

Step Two: The wind-up. I think I heard Lew laughing at this point.

Step Three: The downward swing. Cork, Dale, and I await disaster.

Step Four: Delivery. See what happens when Andy's away for a few days?

Who knows what evil lurks in the hearts of men?

Lew hoisting

Vacation shot

It hit the wall.

TUNED IN
the jesus and mary chain

DARKLANDS

The Jesus and Mary Chain's second album, *Darklands*, strays from the feedback-saturated brilliance of their debut effort, *Psychocandy*, and settles for a more accomplished sound not unlike progressive pop. Brothers Jim and William Reid, while still yielding the skilled guitarwork the Chain is famous for, chose to clean up their act a bit for *Darklands*. Their oh-so-sullen lyrics are still present on the new album, though, and are delivered with simple but catchy chords. "Down on Me" retains much of *Psychocandy*'s sound, as does "Fall". "April Skies" and "Happy When It Rains" ring loud and true of JMC's distinct style. Packed with plenty of downcast views on living, loving, and dying ("As sure as life means nothing/and all things end in nothing/And heaven I think/is too close to hell"), *Darklands* serves as an invitation to deep thought and emotions. *Darklands* is a mellowdramatic follow-up to the Scottish band's first record, and it illustrates The Jesus and Mary Chain's inclination to refine and progress.

— MSD

2 Hip King of Vert
Rockville

Photos by Brett

Here's amateur entrant Mark Eaton boning one beyond belief during the jam. Lung-mustard loves a good halfpipe.

A ramp. A contest.
Beer for sale.
A roaring crowd.
Old faces.
New tricks.
Flatland?
AFA?
Angry promoters.
Stoked people.

Blyther is one BAAAD dude on a halfpipe...

Just look at these famous freestyle figures: Gary Pollak, Jamie "Emcee" Kulik, Eaton (Mark J.), McGoo, Mel, and Steve Giberson. And is that halfpipe enthusiast Hadji lurking in the background? Yup.

A DRUNK MAN

BY L.M. TARD

Wait a minute...There's more.
Bums.
Rollerskate delivery.
Street women.
Gary Pollak?
Raybo.
Flashbacks...A guy with Dia-Compe stickers in hand. He was out for revenge. Another guy named Wilkerson. His run. A ruckus. Team managers, riders and crowd. Pushing and pulling. A drunk man. Call it the "Pinky Scuffle." Pollak trying to hold back. "THUD." A lead chain post is lunged. An "umph" sound is heard. It happens one more time. No one cares. People laugh.

Above: Chris Potts gettin' nutso in the variation department. He crushed his front wheel doing shit like like this. Left: From the U.K. we have Carlo Griggs displaying a wing span bigger than that of an African Lungfish.

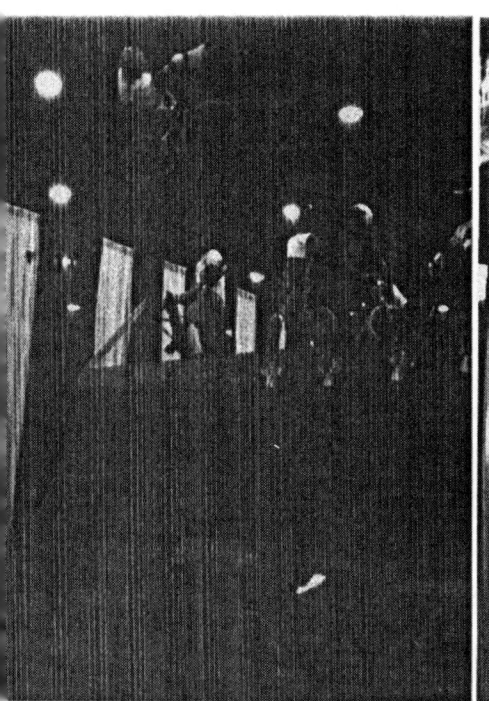

ROCKVILLE BMX

2 HIP

King of Vert in D.C.

Above: Look at the total concentration and determination on the face of Matt Hoffman. Also look at his left leg... Matt's engaged in his candy bar footplant. Nauseating. Top Left: Another one of those candy bar things, this time during a time of practice and a very high air. At Left: How is THIS for inverted? Hoffman. He's riding for Haro now.

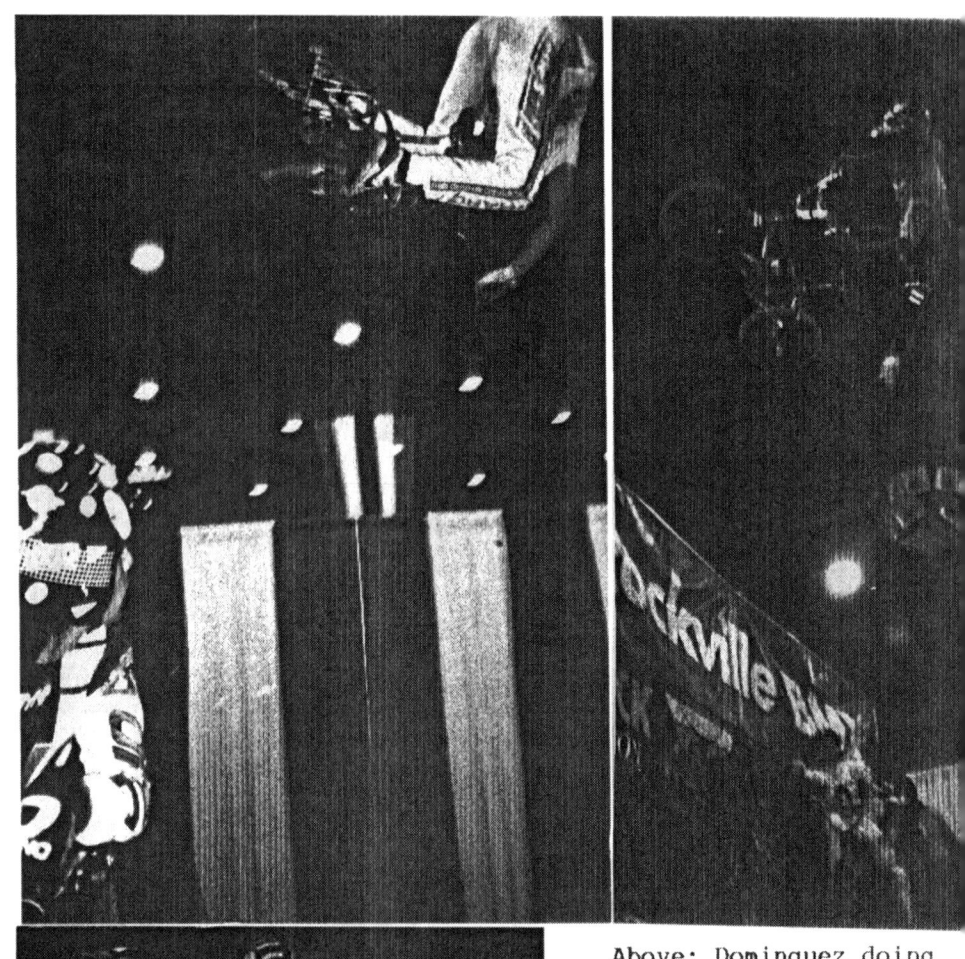

Above: Dominguez doing what he does best...WINNING. Top Left: Joe Johnson working the ramp and Dino DeLuca checking his style. Left: Raybo doing what HE does best...entertaining!

2 HIP
KING OF VERT

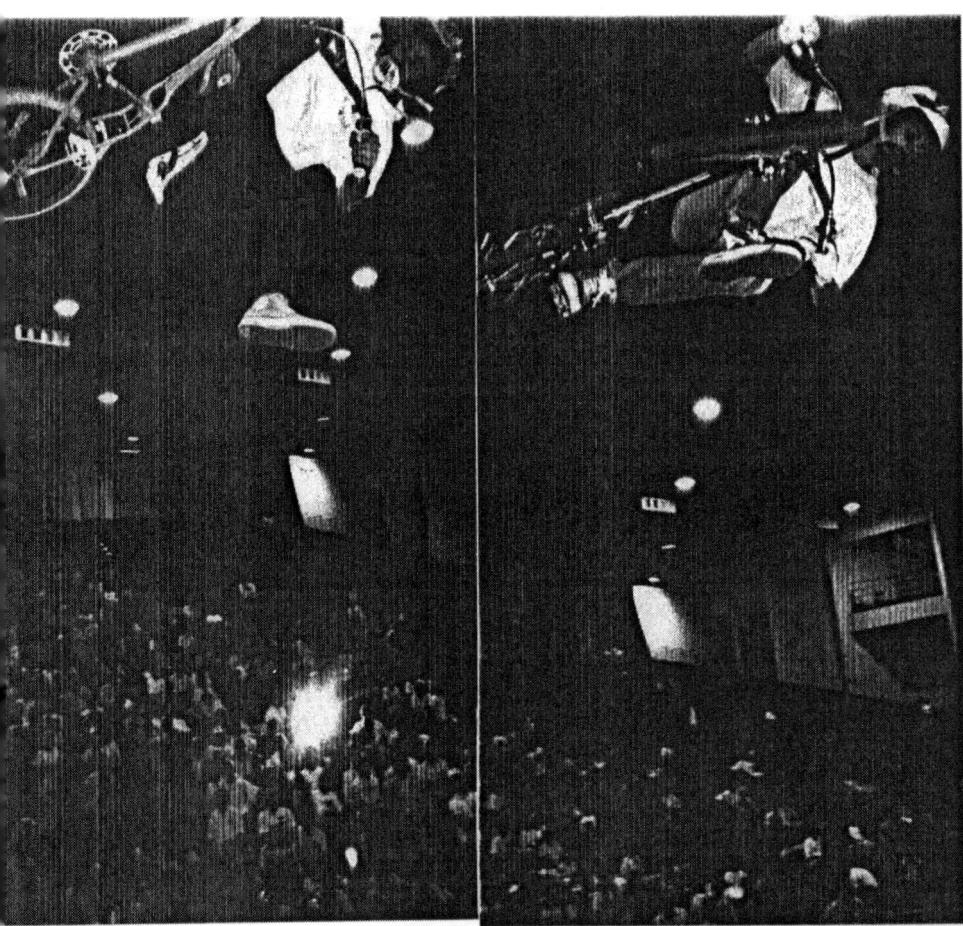

Above: The King warming up with a no-footed can can. Mike Dominguez is very bio. Top right: Brian B. gettin' the feel of the ramp by testin' out a standard can can. At Right: Mr. Andrew Jenkins and 2-Hipster Ron Wilkerson taking a gander at the action.

KOV ROCKVILLE

A non-fictional essay by Michael S. Daily

COURT TIME

When I cruised home from LHU for Christmas break, I was quite eager to ride with the fellas. One unusually warm day, Christmas Eve in fact, the Hoods met at the police station basketball courts, a Grade A practice area officially endorsed by Kevin Jones (Grade K?). We stuck to one side of the courts because about half a dozen youths were playing a game on the other side. There was still more than enough room to go plum crazy on any rolling manoov imaginable. Kev spent most of his time gliding forward in a multitude of different positions. Lung was ripping some mint ground tricks when he wasn't challenging Maverick to some kind of wild and crazy street style stunt. Even Dale was having fun over in the corner.

CONTINUED

Photos by Lunger

Above: A flailing Jones kickin' a caboose. Top Left: The editor engrossed in a backside walkaround. Left: Dale with a modified shrinky squeak.

HAWA?! John Ker conversing with Kev in downtown York, where a hot photo session went down for American Freestyler.

Then a young bearded guy in his late twenties approached the basketball courts with an older man who was probably his father. They wanted to play basketball. Since the courts are public, and we are easy-going guys, we migrated to the center and resumed riding without a fuss. I watched the young guy for a few minutes and concluded that he must have been a pretty good ball-player in his day, perhaps even the star of his high school team. I figured the guy was visiting his folks for Christmas vacation and his old man prompted a "just for old time's sake" session...

    Father: *"Do you still go out and play, Champ?"*
    Son: *"Never. Can't get away from the office."*
    Father: *"Hey, what do you say we head over to the old police station and shoot some hoops right NOW?!"*
    Son: *"(Playfully slapping his dad's shoulder) Sounds great! Let's go!"*

The young guy kept looking at us strangely, as if we were invading his sacred territory. In a sense, I guess we were. He was not impressed by our tricks. Every time we got in his way (or vice-versa), we'd receive piercing looks from him. After about 45 minutes of this, he and his dad left for home. They had enough. The younger man glared over his shoulder at us riding bicycles on HIS basketball court. He did not like us very much.

Undaunted we sessioned on, revelling in the delight of such a perfect place to ride our bikes. I later thought about the bearded young guy sitting behind a desk in an office somewhere, reminiscing about old days of playing basketball with his buddies. Fun days. I imagined him looking back and smiling, but feeling sad and torn inside. I suddenly realized that would be me someday, recalling riding days just like this one. I shook my head and laughed out loud, knowing there's nothing I can do now...but RIDE.

Florida in a Coconut Shell

Aggro Rag correspondant Howdy Riggs crankin' his side order, a trick done to and from many others.

By Howdy Riggs
Florida Correspondant

Florida in a Coconut Shell

I got there Friday night after a semi-long drive and the first thing I saw was a RAX trick team show (we were staying with team Poverty member Mike Gibbion). They said that the "K" was here and we had just missed him. I did not wait around to find out if they were lying or what--I went on to explore the many jam circles going on in the many nearby parking lots (By the way, I was informed by Lew that Jones was not at the contest and I was bummed. What was even worse was that you or Lung or Dale or any of the Hoods were not there. I was twice as bummed.). At those jams there was everyone except the Hoods. I was stoked! It was sooo rad. A cop came up and said we had to leave and no one did. Then the next day was the contest. It was raining but it did not matter because I was stoked. In my opinion, the guys who kicked ass that day were Gerry Smith (a Florida homeboy), Jim Johnson, some unknown guy on a Hutch who won his class, Aaron Dull, and some guy on a Skyway with rims who ripped in the 19 and over class. As far as the pros went, I think Lashua should have placed way higher--he was totally ripped off. Rick deserved the win. McCoy placed too high for as many mistakes as he had in his run (but he did get the crowd going the most). As far as ramps went, the next day was way out of hand!! Wilkerson needs a straight-jacket put on him because he is NUTS!! The same goes for Hoffman. I do not think I've had that much fun in one weekend in sooo long. I wish I was a factory rider and that was my life but don't we all. Soon I hope.

Howdy's bud Paul

Howdy's feet

CRAZY BITS
By Daily

York local Jimmy goin' for broke over some kid doin' a Miami Hopper and the deadly small mogul to large mogul chasm at the now-defunct Thunderdohm skatepark. Oh my gosh.

Crazy bits Crazy bits Crazy bits Crazy bits Crazy bits Crazy bits Crazy bits Crazy bits Crazy bits Crazy bits Jimmy Crazy bits Crazy bits Crazy bits Crazy bits Crazy bits Crazy and Kev bits Crazy bits Crazy bits Crazy bits Crazy bits Crazy bits Thunderdohm Crazy bits Crazy bits Crazy bits Crazy bits Crazy bits moguls Crazy bits Crazy bits Crazy death bits Crazy bits Crazy bits Crazy bits Crazy bits Crazy bits Crazy bits Crazy bits speed Crazy bits Crazy bits no helmets Crazy bits Crazy bits air Crazy bits Crazy bits Crazy bits Crazy bits Crazy bits Crazy bits Crazy bits sailing Crazy bits Crazy bits Crazy bits Crazy bits Crazy bits Crazy bits Crazy bits Crazy bits Jimmy Crazy bits Crazy bits Crazy bits Crazy bits Crazy bits Crazy bits and Kev Crazy bits Crazy bits Crazy bits Crazy bits Crazy bits

Jimmy

Kev

Kevin Jones

PETE AUGUSTIN UNCOVERED

As interviewed by Lungmustard

Videopic by LUNG

When did you first start riding?
Pete: "Way back when Bob Haro started riding. Me and this guy John Swanigan--we used to ride together a lot. And Bob would ride."

Weren't you sponsored by Haro at one time?
Pete: "Just had a co-sponsorship goin' with him. He really helped me out. Bob is real cool. Dyno was my first sponsor."

Who were all of your sponsors?
Pete: "Schwinn, CW for a month, Visage for a week, Life's a Beach, Vision, Rector, Bell Helmets, and Awesome shoes."

Tell me some uncool stuff about some of your past sponsors, like Schwinn...
Pete: "Schwinn were assholes, man. Brad Hughes (Schwinn spokesman) has got his head so far wedged...I get high with the guy and then he tells me my 'image' doesn't fit their team. I design this bike on a napkin and then after I'm off the team they come out with it--the Predator. They still owe me 600 bucks and I want it. And I'm gonna collect. I've been burned by every sponsor. I guess they don't like my attitude but I got 'em coverage. That's all they give a shit about. That's all any sponsor cares about...coverage."

What happened with CW?
Pete: "CW is just a nightmare. They said my contract was all being written up and they'd have it out to me right away. Then I call up there and go 'Man, where's my contract at?' And they're all "McGoo doesn't work for us anymore. You gotta talk to Mike Miranda.' And that guy

was just the ultimate peon."

So that's when you quit?

Pete: "No, I went to Oregon with Mike Miranda. And me and Dizz raged so hard and Miranda just hated us. That was my best contest, man. I tied for sixth with 'World Champion Robert Peterson (laughter)!'"

What was the deal with Visage?

"They were just another ream-job. They wanted me there 40 hours a week, be a pro rider, design this bike with no royalties added in, set up tour, set up ALL co-sponsors...ALL this stuff for 800 bucks a month. So I told 'em to shove it. I was there for a week. I made 162 bucks."

Does Life's a Beach sponsor a lot of people?

Pete: "No, they cut back. The only amateurs they sponsor are Chris Day and Eddie Roman. They mainly stick to pros. All their skaters are all pros. Every other sport that they sponsor--they're all pros and at the top of their sport. I'm not at the top of my sport, but to them I am. They're into anarchy and harsh reality. They're not into this posed-out scene. And plus I've gotten 'em two covers so far so they're really stoked on me. I'm gettin' my own shirt with Life's a Beach. It's called 'Disgust Man.'"

Does Life's a Beach like it when you're in the mags for skating too?

Pete: "Oh yeah. They know I skate too. They're totally into it. They're the coolest people you'll ever meet. The owner walks around in shorts, no shoes, no shirt, dreadlocks goin'--the guy's hella cool, man. He's the best."

Tell me how you used to practice...

Pete: "I never used to really practice. I used to just ride and never thought of the sport as becoming a practice thing that I HAD to go out and practice. I just rode--me and Dave Nourie and Eddie Roman. We'd just go ride, man, just go have fun. It was never anything like 'I gotta practice for this contest.' I used to think that way when I was on Schwinn but that was a big joke and I'm glad I got away from it. I don't practice for anything--I just ride and have fun. That's the main thing. I feel like when you get so pressured that you HAVE to go out and practice, that's when it becomes a job and you have to do it. I don't want to have to do anything. I just want to have fun--I just want to make friends."

How old are you?

Pete: "I'll be 24 in seven days."

Were you riding when you were in school?

Pete: "Yeah. I played hockey for six years. I got kicked out of the league. I got into too many fights. They

PETE AUGUSTIN

didn't like me. Me and my cousin wasted a side linesman. We broke his jaw. They hated us. They kicked us both out of the league."

Who are your favorite groups?

Pete: "Venom, Slayer, Exodus, Merciful Fate, Metallica, Celtic Frost--anything that's hard and fast and violent I like. I like all thrash."

Do you think any of your sponsors thought that you were skating more than biking?

Pete: "I don't care. I was gettin' 'em coverage. And that's all they give a shit about. Flat out. They don't care who you are, they don't care where you live, they don't care what you eat, they don't care how you do anything in your life--as long as you get them coverage. That's why Life's a Beach and Vision are so cool. To a lot of sponsors you're just a number. Look at Tony Murray--that guy was SO ON IT awhile ago, and as soon as he got off of it, he was off Haro, man. They just pushed him aside, you know? They don't remember anything what that guy did for Haro. He was just pushed aside--he was just a number. There's a LOT of people out there like that, man. And it's really sad 'cause there's so much good talent out there."

It seems like they don't even look at how good a rider is--they just look at contest placings...

Pete: "Yeah, contest placings. Which is so lame because a lot of the new guys don't know shit about the background of the sport. They do all these frontyards, sideyards, backyards, funky chickens, pinky squeaks, megaspins...but you ask 'em to do a 180 rollback and they're goin' 'Huh?'"

What do you think about street riding?

Pete: "It dominates. That's what freestyle is--goin' out in the street and havin' fun. Just flyin' down the street as fast as you can. It's raging, man."

Would you like to have street style contests?

Pete: "I don't think they should have ANY contests, man. I think contests are gay. They should have these big jam sessions. See all the top riders ride, pay your fucking ten bucks...you know? Let all these promoters make their money, OK? [Contests are] puttin' down the sport. You got all these guys that are just cuttin' throats over this piece of plastic. And then when it's all over with, it's nothin' but shit-talk goin' on. Why can't everybody just go out there and just be friends and just have fun? Just a big JAM. Why have a contest? You can't fucking judge this sport. There's so many different styles of riding, man. It's like puttin' me against this guy (Joe Gruttola) right here. It'd be totally impossible to judge something like that. The way I look at it, it's impossible to judge something like that. He would blow me away in so much shit and then I'd blow him away in other shit. How can you judge that? There's so many different styles of riding--you CANNOT judge the sport. It's a lame thing to do. Everybody should just have fun and just be friends and not argue and say 'This guy's better than this guy' and 'Well, I made that trick up.' It's lame, you know?"

What type of contests would you like to see?

Pete: "Well, if they ARE going to compete, they should have head-to-head jams. Each rider go out for a minute. Just like in a jam circle--when you're in a jam circle you KNOW who's the best in that circle. Just one person right after another. But then again they should just have jam sessions. Shouldn't even have contests. People would pay to see all the top riders ride--that's all they come to see anyway. They don't care. They're not placin' bets on who's gonna win this contest."

Who are your favorite riders?

Pete: "Everybody and anybody who's into it. There's too many people that are so good--I can't name 'em all. I could maybe name some people I don't like, but then again they wouldn't like that. Even though I don't really care. If I had to like vote for a person who I think is the best, I'd have to say R.L. Osborn. He's done more for the sport than anybody has. If it wasn't for R.L., and Woody, and Martin, guys like us wouldn't even be here today. They're the guys that went out there and promoted the sport when it was NOTHING. R.L. and Mike Buff were the first guys to ever go on tour to promote the sport. And they made it good for us so we could make a living off of it. So I have total respect for those guys."

Ever ride ramps?

Pete: "Yeah, I mess around on 'em. But it's not like I'm a pro on a ramp--I can't do a 540 or anything. I can catch a couple feet of air."

How 'bout on a skate? How high can you get?

Pete: "Just a couple of feet. I just like to do harsh wall rides and slap curbs...break trucks--stuff like that."

Did you ever ride all night?

Pete: "Always. All night long. Last year's Velodrome I rode the whole night before the contest. Didn't sleep at all--me and Chris Day. It was BAD. It was right out here in this parking lot too."

AGGRO RAG FREESTYLE MAG!

UNCOVERED

You're good friends with Chris Day, right?
Pete: "Oh yeah. Me and Chris are like best friends."
What's Jason (Parkes) been up to?
Pete: "Sure hasn't been ridin' his bike. He's a good skater and everything. He's a REAL good skater. Me and Jason were like best friends--we'd ride together non-stop. We used to feed off each other. That's why when we rode together we were ON it, man. The way I looked at it, when we went to jam circles no one would really touch us. We jammed when we rode together. I don't know, we used to tell always think Chris was a total peon. And I used to tell Chris, you know, 'You're lame.' Chris is a bad ass, man.
Where do you live right now?
Pete: "I live in Redondo Beach. I'm relocating. It's a possibility I might be riding for Murray with Rich Sigur. It looks really good."
Anything else you wanna say?
Pete: "Thanks for interviewing me. I've been dying to get this out. FREESTYLIN' won't interview me."
Oh, did you think that was weird when the '86 October FREESTYLIN' had a rivet on it and then the '87 October cover had a rivet on it?
Pete: "Yeah! That's subliminal, dude. The Disgust Man and Lungmustard! Those guys schralp (laughter)! They're our 'October Gods (more laughter)!' What a bunch of dicks...!"

"Rad-Libbing" by Lung

LITTLE ~~RED RIDING~~ *Lung Plywood* HOOD

One day Little ___LUNG___ ___PLYWOOD~~Red~~___ Hood was going through
　　　　　　　A COLOR

the forest carrying a basket of ___GYRO CABLES___ for ~~her~~ *His* grand-
　　　　　　　　　　　　　　　　PLURAL NOUN

mother. Suddenly ~~she~~ *He* met a big ___ANGRY___ wolf.
　　　　　　　　　　　　　　　　　　　ADJECTIVE

"___Holy shit___!" said the wolf. "Where are you going,
　　EXCLAMATION

little ___Lungmustard___?"
　　　PET NAME

"I'm going to my grandmother's house," said *he*. Then the wolf
___BLAZED___ away.
　VERB (PAST TENSE)

Matt Hoffman droppin' a bomb on the Houston ramp.
Photo: Guy-B

whaTEVEr!

Master of unlimited vehicles... The K.

MARK E.

The grim result of being too nonchalant at spinning wheels... one broken finger. "I happened so fast," said Lung M.

COMPLAINTS

My closet has a few Izod shirts in it, but only my roomate and my closest friends know. I own a pair of Vision shoes, but they're not even scuffed. I had a skateboard in '75; a red anodized Bonzai double-kick 24" model with Chitown trucks, stoker II wheels, and 3/4" risers. I learned 180 degree carves on a wedge ramp but very little else. I only skated because my friends hadn't got hooked on BMX yet. I have a girlfriend this week, but we're liable to be on the rocks again by Sunday.

A lot of people stare at me on the streets; it's probably my socks. I wear my pants pegged and an inch too short (for coolness) and my socks are very grey. I separate my whites and colors, but my socks always look dingy. Bleach might help, but whenever I have the extra two bucks to spend on it I always buy Oreos instead. I'm only human.

I have the kind of head that gets noticed at all the Hollywood dance clubs. My hair says "accountant", my clothes say "poser", and my attitude says "fuck you". I guess I'm a rebel.

I get offended when strangers question my involvement in a "kiddie sport" like BMX. It gives me a thrill to tell them how much I make, where I've been, and all the fun I have. I have a friend who hates his job. never goes anywhere, and drives a BMW. Maybe BMX does suck.

I worry too much about the people who worry too much about the people that worry about them. I like to believe I'm OK because all the other people out there think they're OK too and me and my friends aren't. Sounds like EVERYBODY'S fucked up to me. Maybe we should all just relax.

- Hal e. Tosis

FREESTYLE PLYWOOD "HOODS" TEAM

Watch for official Plywood Hoods gear like T-shirts, hats, hooded sweatshirts, and team stickers to develop. New model Aggro Rag shirts are on the way, too. We're also scouting for fun guys to fill out our growing "B" Team. Apply...
"B" Team c/o
Mark Eaton
211 S. Marshall St.
York, PA 17402

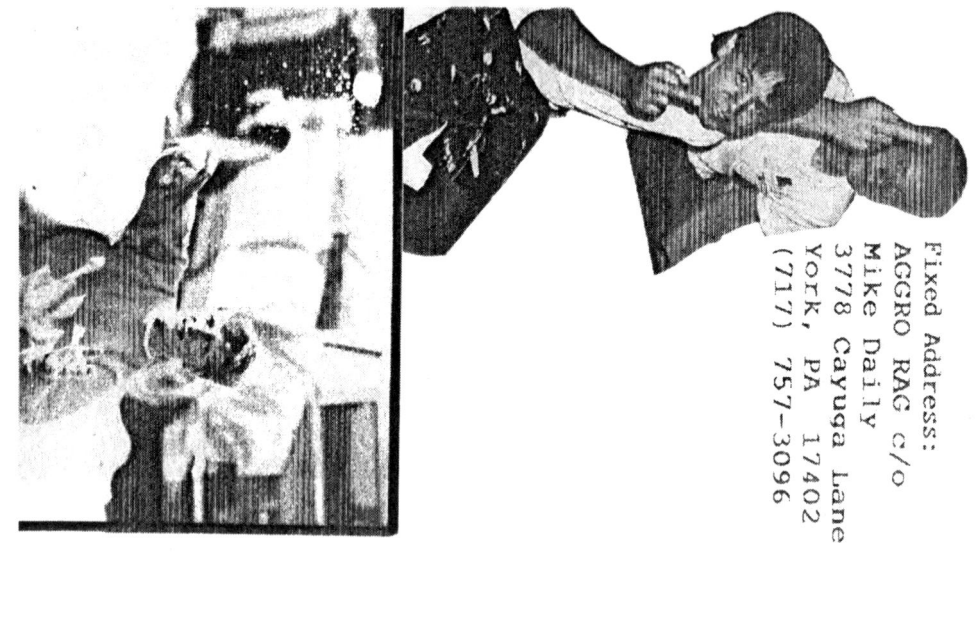

Fixed Address:
AGGRO RAG c/o
Mike Daily
3778 Cayuga Lane
York, PA 17402
(717) 757-3096

Borlando Local and Future "B" Teamer

Howdy Riggs

The Chris Day Fidge: Part I

"The Chris Day Fidge" is a three-part fidge motif that runs throughout *Dorkin' II* (November 14, 1988). Raybo explains the original footage he got at an AFA Masters contest: "Dennis [McCoy] was just like bein' himself—gettin' into the beat and all this stuff—and poor Chris Day was tryin' to be down with Dennis. I was all psyched to watch this run-off [between Ron Wilkerson and Joe Johnson] and somehow I just zoomed in on Chris Day makin' a complete fool of himself. And he didn't know it!"

The Chris Day Fidge: Part II

Standing alongside the flatbottom of Gary Pollak's backyard half-pipe, Dave Pak and Ray recreated the original footage as Gary blasted airs.

The Chris Day Fidge: Part III

General Bicycles riders Pete Kearney and R.L. Osborn (both of them teammates with Chris Day at the time) even got in on it.

I recently asked Chris about the fidge.

AGGRO RAG FREESTYLE MAG!
(Summer 1988)
York, PA/Stamford, CT
5½" x 8¼"

11th ISSUE

Chris Day

Mike Daily: How do you feel about the random "fidge sequences" in *Dorkin' II*?

Chris Day: I think it's all pretty funny. I truly don't take that stuff personally. Back when that *Dorkin'* video came out, somebody said, "Hey, did you see this? They're kind of mocking you a little bit..." I was just like, "Yeah, well, whatever..." [Laughs.] I wasn't upset. I was like, "Oh, they're tryin' to dis me? Oh...alright!" I didn't hold a grudge or nothin'. After a few days, I was like, "Forget about it—it's no big deal." I was really into riding and really focused.[13] Maybe I was ticked a little bit for a day or two, but outside of that, it was just like: "It's Large Ray bein' Large Ray, and they're just tryin' to have fun." And that's all good.

---

[13] "Pete [Augustin] looked me in the eye one time at the apartment and he goes: ' I wanna tell you something: Make sure you don't get a big head. All of this coverage and all of these accolades and people tellin' you you're great, don't let it get to your head. Don't get a swelled head like a lot of these other riders out there do. You need to stay humble and realize that you had a lot of good luck. Don't get all puffed up and arrogant about all this. Always listen to people and *talk* to people. You're still young and growing. I want to make sure that you mature properly and keep a smart head on your shoulders.' After he said that to me, that really shook me up. I was thinkin', 'Do I already have a big head?' That was the smartest thing he could have said to me because from that point on, I talked to every single rider. And after every single coverage thing came out in the magazines, I really tried to make sure that in the back of my head, I just kept sayin', 'Stay humble. Just be cool and don't think you're a big deal.' Because I didn't wanna be that way; I didn't wanna be that guy. And I did see it in a lot of other pro riders. So I really thank Pete for keepin' me straight."—**Chris Day**, previously unpublished quote from transcript of his interview for *Aggro Rag Freestyle Mag!* Number 13 (August 2012).

Roll Hardy and Greg Higgins, 1988
Photo by Chad Johnston

Jason Parkes
Tucson AFA Masters, 1988

orlando
howdy riggs
STREET SMART

SUMMER '88
POOL PARTIES
10

AGGRO RAG
FREESTYLE MAG!

BATTLE THE COMPETITION

"Ride First, Read Later."

welcome to the
Escape From The Planet of The APES issue

TEAM SCROUNGE

DO NOT DROP

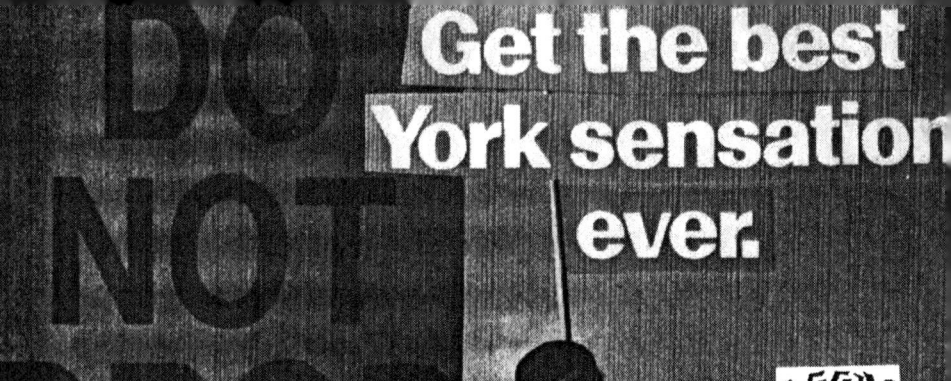

Get the best York sensation ever.

The Thinking Teen's Zine.

AGGRO RAG FREESTYLE MAG!

FRESH

Larry.
Photo by Guy-B

Editor
 Michael Daily
Photography
 Steve Giberson
 Spike Jonze
Contributors
 Mel Bend
 Greg Higgins
 Lungmustard
 Howdy Riggs
 Jamie Smith
Printer
 Chris Daily

"Holy shit," said a man. He tried to interpret what his common eyes just witnessed. He concluded that he saw a boy on a strange little bike do something wonderful. Something gloriously wonderful.
 The boy, aware of the man's fascinated stare, continued riding. He didn't really want the strange man to die for him. Actually the unknowledgable boy would feel stupid if that occurred. So he just rode a bit more, humbly reaping more of the man's just admiration, then silently slipped away, searching...

ON THE COVER

ex·pres·sion·ism (eks-*presh*-un-izm) *n.* Theory or practice of showing or expressing one's innermost thoughts or feelings by the arts or other outward means.--ex·pres·sion·ist *n. & adj.*--ex·pres·sion·is·tic *adj.* See Craig Grasso (photo by Guy-B), Howdy "T-Shirt King" Riggs, Greg Higgins, Spike & A

EDITORIAL

> My merry, merry friends from England in good ol' Lock Haven. This particular night ended with Joe (far left) and I hurling rocks at a moving train. No, I don't just ride...

How much do you weigh? *How old* are you? *How tall* are you? How much *money* do you have?

Thinking and living in numbers and dollar signs, a common affliction of the masses-particularly of my peers. The same peers who have tried to whittle me down in the past with questions like such...

How long are you going to ride that bike around? When are you going to get a car? When are you going to get a girlfriend? How *old* are you now?

I'm 19 years old and starting my third year of college at Lock Haven University. I ride "that bike" more than ever now. I don't *want* a car and I have a great girlfriend (Hi Anne!). Had I "grown up" and listened to the negative words of some of my peers back then, I realize now I'd be just like them...unhappy. I like being happy. I like to ride my bike.

How many megaspins can you do? *How far* can you glide that? *How many* rolling tailwhips was that? How many *hours* a day do you practice? *How many pages* is your new issue?

Don't let numbers govern your riding, your zine or your life. Do you feel good? Is your riding complete? Is your zine complete? Are you HAPPY? Trust in your heart.

Aggro Rag prints the truth in each and every issue. And as they say...the truth sometimes *hurts*. We don't mean to hurt or offend anyone with our rag. You must understand we're not trying to be "cool" by printing bad words here and there or by running a shot of a naked boy riding a ramp on the cover. It just so happens we Hoods admire the honest words and actions of certain individuals who *also* find endless pleasures and pains in freestyling. If you cannot comprehend this reasoning, then perhaps you are not ready to read Aggro Rag. Sorry.

Special thanks is due the following for their support: All of the manufacturers who have stood and continue to stand behind freestyle bicycling, the magazines, Steve Giberson, McGoo, Andy Jenkins, Mark Lewman, Spike Jonze, my mom, my dad, Greg Higgins and Team Scrounge, Howdy Riggs, ODI, Club Homeboy, Putter Brown of Team Oak Street, Yoo-Hoo, R&R Pool and Spa, the Plywood Hoods and YOU.

We're just asking you to *think* a little. Enjoy Aggro Rag #10, ride heartily and God Bless...

Fearlessly,

Mike Daily
Mike Daily
Editor

REQUIRED READING but NOT really

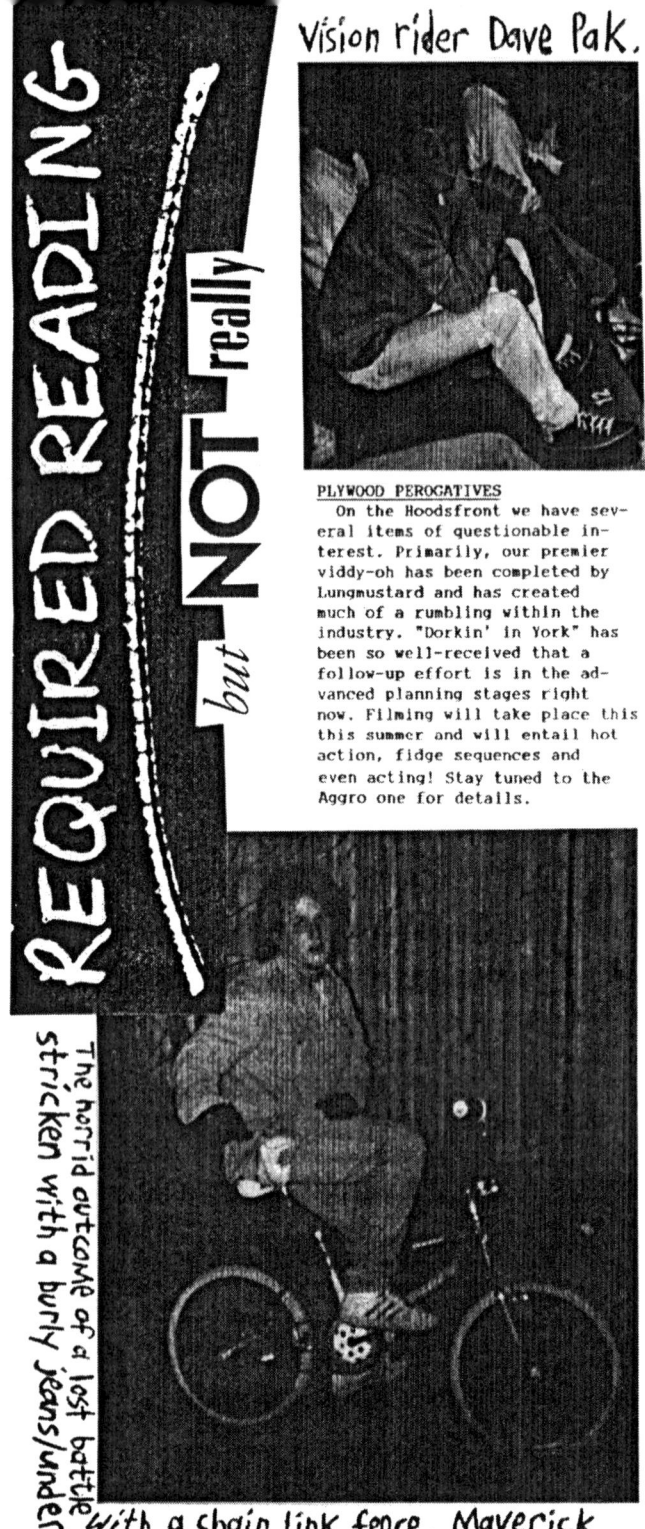

Vision rider Dave Pak.

PLYWOOD PEROGATIVES

On the Hoodsfront we have several items of questionable interest. Primarily, our premier viddy-oh has been completed by Lungmustard and has created much of a rumbling within the industry. "Dorkin' in York" has been so well-received that a follow-up effort is in the advanced planning stages right now. Filming will take place this this summer and will entail hot action, fidge sequences and even acting! Stay tuned to the Aggro one for details.

We are embarking on our first ever tour attempt in August, with intentions of shows in many states. Dale "Twinkle Toes" Mitzel has rented a seven-man van and even a trailor for our launch ramp and scoots. On August 20th we'll be in Chicago, Illinois for a big beachfront show on Oak Street. We'll be modeling Team Oak Street clothing, our new team sponsor. And is a show lined up (thanks to Putter Brown) for that night in one of the hippest dance clubs in Chicago? It's lookin' good. The performances will be composed of music, announcing, plywood schralping and some hectic flatlanding. Come on out and support us why don't ya. The riders for the 2-week tour thing will be: Mark Eaton, Dale Mitzel, Jamie McKulik, Brett Downs, myself and Kevin "The K" Jones, who is joining us after Skyway's Rockville show (which we Hoods may be opening). We plan on having fun no matter what happens.

Concerning this contentedly underground publication, issues will be few and far between but typically packed with goodies. Take advantage of the sub deal described elsewhere in this ish if you wish to stay on top of things.

One last thing.............
Might the editor of Aggro Rag be working on some kind of novel-type short story to be published in bulky zine format? Has the title of said "book" already been conceived? Will it be a long time (years?) before its completion? Does the proposed subject matter actually puzzle Kevin Jones?

QUIPS OF GREATNESS

"Bein' a hero in the United States of America is the shortes lived profession that anybody could hope to participate in. Or hope not to participate in."
- Evel Knievel

"It's just for show, you know?
- Bill Barrett on health food.

"Watch...Mark'll come back with belt marks on his ass."
- Aaron Dull on Lungmustard's "curfew" with Revcore TM Mr. Evans in Arizona (*Aaron Dull Quote #1...1st in a series.).

"Pretty soon nobody's gonna hafta wear glasses." - Some guy Anne Carroll heard once.

"What's your new red row, Brett?" - Daily

"Put it this way-STRICKLER liked red!" - Kev in response.

The horrid outcome of a lost battle stricken with a burly jeans/underwear tear. An' it sho' was COLD out too. with a chain link fence. Maverick

BMX Action Magazine
TRICK SHOW
featuring
R.L. OSBORN and
MIKE BUFF.
July 10th, 1984
at Rockville BMX.
BE THERE!!

FREESTYLE
Redwood Heads
TEAM

THE MAN.
THE INTERVIEW.

Coming Soon...

PLEASE SEND ME A COPY OF AGGRO RAG

— *Jimmy*

FELLOW WALL CLIMBERS
Dear A-Rag,

Just writin' to scam a copy of your latest zine. Heard they're killer. Saw your (Mike Daily) run in Ohio, it ripped. I sucked that day...80 somethingish. Hope to see ya at some other contest. I decide to go to. The scene in Chicago is cool-good for skatin' and even better for money sessions on bikes. BSR is second to none here. Winter is sooo long. I'm glad for parking garages, warehouses too. Well I'm done for now so go catch some hang time on a wall...

Soar Benevolently,
Troy Wroblewski
Schaumberg, IL

P.S.- I put out a zine called "The Wall" but ran out of copies. I'll send ya our latest when it's done (#4).

JUST AN OPINION
'Zine Maker,

Hey! I got your address from Dave's STYLIN' ZINE whose address I got from Roy's UNEXPLAINED zine and now I'm writing to you! Ya know, your zine is to freestyle what the Village Voice was to hippies and I'm glad that I'm getting a copy. I don't expect you to write back or anything. Just keep up what you're doing. There are getting to be fewer freestylers out there. I think the U.S. is going through a transition stage right now. All of the posers are beginning to get weeded out, and only the real dedicated riders are left. Well anyways, that's just an opinion.

Later,
Marr
Crystal River, FL

INSPIRATION
Dear Mike,

Hi it's me again, Michael Rice. The one that interviewed you for Team-X zine. Anyway, after I read your interview I thought why do I ride? Then it hit me-not for the neighbors or to win a contest, for me that's who. My friend Jon and I were so stoked. Our riding has improved in our own eyes because just for the sake of pullin' off a trick for our own personal satisfaction. You have inspired me. It might be great to become good and famous and win contests, but it's only out of hours of practice. My friends and I might make it there one day but for now we live to ride! It's the only way! Oh yeah-do you want those pictures back? Please tell me. I'll send you an issue as soon as it is ready. But we have a problem finding stuff to put in. We put stories in and other stuff. We think that should be enough. Thanks a lot.

Your Friend,
Michael Rice
Crossett, AR

AGGRO ARTIST
Mike,

Hey. I'm John Kopke. Andy said to send you some stuff for an Aggro Rag a long time ago. Now that you're working for Wilkerson, I don't know if you're putting it out anymore. Well, I threw in some stuff that I drew, shot, whatever. Also a stamp. If you have any old Aggro Rags or new ones or a Wilkerson zine or whatever-please send. Thanks fellow freestyler. Oh yah-Congrats on that Cepple layout you wrote that won something.

J. Kopke!
Phoenix, AZ

P.S.- Forgive my ignorance of what it won.

Drawing by John Kopke

Brian Iverson
Photo: Kopke!

ME EQUALS GREEN?
Dear Mike,

Here is a zine of ours that I want you to check out if you have time. A friend and I do this piece of print, which I hope you'll enjoy. It is our third issue, and our first printed and half-toned one. The first 2 were very few and xeroxed. Aggro Rag is an untouchable mag, which I use as a role model. I can't understand how you could have kept it up in the beginning. You say you get no parental support whatsoever. I mean, as of now, my main goal with Whiplash is to lose as little money as possible, forget even breaking even with it. But money has nothing to do with it, right? Kids ask me why I even bother with it if I'm not going to make any money on it, but I guess they just don't understand. Well, at least I think it's worth it. Zines are the perfect way to express anything you feel, with freestyle as their foundations. Why am I telling you this? I'm sure you thought it a million times. I guess I have to tell somebody who understands...but I don't even know you. Oh well, this is our third issue of Whiplash, which we're proud. Even if you just take a look at it, that would be good enough for me. Somebody once said, "A zine is a zine is a zine." Is it you?

    Long Live Zines,
    Darren Kraft
    Whiplash The Zine
    Newton, NJ

2 SKIP SOCIETY
Yo Mike,

Thanx for the letter. I understand the time requirements you have. Sorry about the mag blurbs. I thought you were psyched on it, then when it was too late I got the vibes that you weren't into it. But don't worry about it. Eddie R. and I will be doin' it. We're having a blast! It's gonna be hot. If you're interested maybe we'll get you to contribute once in a while. Keep shreddin' & I'm still a big fan of Aggro Rag.

    C-Ya at a contest,
    Ron Wilkerson
    Leucadia, CA

CANADIAN BAKERS
Dear Mike,

Today (Feb 27th) I received my new issue of FREESTYLIN' (April issue). I always wanted to write you for your zine but I didn't want to just write something lame like "Dude, send me your zine, thanks." I just had my wisdom teeth extracted and my face resembles the Elephant Man. Since I can't do much in this condition I read my FREESTYLIN' issue over and over at least 12 times. The part I liked best was the SCAN section on you and your zine. Since I read the mag enough to memorize it I grabbed a magnifying glass so I could read the small inset of your zine. After reading "Are You a Contest Zombie?" I realized that we are quite alike. You, by far, have one of the best attitudes out there. I like the underground riders because they seem "real" and they are what freestyle is all about. My favorites are Tim Treacy, Aaron Dull, The K, Lungmustard, Jason Parkes, Chris Day and I'm sure if I met you or saw you ride I would include you. In fact, I do include you!

I live in Hamilton Ontario, Canada. There are some hot local riders but most of them have bad attitudes like you explained. One of them, though, is mega-rad and has his head dialed too. His name is Rich MacLean. He is like a cross section between Chris Day and Aaron Dull. I am an ok rider myself I guess (not meant to sound conceited). I can do decades (tons of variations of them, including links to them), Squeakers, Boomerangs (Flails, Anklebusters, Randy Rolls, etc.), Frontyards (no-handed), Miami Hop-Hops and many more. I have been in 2 contests (just local ones). In my first one I got 4th place out of ten guys. The second I got 7th place out of 16 guys. The class I ride is 17 & Over Novice.

There is one thing in life that pisses me off though. When people first meet me at contests or at just an uptown session they look at each other and snicker amongst each other. They have this dumb notion that just because I wear glasses I'm a nerd or a wimp. They also laugh at my bike. It's a well-used, scuffed-up, lime green Skyway Street Beat with chrome Performer bars, blue Hutch stem, chrome Torker II forks and blue Ukai rims. So what if I don't have a fully up-to-date scoot like they have. One guy laughed at my Dia-Compe MX 1000's and said, "They went out 5 years ago." He then proceeded to cut me down for a couple of minutes while his friends laughed. When he was finished attempting to insult me he asked me to do my best tricks. So I cruised up the parking lot and did a squeaker into a grasshopper into a slider into a decade into an anklebuster (my best link trick). Funny thing though, I gained no satisfaction from showing up those posers. Instead I felt like some asshole show-off but I got my point across and left without looking at them. I am sick of trying to prove myself so I only ride with people who accept me when they meet me without expecting me to do a "contest run" for them so they can judge me good enough to be in their acquaintance.

    Yours Radically,
    Cam Severin
    Hamilton Ontario,
    CANADA

P.S.- All your contributions to FREESTYLIN' are totally cool. "A Puppet No More...", "As Authority Sleeps" and especially your contest review "Judge For Yourself." Also, FREESTYLIN's interview with all you Hoods was cool.
P.P.S.- Hey Mike--if I ever meet you I'll do all my million and one Miami Hopper variations and you can cheer me on all the way. (Heh Heh)

Cover of the incredibly-absurd but massively mind-boggling CRIB LIZARD, the zine made by high school rebels to make kids laugh and think.

ZINE FOR THE ECCENTRIC

CRIB LIZARD

BIZARRE LITERATURE

VOLUME ONE NUMBER TWO

2

SUPERMARKET ISSUE!

25¢

Added Bonus!
ACTION MOVIE!

ALSO! Valuable arcade coupon!!

NO WAY!
Dear Mike Daily, Geek-in-Chief,
 Hi. My name is Lawrence. I am a writer for a local zine in the Fort Walton Beach Florida area. I read and bought an issue of "Crib Lizard" at a small yard sale. I stumbled over the Supermarket Issue and promptly asked how they got it. The woman said that her son brought it home from school one day and she didn't toss it out because it seemed kinda demented. Her son suggested that they sell it for the price marked on it (25¢). I picked it up and was a-mazed. What talent! My boss suggested that I write you and ask for permission to print all of it in its own specialized section in our yearly special. You and the other off-their-rocker writers will receive full credit. How does such a small magazine from Pennsylvania have such a wide circulation? And we've never heard of it before. We are lucky if ours reaches Atlanta, GA.
 Please respond soon so we can learn more about you radical-assed Ya hoos.
 Sincerely,
 Lawrence A.
 A.W.S. Productions
 Hurlburt Fld, FL

"J.P." SALINGER?
Dear Mike,
 The money I sent with this letter is for a subscription to Aggro Rag. I hope the money I sent doesn't get stolen because I need some inspiration from your zine. This winter really sucked, none of my friends have been riding. I was thinking of just going to some place where there is a lot of hot riders, some place like NYC or California. I figure I can sleep in the streets or on a beach and hang out with all the cool guys. I could just ride all day and be a scumbag. That would be great. I just can't handle school. I hate all the kids there. My friends are all jerks to me. They want me to be on their team now but all they want to do is these lame shows for the Boy Scouts. They don't even want to go to comps. They say that the team I'm going to put together is going to be lame, fuck them, all the kids on my team are better than most of the kids on theirs. Your hair is cool. You, Kevin, and Mark are all gods. Also so is Joe G., Chris Day, Rick M., Dennis, Jason Parkes, and Daren Pelio. Daren rips. Did you ever see him ride? He's bionic. I don't know why he doesn't place at the AFAs, maybe he doesn't go. He didn't touch during his 3 minute run. It was the most perfect routine I ever saw. It was the most perfect thing I ever saw. He timed all his tricks to the music, he was everything. You know at shows how people clap but they don't really mean it? At that contest we were all relaxed then he came on, and nobody told us to clap, he just got us so psyched. Everyone was screaming and crying. My mother even thought he was a god. You know like in football when someone gets a TD everyone claps but do you think to yourself, "Boy wasn't that a great pass" or "That was a superb catch." When I saw Daren ride I wanted to clap for him. He was probably the only person I have ever wanted to clap for.
 Would you write me or somehow tell me that you have read this letter. People like you are really great, who would do something as great as making a zine with as little time as you have and ask for so little in return. If

...ou don't read this letter
...at's okay. I know how real
...ittle time you have.
         A friend,
         Jean Paul Paquette
         Pittsfield, MA

MASTERPIECE MISSIVE
Hey Mike,
  Thanks for writing me back.
Keep my money and send me a
few old rags and a few new.
I'm watching figure skating
right now, Debbie James
should kick ass. I get into
figure skating, maybe because it's so much like
"stylin'. You were right about that scene business. The
new issue of FREESTYLIN' just
covered the King of Flatland
and all these people there
got their picture in.
  Did you see that Daren
Pelio got second? He's so
good. I knew he would place
sometime. He did it with
kind of lame tricks too.
I'm not crackin' on him,
it's just that he could do
tricks twice as good. In
Florida he'll really rip
cause he'll have seen the
phenomenal tricks. I'll get
to see him March 27th in
the New Hampshire contests,
he'll get me psyched for a
year.
  I'm going to that contest
in a month and I'm practicing hard. I hope I don't
jell this time. I'm gonna try
and go out in the jam circle
more and get myself some respect so I don't get so nervous.
  Your advice was cool about
the trick team but you don't
know those guys. I'm starting a team with my good
friends and my mom will try
to get us shows. She's cool.
She drives me to contests.
The team's gonna be called
Cycle Bionics. Do you
think that's a cool name?
We're gonna go to the New
Jersey and Ohio contests or a
at least try to make it
there. We're gonna try to
get a place to ride for the
winter. Everyone will be able
to ride there and everyone
who is serious about stylin'
can be on our team.
  The girl from Japan just
finished her run. People were
giving her a standing ovation.
She hit a triple that made my
grandmother scream.
  I'll check out some of
those tapes you mentioned. I
like everything besides metal.

My name is pronounced like
John and my first name is
Jean Paul so you'll know just
in case you get to talk to me.
(Debbie screwed up her first
big move-a double triple-theff
she screwed up 2 more triples.
She got the bronze though.
She'll get 'em next time.)
Thanks for writing me, again.
I'd like to hear from you again.
         See you later,
         Jean Paul Paquette
         Pittsfield, MA

REDNECK RETALIATION
Fellow shredder,
  I got the magazine and I
thought it was well worth
sendin' just a stamp for!
You probably don't remember
me. I'm Peter Hendrix. I
sent for the "Aggro Rag"
copy. I didn't really expect
to get anything back. I think
it's great that you're in
college. I know some really
snobby kinda-screwed adults
that consider freestylers
irresponsible jerks. People
like yourself prove them
wrong. I have enclosed a
dollar for the issue of
Aggro Rag. By the way, Led
Zeppelin is very shreddin'
kinda music! I just got
"Led Zeppelin II". You
should get it if you don't
already have it. I think I can
relate to your magazine more
so than any other.
  What kind of bike do ya
got? I have a Hutch Trick
Star. I like them because
they're light, exotic, and a
supreme status-getter. I
have faith that your magazine
will be a success. I've been
tellin' my friends to get
Aggro Rag. I must admit I was
very impressed with your letter. You may hear some bad
stuff about freestyle in
Georgia. I admit it does
have a lot of bad points but
freestyle does exist down
here. In my school there is
four classifications of
people: Preps, Rednecks,
Heavy Metalers, and Freestylers. I have nothing against any classification of
the human race except rednecks.
  More than one bike has been
keyed by an inferior group of
people referred to as rednecks. More than one redneck
has gotten into his pickup
truck before he has realized
the right two tires have been
slashed in retaliation.
  I guess I better end the
letter here.
         Rip it up,
         Peter Hendrix

HOODS HEARD OF IN HOLLAND
Dear Aggro Rag,
  This letter might have
reached you a long time
later than it's written but
I'm glad it has reached
you. This letter comes all
the way from Holland (The
land of the tulips, windmills and wooden shoes).
  My brother Paul (age 20)
and I (Bart 18) make a little magazine of our own,
and so we confronted with
Sterling Ruby who was on
holiday in a place 15 minutes away from here. A skater from that place called
me that he was there and so
I took my camera and a piece
of paper and headed to the
place where they would go
skate.
  When I wanted to interview him, he told me he was
from Pennsylvania and so I
asked him if he knew "the
Plywood Hoods." Yes, those
guys live 15 minutes away
from where I live!!!! Oh
man this couldn't be true!
The world is small isn't
it? So we talked a little
about you and the guys when
you were breakdancing and
started freestyling.
  Maybe you wonder how I
know you, but that answer
isn't difficult. You know,
we read FREESTYLIN' too and
so we read your article in
the October '88 issue. I
really liked that article
because it's about the same
over here. From that issue
I wanted to reach you but
I didn't know how. I'm glad
I found a solution. I hope
you'll be glad to send us a
magazine, we'll send you a
F.A.T.-magazine back.
  If you send us a mag,
please write a letter with
that with the latest news
from America so we can put
it in our mag. Maybe Mark
Eaton knows my brother,
cause they met in Washington D.C. October 24th during the K.O.V. series. If
so say hello to him.
  Our magazine includes
skateboarding as well as
BMX freestyling. In our
last issue we had an interview with Mike Loveridge.
Cool huh? We like to get
post, especially from America, so please send SOMETHING to us.
         We hope to meet you
         sometime,
         The F.A.T.-boyz.
         The Netherlands, Europe

ESCAPE FROM THE

Photo by Guy-B

ESCAPE FROM THE PLANET OF THE APES

    The portly woman decked out in navy blue haughtily sauntered past the entrance doors, her mock badge catching a glint of artificial lighting. Her immediate goal was to put a halt to a small group of teenagers who were dangerously pedaling their bicycles down an empty corridor. She liked to believe she was protecting law-abiding citizens from harm.
    "I told you to WALK those bikes! Now get out of the building and don't come back!," the hired hand of authority growled. She boldly stood in their midst, hands on hips, waiting for them to follow her orders. And depart they did.
    The incident colorfully described above took place in Tucson, Arizona at the AFA Masters this year, and it caused me to render the following revelation unto the Hoods: "Forget the *fictional* story-- This IS the 'Planet of the Apes'!"
    Conflicts with cops in the past have produced bitter undertones in ALL of us. That's a fact. It's not that freestylers are overly resentful of authority for authority's sake, but many bikers feel their rights are often times violated and overlooked by police officers. And on many occasions they are. However, I see the purpose and duties of the police in a different light now.

Why do you think there IS a force of individuals specifically trained to maintain law and order? Not to keep you from having fun riding your favorite bank...THAT I can assure you of. To put it bluntly, because there is no law and order on the Planet of the Apes. Murdering, stealing, raping, cheating people inhabit the earth. Humans in form but not in behavior. A race of apes *thinking* they are advancing while actually regressing with every selfish step. A people governed by fear and hate. Attempts must be made to control and protect them from themselves.

Freestyling also occurs on the Planet of the Apes. Most people who freestyle today correspond with the trapped human astronauts in the "Planet of the Apes" saga. They strive to escape the animal-like restrictions placed upon all inhabitants of an ape-infested planet. Ideally, we ride to demonstrate a free, limitless lifestyle not harmful in any way, shape or form to anyone or any thing. The love of this freedom is what drives us to constantly improve and create.

Now...if one chooses to "rogue" around town and intentionally create disorder, he is nothing but an ape on a bike in my eyes. In Arizona, as we were being chased through the near-empty streets by police helicopters, I felt like an animal. I didn't like that feeling too much. Those captured (I was) were released after the cops got the situation under control. The Tucson police were doing their job of maintaining law and order, which we were temporarily disrupting. I can wholly accept that.

This is what I'd like you, the reader, to accept: Whenever a figure of any authority comes down on you for riding somewhere or somehow, try to listen and silently move on--Even if the figure seems fake like the "guard" at the contest. The apes are showing you, the trapped astronaut, how you can escape. Thank them and cruise.

We're called the Plywood Hoods, but destructive hoodlums disrespectful to society we are not. I choose to think of our team as a brotherhood of thinking, responsible riders. There is no place for an ape on the Hoods.

Think before you act, or react. Stop hiding and start riding. It is time to *demonstrate*, my friends.

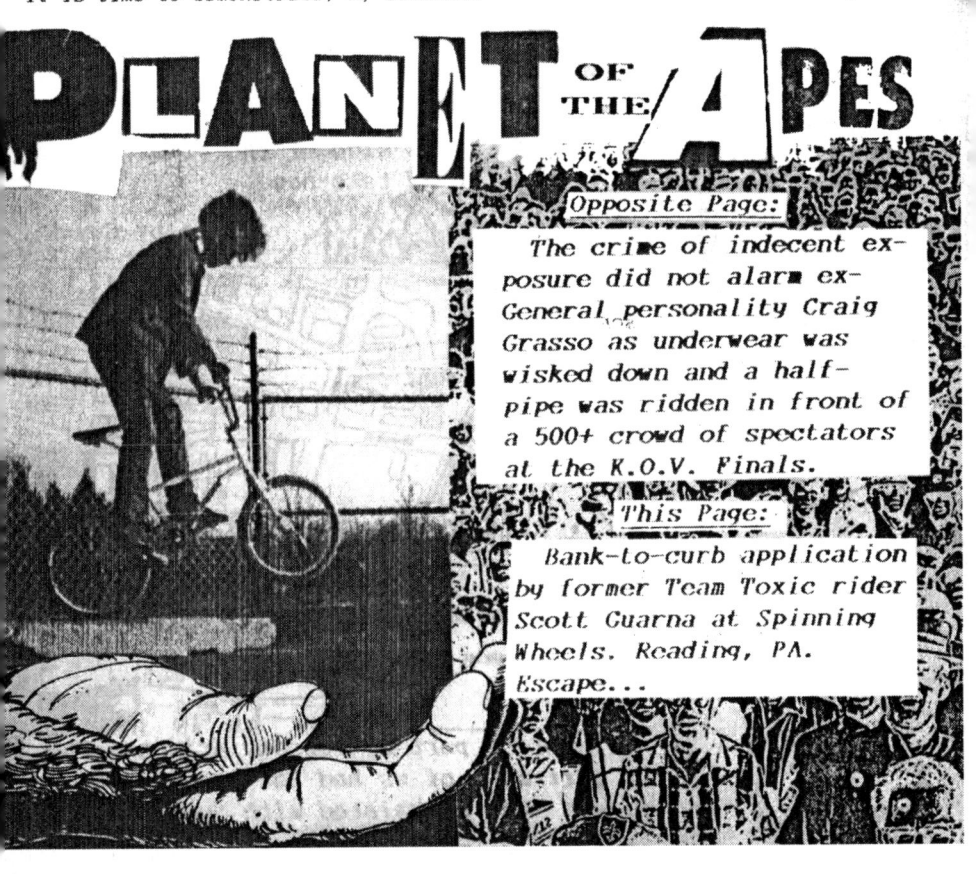

PLANET OF THE APES

Opposite Page:

The crime of indecent exposure did not alarm ex-General personality Craig Grasso as underwear was wisked down and a half-pipe was ridden in front of a 500+ crowd of spectators at the K.O.V. Finals.

This Page:

Bank-to-curb application by former Team Toxic rider Scott Guarna at Spinning Wheels, Reading, PA. Escape...

NO SKATEBOARDS BIKE RIDING or LOITERING
GLENDORA V.C. 9.20-010

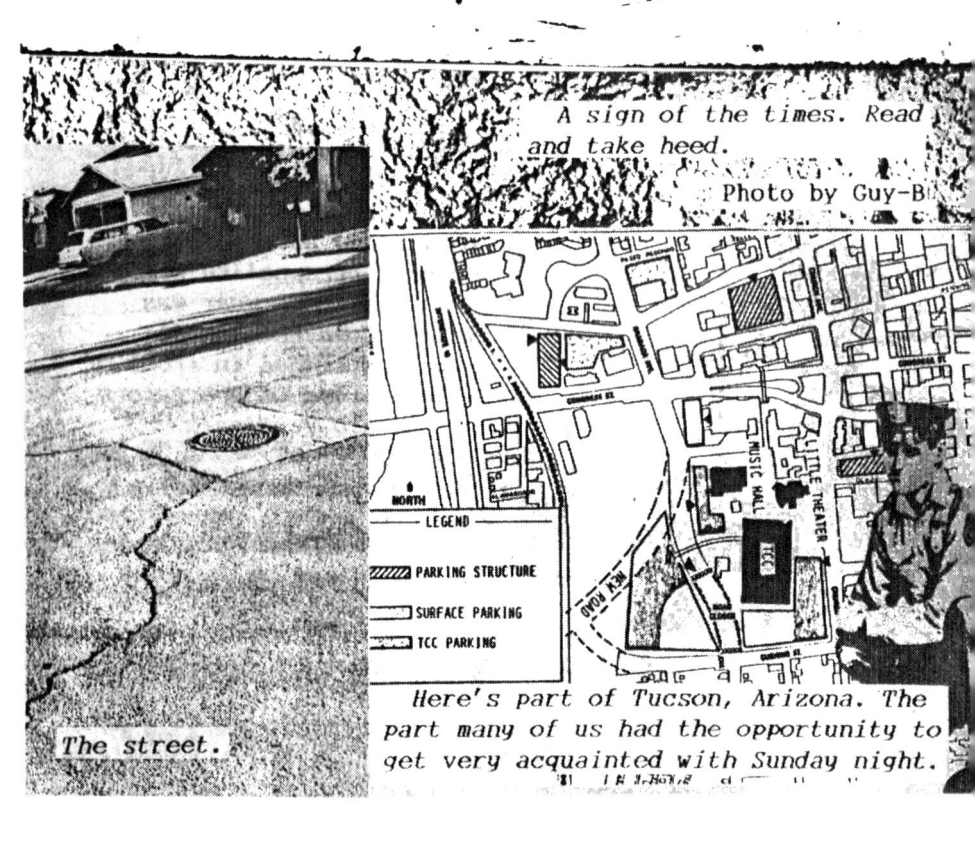

A sign of the times. Read and take heed.

Photo by Guy-B

The street.

Here's part of Tucson, Arizona. The part many of us had the opportunity to get very acquainted with Sunday night.

LEGEND
- PARKING STRUCTURE
- SURFACE PARKING
- TCC PARKING

Escape FROM THE planet OF THE Apes

Chris Day has had his share of run-ins with the police in the past. Ask him sometime if he thinks riding from the cops is advisable.

Photo by Guy-B

AGGRO RAG FREESTYLE MAG!

One who tends to escape every time he rides his bike...Grassroots. Fastplant boost over agua in Tucson, Arizona. **Photo: Lung**

Aaron Dull with a squeaky-clean funky chicken in AZ. Shot by Eaton.

Aggression in progress by pro Pete Augustin. The rage of an Augustand in Arizona. Lungpic.

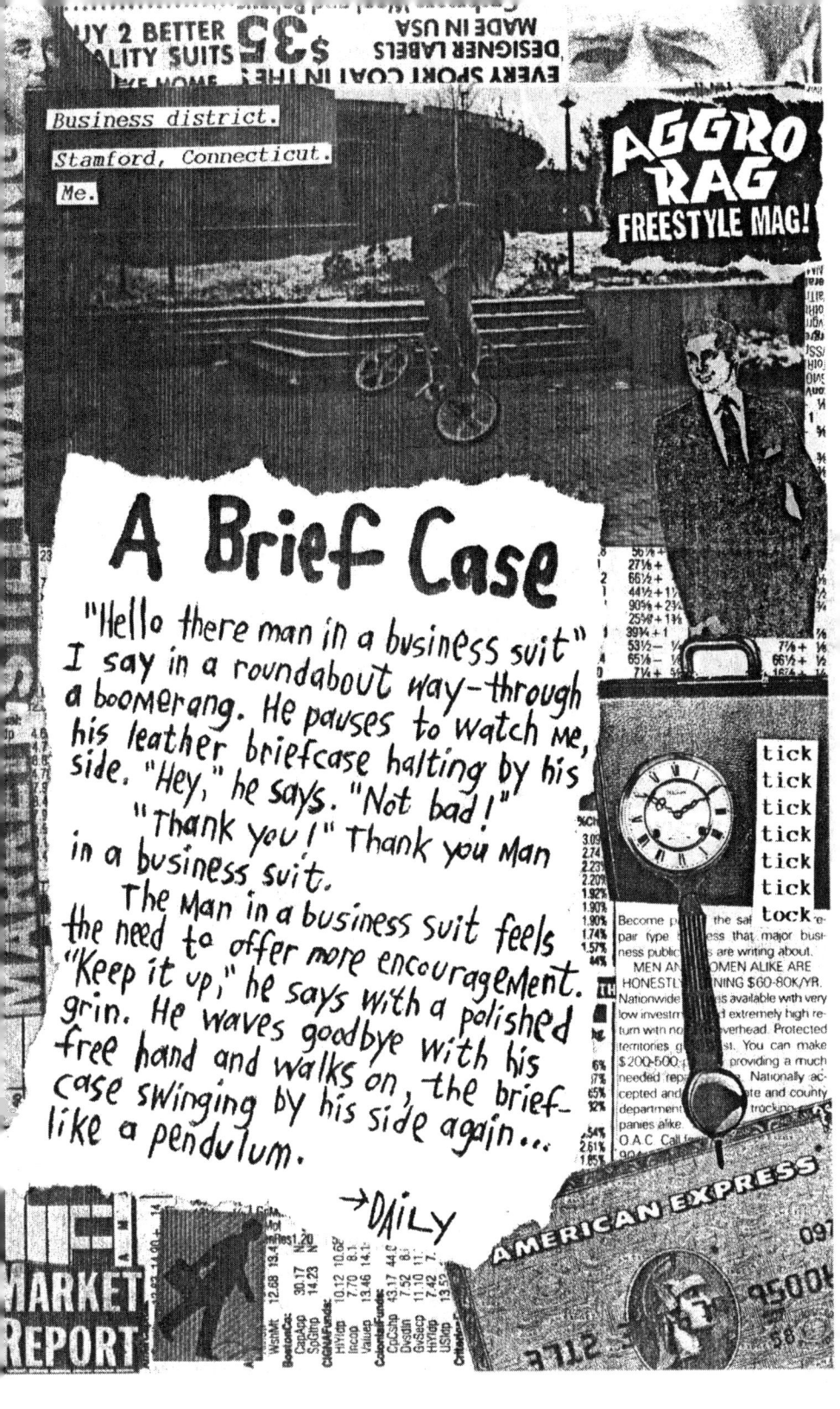

BUY 2 BETTER QUALITY SUITS $35 EVERY SPORT COAT IN THE... DESIGNER LABELS MADE IN USA

Business district.
Stamford, Connecticut.
Me.

AGGRO RAG FREESTYLE MAG!

A Brief Case

"Hello there man in a business suit" I say in a roundabout way- through a boomerang. He pauses to watch me, his leather briefcase halting by his side. "Hey," he says. "Not bad!"

"Thank you!" Thank you Man in a business suit.

The Man in a business suit feels the need to offer more encouragement. "Keep it up," he says with a polished grin. He waves goodbye with his free hand and walks on, the briefcase swinging by his side again... like a pendulum.

tick
tick
tick
tick
tick
tick
tock

→DAILY

MARKET REPORT

AMERICAN EXPRESS

PooL

Much to our delight, several nearly-empty pools awaited our fervent shredding in Tucson, Arizona. Two locals (Rich and Courtny) were appointed as tour guides and we succeeded in conquering the beasts of plaster and concrete.

Top: Pool grafitti and riding directed by Kevin Jones-differing forms of artistic expression. Bumhead Pool. Below Top: Aaron Dull Quote #2..."What are they gonna do-*arrest* us for cleaning out their pool?"

PARTIES

The session halts for a moment as Eaton, Dale, Kev, Aaron and Tour Guide George, er uh Rich take a lil' breather.

Jones attains tiles of blue and a happy feeling in his abdomen with this big carve. The wall on this particular pool was *very* vertical, which regardless failed to stop Jon Peterson from riding out. Arizona.

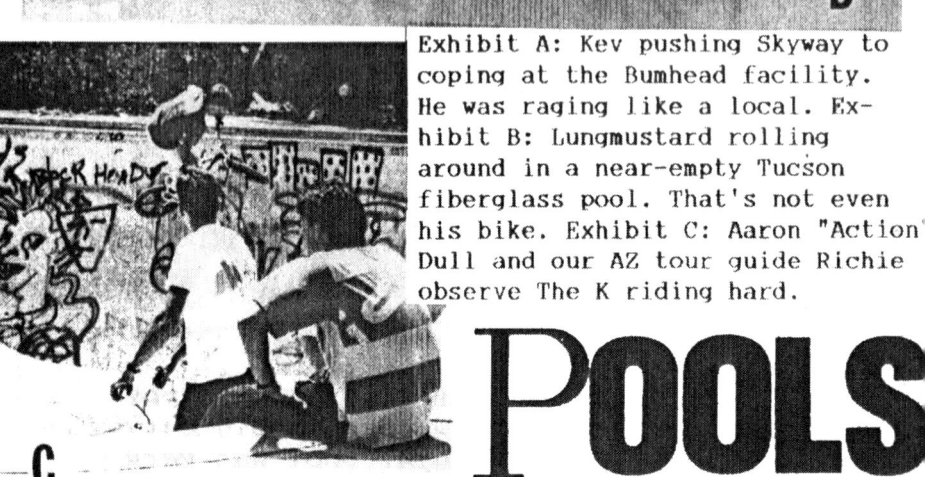

Exhibit A: Kev pushing Skyway to coping at the Bumhead facility. He was raging like a local. Exhibit B: Lungmustard rolling around in a near-empty Tucson fiberglass pool. That's not even his bike. Exhibit C: Aaron "Action" Dull and our AZ tour guide Richie observe The K riding hard.

POOLS

This looks like a job for...

Model 180

RALPH ?

Aaron Ralphin' it.

Ross Bicycles went bankrupt and dropped our tour but I still ended up getting hired by Ross for the summer—Philip Ross to be exact. Phil is one of the owners of R & R Pool & Spa, INC. in Greenwich, Connecticut. I work as a service guy. We cruise around to area pools and fix pumps, acid wash, paint or whatever. It's a cool job, plus I get to scope each pool for riding potential (even if I can only shred 'em in my mind). And man, some of those transitions...

The other day Matt (plumbing expert/driver) and I (toolbox carrier/radio programmer) were on a job and he introduced me to Ralph. Ralph's technical name is "Polaris Vac-Sweep." Home owners come up with their own monickers for the highly-specialized vacuums/sweepers. Basically it's a bike-like device which is hooked up to the return line and scoots around the bottom of the pool, catching debris in the attached bag. A long hose allows it to cover the entire surface area. A short hose trailing off the rear of the vac propels it like a flagella. The steadily-thrashing hose uplifts dirt the bag misses, which floats to the surface and goes into the skimmer. It looks funny but it works. The things are "handy as hell" as Matt put it.

I watched as Ralph slowly pumped the transitions, carving crazy lines wherever he pleased. "He's gettin' UP there!," exclaimed Matt. I laughed and cheered as Ralph emerged from the water to grind coping. A few times he got too rad, though, and one of his wheels fell off. Matt and I were only too happy to fish him out and repair him for more action. I wanted to ride with Ralph.

Ralph was working the shallow end then. He carved the wall low and I went "Awwwww!!" Ralph instantly rebuked me with a spray from his lashing tail and slowly headed for the stairs. What was he gonna...

"O.K., we're outta here Mike," said Matt. Awwwwwwww. Bye Ralph.

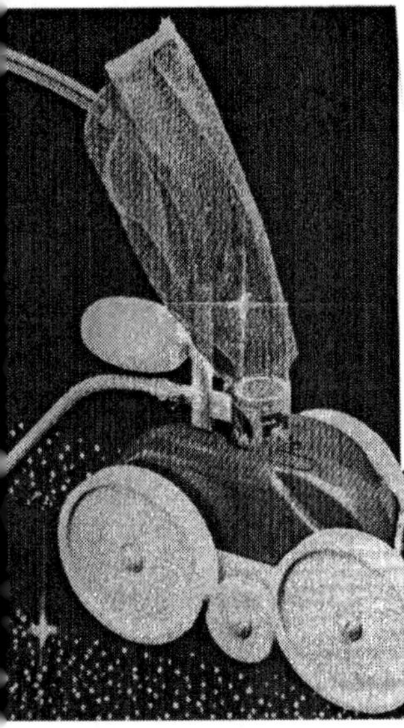

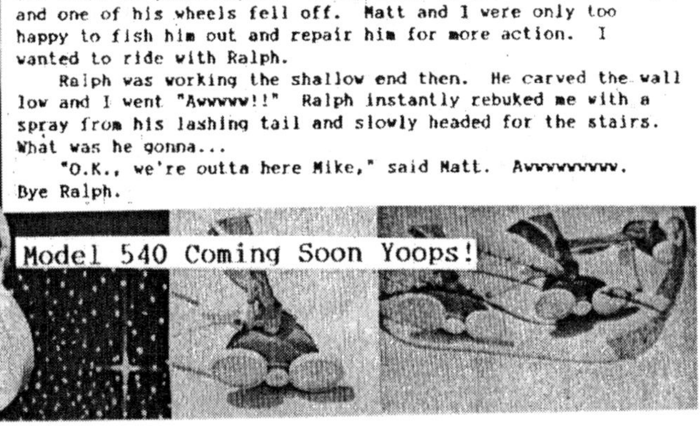

Model 540 Coming Soon Yoops!

POOLS

UP: One of the most classic Hoods photos ever snapped by an amateur. Dale took this aggro shot of The K aerialing in past-flat formation at The Nuclear Pool at Spinning Wheels. A few airs after this very one ended with Kev's GT bars breaking in half and deeply gashing his forearm, requiring many stitches. Heroically, Dale removed his brand new Rockville BMX T-shirt to stop the bleeding. Kev said Dale was feelin' mighty woozy. DOWN: Brian Peters cuttin' a flat one himself at the same pool. Early 1986.

Jym !

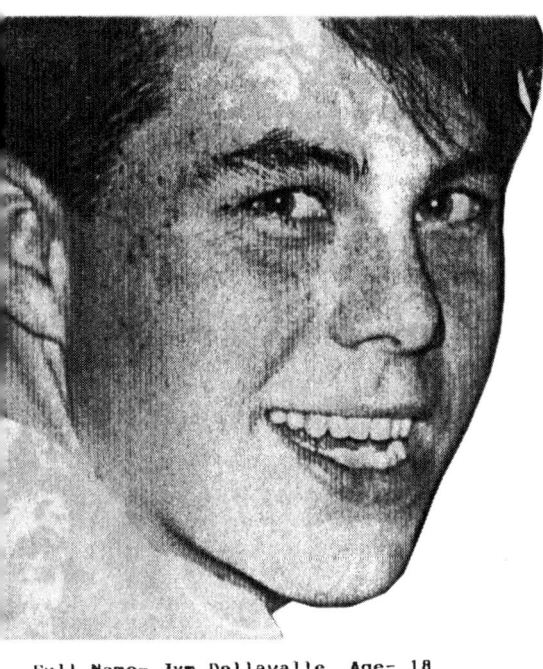

Full Name- **Jym Dellavalle**   Age- **18**
Hometown- **Marshalls Creek, PA**   Bike- **Dyno Compe**
Ambition in Life- **The greatest pleasure in life is doing what people say you cannot do.**

1) What is your favorite trick? My favorite trick is the one-handed surfer and the rolling perverted boom I invented.

2) Who is your favorite rider and why? My favorite riders are the Hoods because they've inspired me to ride more than anyone, especially Jamie. And the kid next to Gary Pollak's house. Adam is fun to ride with too.

3) What do contests mean to you? Contests are where you may see a juvenile get caught taping pros throwing bicycles off the corners of quarter pipes, throwing objects into the roaring crowd and becoming nervous as shit when I mess up on my first trick. Oh yeah, I still owe Jamie from Wayne. I'll get ya...

4) Who are your favorite bands? My fave bands are The Cure, Screaming Brocolli, Cocteau Twins, Minor Threat, and Little Richard (Tutti Frutti). Also, no one can defeat Hip Hop says Cool Ass Jym.

5) Describe your ramp. My ramp--it's 8 feet high, 16 feet wide, 40 feet of flat and can be shredded on heavily now. My brother is too good on it. In the summer that's where I dwell so it's great.

6) Complete this sentence: Socks are important to me because...? They keep the liquids which excrete from the pores of my feet away from the soles of my shoes so I don't say pew...

7) How much do you practice and who with? I practice everyday for 2 hours except Tuesdays (that's when I swim). I like to try new stuff but never plan on putting it in my routine. Like Kevin in Wayne. The Caboose-- that made me angry. I wanted him to pull that off so bad...

8) Evaluate your riding style (essay question-25 pts.). My riding still is somewhat scary. It makes whoever is watching wonder if I'll pull it off, It's a sketchy way of riding but still non-stop. Kind of like putting your left shoe on your right foot and trying to do the smurf.

9) What is fun? Fun-that can only be when you're around Jamie's house when Arreste is home, or when all the Hoods are together. Or watching "The Young Ones."

guest writing

picture sent by mark lewman

A MIND WITH A VIEW

You delve into my mind because you don't understand it. You discuss how my brain is abnormal. Why? Because it's not like yours? Your observations are relative, not discerning. Perhaps I'm too clever for you. I am your hidden leader. The scars on my wrists prove my immortality. My thoughts wander because your trivial questions bore me, yet you think you're superior. Fools.

So I ignore you. I am satisfied to know it myself; to realize I am above you. I act, to toy with you, at times. I play the role you have set for me, then laugh at you. Within these walls I am larger than life, but you think I am trapped. My knowledge is incomprehensible to you. You label me insane.

jkas.

On the ragged edge

ZINE ALERT!

NOTE: When sending away for zines, it is highly recommended you write an accompanying letter about yourself, your scene, etc.

"The Wall" is the kind of rag venture made not for the glory of its writers but for the purpose of establishing creative statements on riding. BSR and ideals concerning street dominate the nature of its well-written stories. Music preferences and info on some choice bands is proudly built into "The Wall". If you consider yourself a veteran of the street game or just an eager beginner, do yourself a favor and try to get this zine. Send money and ask for #4, because it's great.

THE WALL
814 Knightsbridge
Schaumberg, IL 60195

Jamie Smith, who writes under the pen-name of "jkas.", is the author of this gem of a Xeroxed storybook. Filled with colorful vision, "STOKE 'Zine" gives one that "feeling" of cruisin' the streets. All stories do not deal with biking and skating though. Take a chance and broaden your horizons...Send for STOKE. Now mister.

STOKE 'Zine
43 Commissioners St.
Embro, Ontario
CANADA
N0J 1J0

some HoOdS HISTORY!

Knowing and riding with Brian Peters has been a major joy in my life. We went to California in 1985 and learned a LOT together from that. Brian was bitten by the freestyle bug in '84 at the East Coast Nationals in Harrisburg, PA, where he saw Brian Blyther do a demo for Huffy. He quickly built his own quarterpipe and began practicing. Soon Brian had a very impressive array of variations. His ground riding was improving rapidly and we decided to go full-bore with the Plywood Hoods. We had a blast doing shows and just ridin' around. But Brian never liked competition (he was *always* in it for the fun of it) and contests were becoming a big deal. In '86 satisfaction from riding began decreasing for Brian so he called it quits. I've heard Brian has been riding again.

FREESTYLE PLYWOOD HOODS TEAM

Mike Watert flinging himself into the air at Brian's. Now he flings himself into a fury every day practicing on his drums. He's good.

Founding Fathers Daily, Peters and Downs. It's been a fun time ever since.

This guy's mental stability was highly questioned after this mid-ramp-jam "wild man air" which he actually lived to talk about. Ron Caez.

Today's Tom Sawyer
He gets high on you,
And the space he invades
He gets *by* on you.

… from MEL…

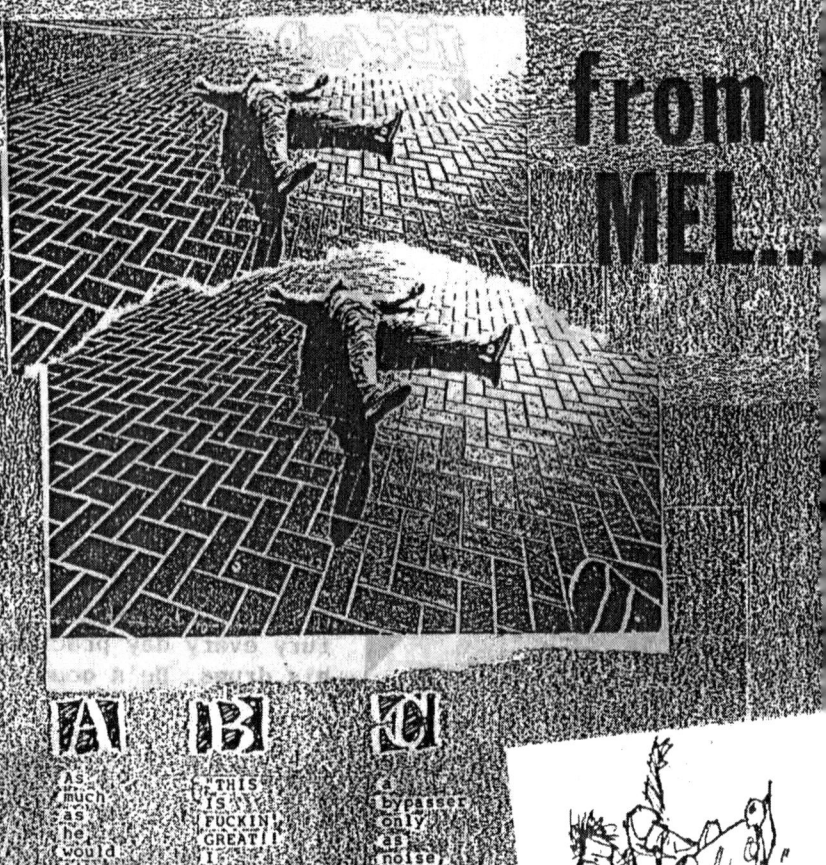

A B C

A
As much as he would like to yell it, he couldn't. He was alone. He could only grin and bear it, barely restraining from jumping up and down. He wanted to scream it so all could hear.

B
"THIS IS FUCKIN GREAT! I JUST SLAPPED A 50/50 FOR 15 FEET DOWN THE GROMMET CURB!!! DID YOU SEE THAT??! NO ONE DOES THAT!!" His interior exstacy and the actions that made them possible are visible to

C
a bypasser only as noise, or disrespect for society. "SHIIIIT YEAH!!" he thinks throwing his fist in the air. He shakes his head and pushes off, a low "Haaaa..." escapes his lips.

DORKIN' in york

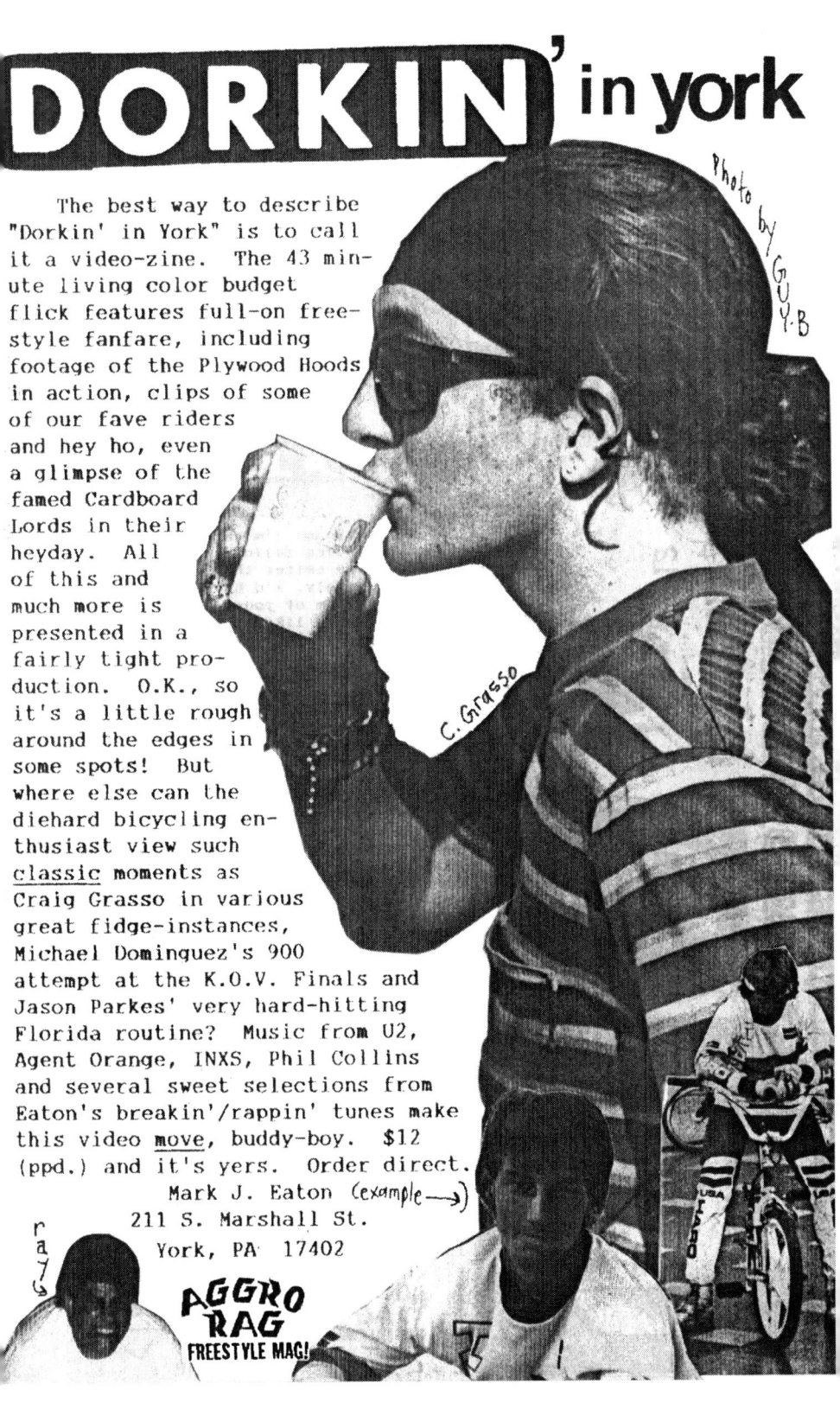

Photo by GUY.B

The best way to describe "Dorkin' in York" is to call it a video-zine. The 43 minute living color budget flick features full-on freestyle fanfare, including footage of the Plywood Hoods in action, clips of some of our fave riders and hey ho, even a glimpse of the famed Cardboard Lords in their heyday. All of this and much more is presented in a fairly tight production. O.K., so it's a little rough around the edges in some spots! But where else can the diehard bicycling enthusiast view such <u>classic</u> moments as Craig Grasso in various great fidge-instances, Michael Dominguez's 900 attempt at the K.O.V. Finals and Jason Parkes' very hard-hitting Florida routine? Music from U2, Agent Orange, INXS, Phil Collins and several sweet selections from Eaton's breakin'/rappin' tunes make this video <u>move</u>, buddy-boy. $12 (ppd.) and it's yers. Order direct.

Mark J. Eaton (example →)
211 S. Marshall St.
York, PA 17402

C. Grasso

ray

AGGRO RAG FREESTYLE MAG!

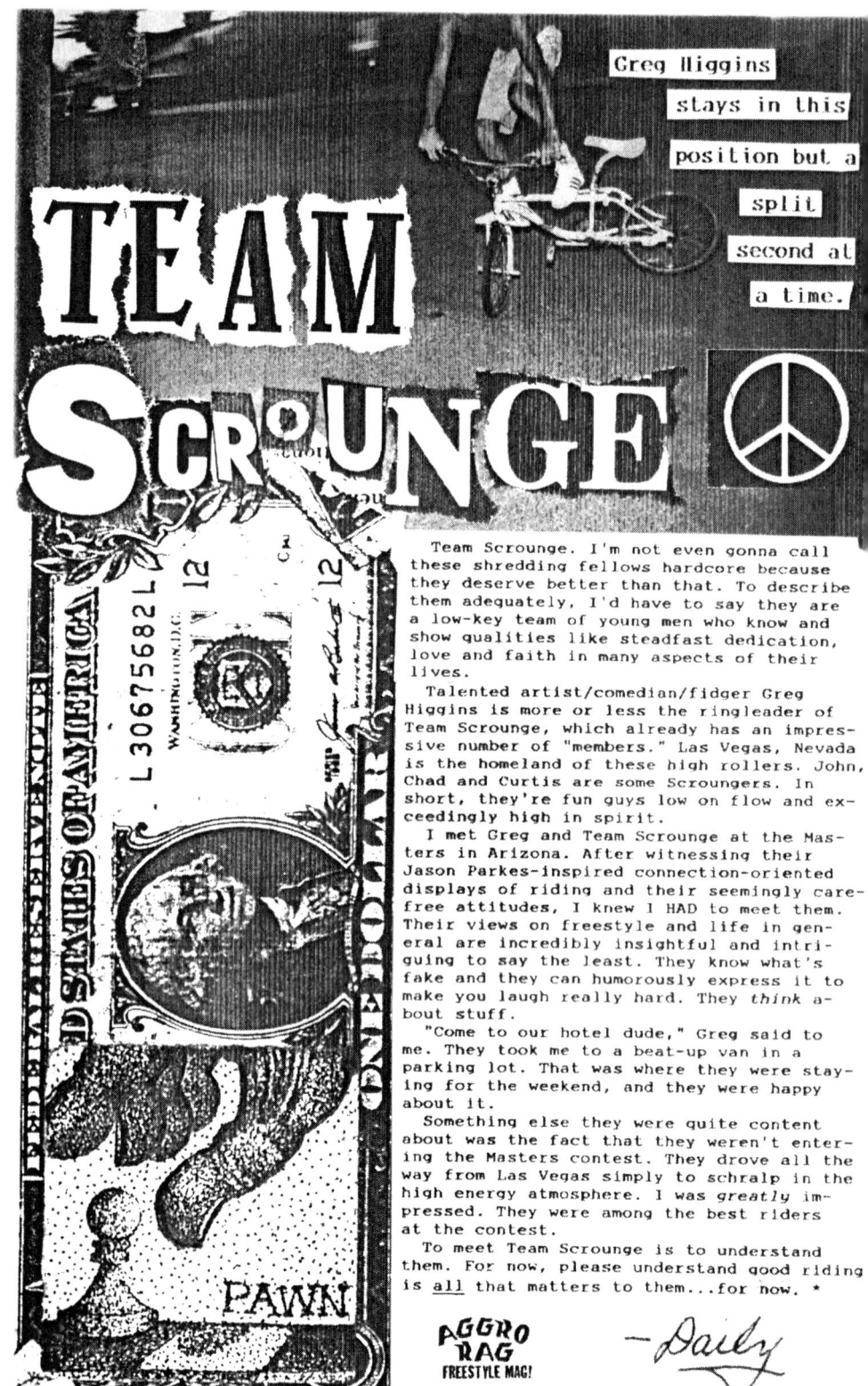

TEAM SCROUNGE

Greg Higgins stays in this position but a split second at a time.

Team Scrounge. I'm not even gonna call these shredding fellows hardcore because they deserve better than that. To describe them adequately, I'd have to say they are a low-key team of young men who know and show qualities like steadfast dedication, love and faith in many aspects of their lives.

Talented artist/comedian/fidger Greg Higgins is more or less the ringleader of Team Scrounge, which already has an impressive number of "members." Las Vegas, Nevada is the homeland of these high rollers. John, Chad and Curtis are some Scroungers. In short, they're fun guys low on flow and exceedingly high in spirit.

I met Greg and Team Scrounge at the Masters in Arizona. After witnessing their Jason Parkes-inspired connection-oriented displays of riding and their seemingly carefree attitudes, I knew I HAD to meet them. Their views on freestyle and life in general are incredibly insightful and intriguing to say the least. They know what's fake and they can humorously express it to make you laugh really hard. They *think* about stuff.

"Come to our hotel dude," Greg said to me. They took me to a beat-up van in a parking lot. That was where they were staying for the weekend, and they were happy about it.

Something else they were quite content about was the fact that they weren't entering the Masters contest. They drove all the way from Las Vegas simply to schralp in the high energy atmosphere. I was *greatly* impressed. They were among the best riders at the contest.

To meet Team Scrounge is to understand them. For now, please understand good riding is <u>all</u> that matters to them...for now. *

AGGRO RAG FREESTYLE MAG!

—Daily

BEFORE YOU IS AN EXCERPT FROM THE NATIONAL BESTSELLER, "101 USES FOR A HIP-PACK" © by REKNOWN LITERARY GENIOUS, Greg Higgins, READ ON...

EXCLUSIVE!

USE #63: SELF-DEFENSE...

THE HIP-PACK, WITH IT'S VERSITILITY, CAN BE USED (PREFERABLY FULL) TO STRIKE ANYONE (i.e. ANYONE) WHO WISHES TO POSE A THREAT TO YOU OR YOUR BIKE (OR SKATE). AS SHOWN IN THIS VIVID DEPICTION.

THWACK!

NOTE: DUST STIRRING IN BACKGROUND, AS A RESULT.

TEAM $crounge!

now sit your ass down

GREG HIGGINS FLOATS THRU A WAY GRACEFUL MANOOV WHICH HAS BECOME VERY MUCH FOR GOTTEN OVER THE YEARS. THE G-TURN

$ $ $ $ NO $ $
$ $ $ $ $ $

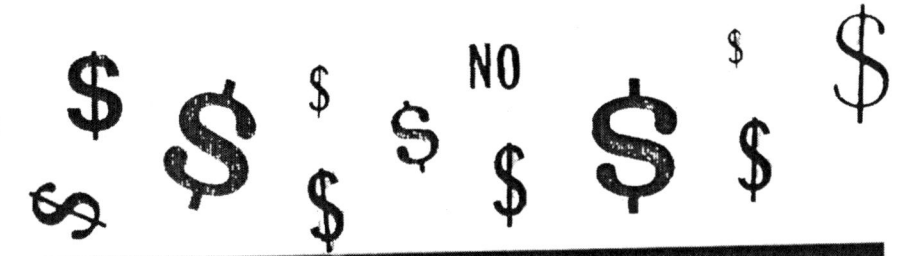

Please Buckle Up

Gregory Higgins can-canning a G-Turn. Greg and tEaM SCRoUNJe rage so hard yer eyes will bleed. ON any given street session they have been know'N to manual over excessively sick terraiN But schralping up the ground in quick coNNectioNS is their first LOVE.

TEAM SCROUNGE

greg

For more information about Team Scrounge or any of the aggro members therein, write to:

Greg Higgins
4458 E. Philadelphia St
Las Vegas, Nevada 89104

THEY RIDE.

Photos by Lungy

Chad Johnson. Look at his left foot. Look at his bent cranks. Try to imagine the twisted trick he is pulling with precision. He shreds.

John

AGGRO RAG FREESTYLE MAG!

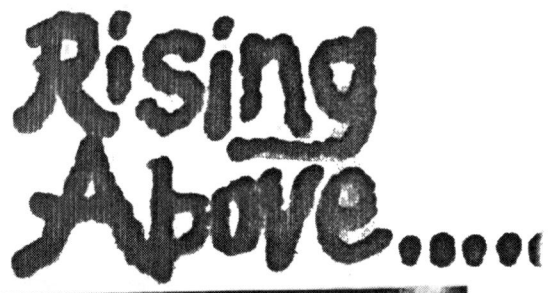

Rising Above......

His first air.

360° through his pulled 540.

The attention of every human at the '88 Austin, Texas contest is intently focused upon the gifted one as he fulfils righteous thoughts of ramp riding. A single hand is not raised as they look up in the air to watch knowledge. A subdued crowd...subdued by the spectacular gift they are receiving through Michael Dominguez.

Photos by Eaton

MUSIC to JaM to.

By Daily

Photo by Guy-B

Tuned In

"NeVeR GET OLD"

"When did the Light die?" bewails Sinéad O'Connor on "The Lion and the Cobra", a work which beautifully combines lyrics of unbridled Truth with a brilliant symphony of moving sound. Sinéad releases her strong vocals in such a manner that girlish innocence clashes and contrasts with emotional eruptions from the depths of her heart. The simplistic, hard-hitting harmonies within cuts "Jerusalem", "I Want Your Hands on Me" and "Troy" invariably lead the listener *"away to unseen shores"*. "The Lion and the Cobra" offers food (faith?) for thought and its power is sure to engross you. Do not be surprised if you too find yourself expressing *love* for this gifted young artist from Ireland.
— Mike Daily

Sinéad O'Connor — the Lion and the Cobra.

TEN REALLY GOOD ALBUMS

1) **New Order**-"Low Life"
2) **Midnight Oil**-"Diesel and Dust"
3) **Tears For Fears**-"The Hurting"
4) **The Jesus and Mary Chain**-"Barbed Wire Kisses"
5) **The Mission U.K.**-"Gods Own Medicine"
6) **Def Leppard**-"Hysteria"
7) **Skinny Puppy**-"Cleanse Fold and Manipulate"
8) **The Cure**-"Pornography"
9) **Big Black**-"Songs About Fucking"
10) **U2**-"The Joshua Tree"

Once upon a time, in Apopka, Florida, there lived a young boy by the name of Howdy who liked to ride a Hutch Trick Star and make his OWN t-shirts. And he lived happily ever after.

Howdy!

It is constantly Howdy's duty to go marauding around Florida, attacking anything that does not move (or attack him first).

Mitch Collins kind-of-grinding a ditch ramp. Howdy says Mitch is now "Mister Street" and doesn't ride ramps anymore.

"Is this kid on acid?" -girl at school.

Mitch and some local homeboys-to-be.

"Who says we can't ride here?!" - Jim Norman

THE LOCALS OF BORLANDO

Right: Mitch Collins bonelesses one at a local ditch ramp. Is it not refreshing to see some guys still wear trusty VANS?
Bottom Right: Brian "Homeboy" Homes topsiding a can can on his ramp. An original Borlando local fer sure. Below: Bar-spinning bank abubaca by Jim Norman. Hutch pedals?

Right: Jim Norman riding the Park Street wall..... bricks or no bricks. _Lower Right_: Paul tweakin' a big grin. _Lower Left_: Mike Lombardo airborne. Howdy says Mike is an all-around swell egg. _Directly Below_: Orange Cycle, a helpful sponsor of Riggs.

paul

The exciting conclusion to the famous Ken Mann interview, which our readers have been on the edge of their Tioga seats waiting for. Enjoy...

PART 2

Lung: "What's TRP stand for?"
Ken Mann: "Taufique Recreational Products."
Lung: "Name some main guys TRP has sponsored."
Ken Mann: "Uh...R.L..."
Jamie: "Was he the first one?"
Ken Mann: "He was the first rider. The first sponsored rider. We gave 'em away before but that wasn't sponsored. Denny Howell was pretty early. Joe Gruttola we had from the beginning. Then Brian Belcher--he was in there. Krys Dauchy...she isn't on anymore."
Jamie: "Why is she off?"
Lung: "GT seatposts."
Jamie: "Oh."
Ken Mann: "Carlo Griggs,..."
Lung: "You have Kevin on there don't you?"
Ken Mann: "Kevin who?"
Lung: "Jones."
Ken Mann: "Oh yeah, he's on there.
Jamie: "He doesn't have one (TRP seatpost) though."
Lung: "Yeah--that one's his."
Jamie: "Oh."
Ken Mann: "We're probably gonna have Dennis but he doesn't know if he's gonna be on Haro so he wants to wait."

Lung: "What if he IS on Haro?"
Ken Mann: "Well then we're gonna give him a layback but he doesn't know what kind of post he wants to be sponsored for."
Lung: "Oh...OK."
Ken Mann: "Rick Moliterno's gonna be sponsored in '88. Lots of people."
Lung: "It's lookin' big, huh?"
Ken Mann: "Yeah."
Lung: "Where do your seatposts get made?"
Ken Mann: "MCS."
Lung: "What...you got it goin' with MCS or what?"
Ken Mann: "Simon has a friend in MCS and they get it all made. He gives 'em dimensions and they make it. But right now we're probably gonna try to get it made somewhere cheaper so we can sell more."
Lung: "What was that thing in FREESTYLIN' about Simon's trip to Japan or whatever?"
Ken Mann: "(Sigh) Simon was gonna go to Taiwan to get a maker for the Gorker (i.e.- Buffguard) and he decided not to go and they already printed it so it was just like free publicity."
Lung: "Does Simon like free publicity?"
Ken Mann: "Yeah." •

COLLEGE CAN BE FUN

Me lofting my bike overhead at the end of my act in our school's talent show.

Quite a rare (believe me) photo...Kev at LHU. We did a show once.

George, my dad, in the midst of making some dirt disappear from the front of our house. I thought ol' George was trying to make ME disappear two years ago when he sent me off to college. Now I see that move as being one of the best ones of my life.

Lock Haven University has an *excellent* exchange program, which is how I met these fine friends from foreign lands... Manuel from Mexico, my roomie Volker from Germany, Darko from Yugoslavia (looming ominously in background) and pool shark Avinda from India. A very learning experience <u>for sure</u>.

Oh "K"!

Kev-Texas '87

I remember things. I remember riding to Thunderdohm one day and seeing a guy named Barry who rode a gold Race Inc. pedaling in the opposite direction with only half of his handlebars left. He was smiling. I also remember watching Kevin Jones' 1987 Texas routine on videotape. He ripped so hard. But I thought the best part of his run was the stall lawnmower he did into Trolley. Why? Other than it being the only one of the contest, that stall lawnmower was so STYLISH.

Kev-Arizona '88

During this year's Skyway tour, The K sent me a cool letter and this photo to drool over. "Sick or what?!?" Florida.

BE TEAM

The "B" Team of the Plywood Hoods is hungry for more members. John Huddleston, Jym Dellavalle and Jason Parkes are the first three history-making inductees to this special team. Would you like to become a "B" Teamer? Welp, here's the low down: It costs nothing to join (it's not a matter of money). T-shirts are readily flowed. The opportunity of appearing in Hoods videos. The only qualifications for "membership" are humbleness, originality and radness. We are not judges of any kind so please don't apply. Just keep it up and we'll find you.

On a silver platter...

AGGRO RAG FREESTYLE MAG!

"Ride First, Read Later."

WALL RIDES

Blockbuster ISSUE!

October 1987
Volume 2 Number 8

60 pages!

**BIG INTERVIEWS
SOME CONTESTS
AND OTHER GOOP**

Guaranteed by Good Housekeeping

Subscriptions?
Not exactly, but close enough. Send five dollars and for awhile get lots of Aggro Rag-related things (rags, stickers, flyers, whatever). Not for the impatient customer. Satisfaction Guaranteed.

CAN YOU FIND: Dick Van Patten, Gavin McCloud, Brett's dad

AGGRO RAG FREESTYLE MAG!

Exclusive Photos!

Ride First, ead Later.

NO.9

Kevin Jones Sleeping in a Hotel Room!

Inside:
- Contests!
- Interviews!
- Buddies!
- A Star Pin-Up!
- No Skating!
- One Ad!
- PLUS TONS MORE!

OHIO!

DEAL?

Offered for the first time ever to the underground...the last two raging issues of Aggro Raggro (120 pages of hella radness) for the cost of six dollars (postage included). **TWO BUCK!** Read the much talked about, uncut interviews of riders Pete Augustin, Dizz Hicks, Jason Parkes, Craig Grasso, Ken Mann and Ceppie Maes. See some contests from OUR point of view. Indulge **60 pages** in the many stories written with more than a grain of imagination. Learn what fidgin' is really all about. Six bucks should sound like a large sum to ask for these back issues. Maybe it is and maybe it isn't. That you must decide for yourself, spagmumpola.

---- cut here ----

AGGRO RAG FREESTYLE MAG!

Send to:

Mike Daily
3778 Cayuga Lane
York, PA 17402

(Check appropriately)

____ A. Rag Sub Deal...$5.00
____ Back Classics.....$6.00

Name_____

Address_____

City_____ State_____

Zip Code_____

Photo by SPIKE

AGGRO RAG
FREESTYLE MAG!
3778 cayuga lane
york, pa 17402

Enjoy

AVOID BREATHING FUMES

DAVE MIRRA

**AGGRO RAG FREESTYLE MAG!
(Summer 1989)**
York, PA
5½" x 8¼"

12th ISSUE

As Mark "Lungmustard" Eaton says in the Director's Commentary[14] for *Dorkin' III*: "Dave [Mirra] came down for two weeks in the Summer of '88 to ride with us. He wanted to brush up on his flatland skills at the time and we just hung out and we rode every day. And the funny thing was: He stayed at Jamie [McKulik]'s house and Jamie was like, 'This kid is driving me crazy! He wakes up at 8 o'clock every morning: "Come on! Let's go ride! Let's go ride!" Jamie was like, 'You gotta take this kid off my hands.'" I interviewed "this kid"—the man we used to call "Little Buddy"—for *Aggro Rag Freestyle Mag! Plywood Hoods Zines '84-'89: The Complete Collection*.

Mike Daily: The caption for your no-hander at Woodward in this issue says: "Dave Mirra making it to the amateur finals was a BIG achievement. Dave is 14 years old."

Dave Mirra: Yeah. Nuts. Just to make it to the finals. There were no age groups. I had just turned 15. All the guys were way older. I was really just getting into ramps—quarterpipe stuff and ridin' my buddy's indoor eight-foot-wide half pipe. To cross from flatland to ramps, it was awesome. I got so into ramps. It was just a whole 'nother time. Ramps were so scarce back in the day. Back then, flatland was huge because you could do it anywhere you wanted—any time—where with ramps, you could find a ramp once in a while. You know how it was: It wasn't like there were skateparks or anything. If there were, it was rare. Very rare.

---
[14] "Those commentaries were done during many 3am benders."—Lungmustard

In *Dorkin' II*, you're bustin' out lots of great flatland tricks—and dialed, too. Flatland was the main reason you came out that summer to ride with the Hoods for that week. Your flatland skills must have helped you later on with ramp riding.

It did. I think—to this day—flatland's the most technical...well, ramp riding's getting pretty technical now, I'd say, with these new school guys incorporating brakeless flatland stuff. It's so technical.

I'm thinking of tailwhips. I don't know if there's any correlation between the flatland and ramp tailwhips, but you've always had both so dialed. Tailwhip airs...

Yeah. I don't think it directly feels the same because you're in the air—but I know that anything in your foundation that you do—whatever you've done in your life—it works out some way down the line. It never hurts to be better in a lot of things, and great at one thing. You can try several, several things, and then you can be great at one because of all the things you've done; things you've learned.

That makes me wonder what things you've done on bikes that you've adapted to rally car driving and boxing.

I would say rally cars for sure because the guys that I compete against have done it for a lot longer. BMX has helped me a ton. Peripheral vision, you know? There's things where you go by feel—you don't just go by eyesight. In BMX, it's definitely been that: 540s, flairs, things where it's really commitment. Boxing as well. Being quick and being accurate. I love it. Boxing may have been as technical as BMX—and particularly car racing. I think that's why I love it so much. If I could go back 20 years, I'd be into it a whole lot harder.

Photo: Jared Souney

Are you still involved with video games? Does the company still put those out?

No, they're not. I haven't had a game since 2001. It's been a long time. The BMX market's a little bit dried up for video games, as far as I know. It's probably the last one the scene has had out there.

I'm sure there's still a diehard fanbase for that game. Guys who still play it?

Oh, there's so many people who still are like, "Dude, when are you gonna get a new game? When's it comin' out?" It is what it is. All that stuff was fun while it lasted. I think now it's time to move on a little bit. I think I'm definitely done competing in BMX. I made that call in 2011. I went to Oceanside and that was the last straw. I said, "I'm just not into it."

You still have the Mirraco bike company and the full team.

Yes. It'll still remain that way. But I just don't choose to ride anymore. I think it's a different sport than it used to be, Mike.

Is it?

Yeah. It's definitely not the same. It's not the same at all. It's great—the riding's amazing. I love watchin' it. I do love goin': showin' up and seein' what these guys can do. I know what it takes to win. It's great to just sit back and watch the guys just kill it.

Are a lot of the guys who are killin' it 15 years old?

Oh, there's some great, amazing riders—better than I ever was at 15. A very few, but there are guys.

What do you remember about being featured in the early *Dorkin'* videos? Because at that time, not tons of people had seen footage of you really. Is that right?

Yeah, for sure. When the Haro team came through Syracuse in '87, they co-sponsored me and sent me some free bikes. [Ron] Wilkerson, [Dave] Nourie, [Brian] Blyther, Bill Hawkins…that was amazing. To be from the East Coast and get a free bike, even that much. It was like, "Wow!" Then I met [Mark] Eaton and Kevin [Jones] and Brett [Downs] down at that Charlie's contest in Levittown, Pennsylvania, in 1988. They invited me and I went to York in '88 for a week that summer. That was insane, you know? Even riding with Kevin and Eaton and everybody—all you guys, all the Hoods. And to be in that video, that was like the first real break—to get my name out there. It motivated me. It was a huge, big push. I was part of a scene outside of my scene. Well, we didn't really have much of a scene. It was a sport that nobody even really considered a sport. Especially where I was from. It was like, "Oh, you're gonna ride forever? Sure." You know what I mean? It was really a rebellion kind of feel, as well. Then getting on Dyno in '89, that was huge. That's a big reason why I got there.

Was that after the Woodward contest?

I was ridin' a GT, a frame that I got from Kevin. Yeah, shortly after that is when I got on Dyno. It was after the 2-Hip in Long Island. That was where I got fourth. It was really amazing. That was when I really made it to the Dyno factory team. They flew me to Orange County for the first one in 1990. Just unbelievable. There was all the superstars and the guys you knew were amazing, but still, I was 15. It was an unbelievable opportunity to go to these events and hang out with these Pros that I saw in the magazines. It was mind-blowing really, more than anything.

Contests were always the get-together time. Did you kind of consider yourself one of the Plywood Hoods, ever? You were credited as a Hood in the videos...

Yeah, I did. When they did those videos, it was huge. It was amazing that I was so young and part of a group that I read about in the magazines. Mark and Kevin with all the rolling tricks, they were the guys doin' it. They were the ones that were changin' the whole sport. All of you guys, but they were the ones in the magazines, doin' rolling tricks. You guys were the first—think about it, Mike—the first group—the first *gang*, in a sense, in the sport—that people talked about and people followed. The videos and the riding, that was awesome. For me to be a part of you guys and the group, that's just awesome.

Mike Ness[15] & Dave Mirra

[15] Social Distortion.

AGGRO RAG
FREESTYLE MAG!

Craig Grasso

Interview

"Ride First,
Read Later."

SUMMER 1989

2 HIP

BIG Interview:
MAD DOG

Smokin'
Issue!

summer '89

AGGRO RAG
FREESTYLE MAG!

This paragraph includes: No bullshit editorial. No flamboyant fiction. No snow job or cover-up. Nothing about this issue. No harangues about 'zines. No propaganda to feed fading images. In short, absolutely nothing.

You're welcome.

Editor: Mike Daily. Contributors: Mark Eaton, Steve Giberson, Greg Higgins, Spike Jonze, Shayne Karas, Lew, Maverick, Matt Pingel, Chip Riggs, Scott Towne.

ON THE COVER: Grassroots, John Byers, Kev, Mad Dog, Indian lady. Printing by Ray Bo.

Photo: LEW

list of things to do:
1. finish loft 6
2. check on those curbs after work
3. withdraw $40⁰⁰ from the bank
4. prank call Eddie Roman
　　　　　— LEW

Spike Jonze is to be thanked profusely for sharing his rad photos with AGGRO RAG. Thank you Spike!

amazing DALE M. look alike!

Dale. **Shayne.**

Surprise gripped Dale when he was first shown these remarkable pictures of Shayne Karas. Said Mitzel with a start, "He DOES look like me!"

Dear Occupant (Mike Daily),
Greetings and salutations dear sir. Okay, okay-- enough on the formalities. My name is Shayne Karas from Bloomington, MN if you haven't guessed by the envelope. I've never written to you but I just felt the urge to see what the heck is this publication referred to as Aggro Rag all about. I don't hear much about ya in the mags, do you still ride? College tends to put a damper on things that are fun. I only take a few classes at a community college. Don't feel the need to "jump right in."

dALE get it!

Lots of people give me crap up here about my striking resemblance to Dale Mitzel. There's a small chance that I may be moving to PA. That would be way bitchen to ride with the Hoods on a DAILY (pun intended) basis. You should check out our scene cuz it's way happenin'.
--Shayne Karas

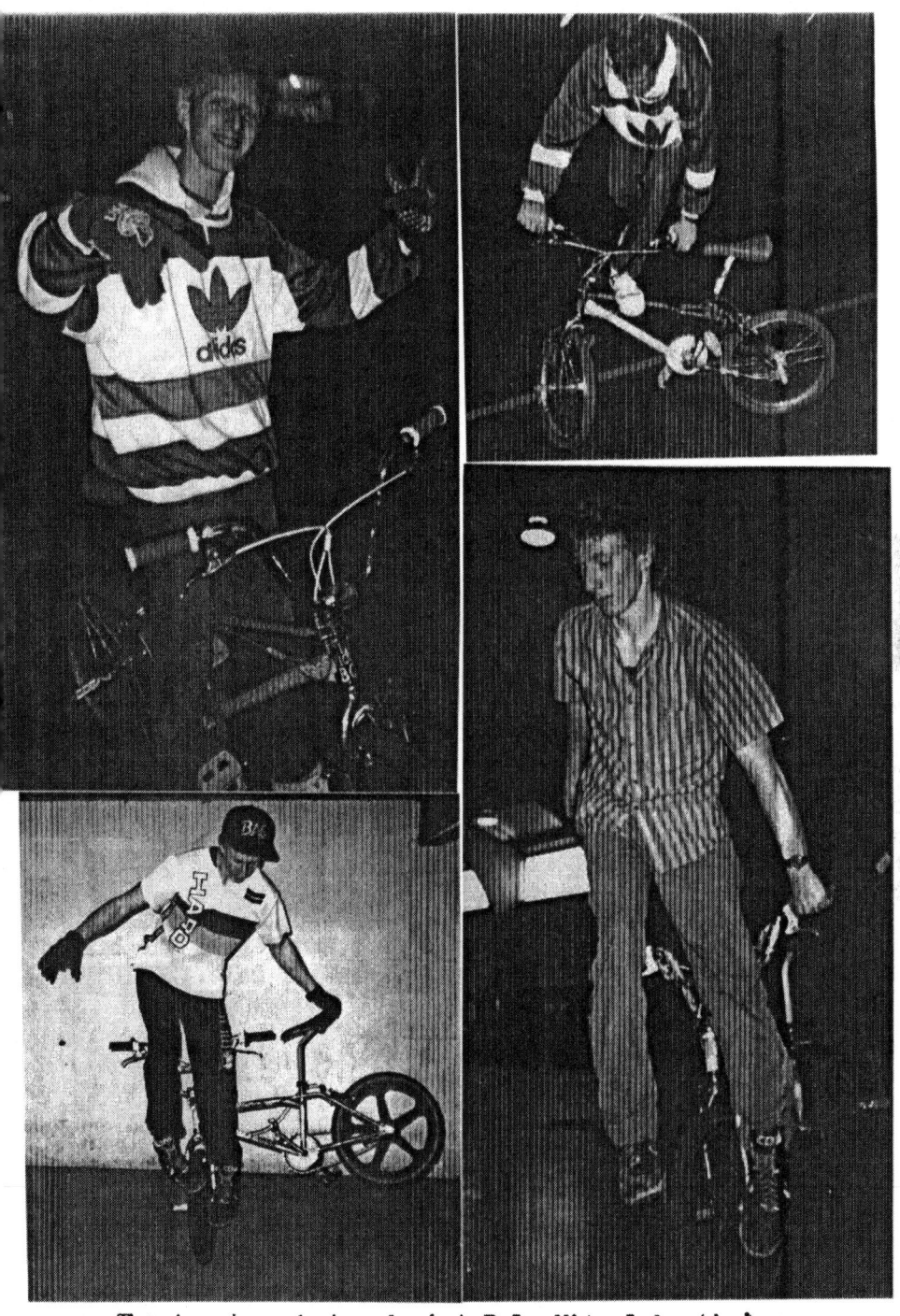

The top two photos depict Dale Mitzel bustin' out with his inborn jiveness. Below him see startling look-alike Shayne Karas do the same.

Here's Dale's common view of the bikes packed in his hatchback...

That grin of deep satisfaction graces Dale's face every time the bikes are on tight and secure, ready for transportation.

...and here's the bikes' view of Dale.

Photos: Brett

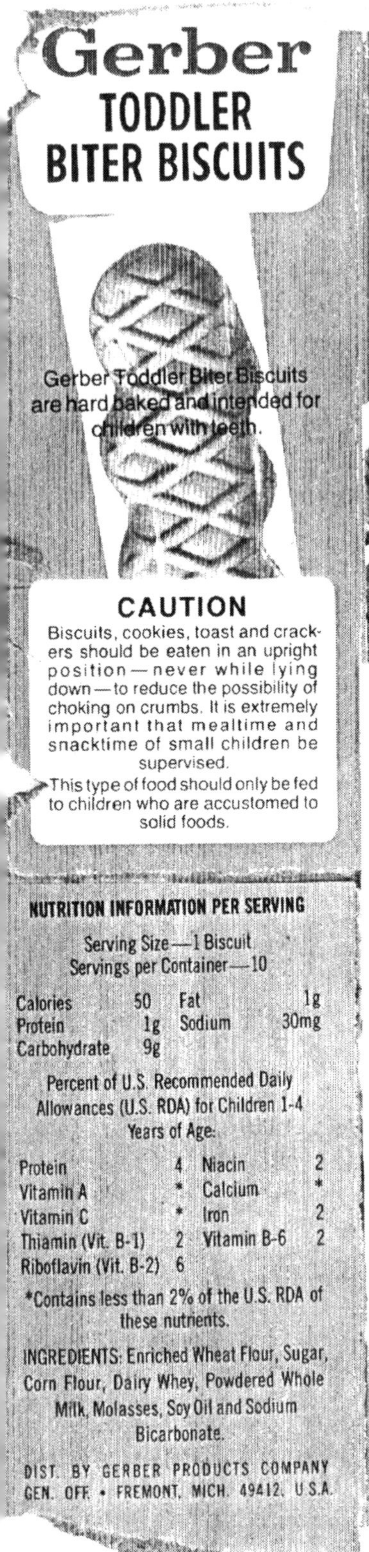

Gerber TODDLER BITER BISCUITS

Gerber Toddler Biter Biscuits are hard baked and intended for children with teeth.

CAUTION
Biscuits, cookies, toast and crackers should be eaten in an upright position — never while lying down — to reduce the possibility of choking on crumbs. It is extremely important that mealtime and snacktime of small children be supervised.

*This type of food should only be fed to children who are accustomed to solid foods.

NUTRITION INFORMATION PER SERVING
Serving Size — 1 Biscuit
Servings per Container — 10

Calories	50	Fat	1g
Protein	1g	Sodium	30mg
Carbohydrate	9g		

Percent of U.S. Recommended Daily Allowances (U.S. RDA) for Children 1-4 Years of Age:

Protein	4	Niacin	2
Vitamin A	*	Calcium	*
Vitamin C	*	Iron	2
Thiamin (Vit. B-1)	2	Vitamin B-6	2
Riboflavin (Vit. B-2)	6		

*Contains less than 2% of the U.S. RDA of these nutrients.

INGREDIENTS: Enriched Wheat Flour, Sugar, Corn Flour, Dairy Whey, Powdered Whole Milk, Molasses, Soy Oil and Sodium Bicarbonate.

DIST. BY GERBER PRODUCTS COMPANY
GEN. OFF. • FREMONT, MICH. 49412, U.S.A.

STRAINED • VITAMIN C ADDED
BANANAS WITH PINEAPPLE AND TAPIOCA
NATURALLY SWEET
NO SUGAR ADDED
Gerber
NET WT. 4-1/2 OZ 128g

JUNIOR • VITAMIN C ADDED
RICE CEREAL WITH MIXED FRUIT
FORTIFIED WITH IRON
Gerber
NET WT. 6 OZ 170g

* * * GOOP * * *

Daily: "Dude! This is SO cheap!"
Kev: "You know why, don't ya?"
Daily: "Not really."
Kev: "You know, 'cause baykestools (babies) don't have tons of money!"

So the conversation went as we stood before the baby food selection in a grocery store. We were just about to see "My Stepmother is an Alien" and some serious goop was in order.

Being on a shoestring budget was not a new thing to me and neither was picking up some all-natural, vitamin-fortified, CHEAP Gerber products for snacking.

Biter biscuits are gnarly and are great raw or dipped into a jar of your fave flavor of baby food. Baby food is totally tasty and nutritious PLUS it's already chewed! You can't beat it!

As I heartily munched on a biter biscuit Kev turned to me in the movie theater: "You're jus' teethin', right?!? *

tHe 2 hip

WOODWARD, PENNSYLVANIA

King of Vert
AND MEET THE STREET

Ron Wilkerson.

Many crucial questions were left unanswered after the 2-Hip contingent turned Memorial Day weekend at Woodward BMX Training Center into 2-wheeled apocalyptic insanity. Do the pros really need money THAT bad or are they just all completely crocked? How in the world did Joe Johnson almost pull off a TRIPLE tail-whip air? Has Coors actually extended their sponsorship program? And was that really DALE giving Jamie a back massage in the hotel room?? WithOUT a shirt on?!??

Photos by Daily

"Super Dave" Voelker.

Craig Grasso steered some smooth lines. ASTplant.

they call it street...

Wilko

Campbell

Mr. Joe Gruttola.

Danny Schow...the guy grows moss on his bike.

MAD DOG

Chris "Mad Dog" Moeller chewed gum and casually took care of business in the Great class. His runs for the finals were screaming. Above left illustrates Mad Dog's consternation after chewing from his grip popping off in mid-air. On the right see him X-up and can can.

To say Dave Clymer was goin' for it would be a drastic understatement. He went CRAZY! Clymer did a wall jump (!) and a care-free car jump.

360's ↓

Eddie Roman.

Vic Murphy

C. Day

Danny Meng.
roly poly

Lung.

Kevin Martin and Craig Campbell

Dave Voelker topped the Greats this day with leaps like this lookdown.

Some PA boys gettin' a lil' rambunctious here. Above, Kevin Jones Learies one. Above and left Gary Pollak does a 180 rock and roll out cruncher o'er the spine. And left over is Jym Dellavalle rolaid jumping.

John Byers

Dave Mirra making it to the amateur finals was a BIG achievement. Dave is 14 years old.

Jay Miron

...and the RAMPS

Cooler than Duckie from "Pretty in Pink," Lew...

Jamie with a tabletop disaster on the ditch ramp. He rode the thing non-stop...all day.

Here is Brian Blyther doing an air on the ditch ramp. On the DITCH ramp. I repeat, on the DITCH RAMP! Versatility is a virtue...

KOV ACTION

Jess Dyenforth rode impressingly well all weekend. His forte is the art of lip tricks. Top sider.

Voelker's 900 attempts were high. And close.

2hip

1

2

You can call this kid a Cracker Jack-- Joe Johnson won Pro. Pro practice is when Joe knew railing plants were in his run.

Craig Campbell. Tailwhip disaster.

MATT HOFFMAN...

Flip dismount to deck

No hander

Blyther X-up

Joe J.

2X tailwhip

wacky CELEBRITY RACE!

(From L to R) Gary Pollak, Dave Voelker, Ray, Ron Wilkerson, Dennis McCoy, Joe Johnson, Brian Blyther and Pete Augustin entered the "Freestyle Celebrity Race." If you want to know who crossed the finish line first...

...check out the Disgust Man down at the end, Pete Augustin. He took a dastardly detour and proved the old "shortest distance between 2 points is a straight line" theorum. Joe J. crossed the line 2nd. Note Voelker's unique starting technique!

MAD DOG

Photo furnished by SPIKE

Greg Hill's Nora Cup.

Professional BMX racing and freelance writing in conjunction with selling and bartering all kinds of products keeps Chris Moeller alive...literally. Continue reading as Mad Dog spouts off about ODI jackets, BSR, pro BMX, S & M and safe sex.

Interview
by Howdy Riggs

Say something for Aggro Rag, Chris.
Chris: Would you like to buy an ODI Mushroom, John Ker signature, affro sheen jacket (laughter)?"

How did you get your nick name?
Chris: "I was in a rainforest with a group of boontang gorillas and I was fighting off the females because it was breeding season and I was fighting them off left and right and the natives called me Mad Dog."

How did you get hooked up with the guys at BMX Action?
Chris: "A long time ago I did a 'Local Thrashin", and I was there and they were. And they needed a test rider, a medium-sized test rider, and I was medium- sized, so they got my phone number from my friend Mike Smith and they called me and then I test rode for them. But I had never subscribed to the magazine before that."

Now do they send you free magazines?
Chris: "No, but I can go down there and get as many as I want."

Do they give you free clothing?
Chris: "Yeah."

Do you enjoy it?
Chris: "I enjoy the profits."

So you sell the clothes?
Chris: "Sometimes. I sold my BMX Action t-shirt in Colorado. I laid out all my clothes on the bed for the Canadian people. Do you remember that, Dave (Clymer)? What'd I get for it, five bucks?"

Dave: "I don't remember."
Chris: "But it was faded so it was only worth five dollars."
Dave: "All I know is you made more money in Canada selling stuff than you did winning races."
Chris: "I sold my bike, $250.00 for just the frame."

Do you have a real job or do you consider BMX your job?
Chris: "Um, yeah BMX is my job I suppose. I also write stories for the ABA and for BMX Action and I freelance and stuff. Like this weekend, I never pay my entry fees for the ABA because I write stories and that's how they pay me. They pay my entry fees. So that saves me eighty bucks a weekend. I can go to a race with like twenty-nine dollars like I did this weekend and I'm O.K."

Who are your sponsors?
Chris: "S&M, Airwalk, Life's a Beach, and Dyno. Dyno's good because I can get Dyno stuff and GT stuff. Oh yeah, ODI sponsors me now too."

You love those jackets don't you?
Chris: "Ah, you mean the affro sheen jacket. I tried to get them to put studs and crystal beads on there with some fringe but they didn't go for it. But they do have these little handles here on the shoulders and I bet you don't know what they're for."
Various people: "Holders for hats, holders for back packs..."
Chris: "No, this is a racey rally car jacket and this is where you put your X seatbelt thing."

Holy, so you hook it in there so you're stuck when you wreck and you would

Pic: Riggs

have to rip your jacket to get out?

Chris: "No, it has these handy dandy snappy rappy things so you can pop right out. It's kind of a convenience jacket. It's also got this strap on the top here. Herb (Guerr) is a good guy. Herb used to own ODI. He must have designed this jacket."

What do you think about this BSR dilemma going on right now?

Chris: "I don't even want to talk about it."

Did you start it?

Chris: "No, I didn't start it. All the people at General started it, and then Hammer came along and they were really the ones who got it moving. They got the ball rolling. Hammer got it rolling, General started it and Fred Blood helped it out, with a lot of help from Hugo Gonzales 'cause he's in the circus. It's kind of an industry thing, BSR is. They made it up. It's really fake, it's not for anyone."

Deadland Wayne: "Bicycle Silly Riding..."

Chris: "No, it's Bicycle Street Riding, don't you know? Bicycle Street Riding, that's what it stands for because it's just BSR. It sells a lot of bikes for General and Ozone."

So what is an average day in the life of Chris Moeller?

Chris: "There is no average day. I wake up late. I used to go to school. When I was in high school, that was it, I went to school until twelve o'clock then I went to work at BMX Action and came home at five-thirty every day. And I did that five days a week and I raced on the weekends. But now I'm supposed to be going to college but they kicked me out because I missed the first two weeks of school. See, I went to a race and forgot about it and when I came home I was kicked out. So now until the beginning of next semester I just wake up around eleven o'clock and eat then usually if I have a story to write I just do it in a few hours and then I send it out real quick. Now I usually FAX them out because I'm so late there's no time to mail them. And then I ride a lot. I ride my mountain bike a lot now."

You get into mountain bikes?

Chris: "A little bit. I just got into it because I broke my foot and I couldn't ride a twenty inch bike because I had this big cast on. So I wanted to ride because that's the only thing I wanted to do so I figured with a mountain bike I could at least ride. And I didn't have a car at the time either because I had sold mine."

How much did you get for it?

Chris: "Eight-hundred dollars, but I bought a new car now. I traded my motorcycle for a car. It's a Volkwagon diesel truck. It's quite a machine. It's equipped with a spare gas tank, it's got an AM-FM cassette radio, and new tires. But it doesn't run because the electric fan won't come on so it overheats and I can't drive it. So I have to find a ride home from the airport when I get home."

So what's the deal with S&M?

Chris: "We're out of bikes right now. As soon as we get them they always sell real quick, they're gone. But the people who make them, Revcore, are really slow. And I hope Roger Worsham reads this because he always hangs up the phone when we try to call him, and he never makes our bikes! And then when he does make our bikes he makes the chain stays too close to the tire and they rub and then he makes the bottom brackets too small so the cups don't fit in them. And then he puts ball bearings inside the forks just to drive us to hell, and then he makes the brake slots off so we have to put fuckin' adaptors on our brakes. And not only does he do all that but every bike is different, so it's kind of a 'custom' frame. You have to look around and find the one you want. I think it's got an adjustable jig, it adjusts as they make 'em. GT might make them soon though, and that would be good because GT is in Huntington Beach and we're in Huntington Beach. They could make a lot of frames and we could get things going. But we have a new S&M bike coming out in two weeks called the Holmes. It's extra long, the Holmes extra long. It's in memory of John Holmes. It's going to be three inches longer than our bike because people want long bikes now. It's going to be really, really long and it's going to come in chrome and it will also come in flesh tone with blue veins, and it comes with a condom attached to the seat post. It's going to be a real good bike to practice safe sex with. And now we're gonna have handlebars too. They're going to be called nude bars and you won't have to be 21 to enjoy our nude bar. Then we're also going to make a seat post called the base pipe which is going to be good because you can smoke crack with it if you put all the proper paraphernalia on the post."

(More selling takes place with some racers who come up and Chris manages to sell some number plates to them for five dollars...)

What made you cut off your curly locks?

Chris: "I had dreads ya know before I got it cut off. I had dreads for about a month but I started getting zits because they were rubbing all over my forehead and my back so I got them cut off. But they were allright when I had them, I liked them. This is a real clean hair cut.

Do you like R.L.?

Chris: "R.L. is actually a cool guy. I like him, he's allright. He gave me a lot of stuff at one time but I did a good job. Even though I may say bad things or whatever I think I did a good job for Hammer. Didn't you see a lot of pictures of me with Hammer stuff on?"

Yeah. What's your theory on winning?
Chris: "Winning, that's winning. A winner can win, a loser loses, skinny people can win."

Do you need big muscles to win?
Chris: "They help I think. I think all you need to do is come out of the gate thing good. If you come out of the gate good you do good but if you don't, like I don't, you usually blow it. But I have excuses though. I have a lot of excuses. Do you want to hear them?"

Sure...
Chris: "I've been hurt for a long time. My foot was broken and I was in a cast for about two months."

What caused that?
Chris: "I was racing in Canada and I got my foot caught in someone's wheel and I broke three bones in my foot."

Was it extreme pain?
Chris: "No, it didn't even hurt. I didn't even go to the hospital for a week. It just stayed swollen and then I had a ticket to go to a race that weekend. I couldn't ride so I had to get a doctor's note so I could get my money back from the airlines. When I went to the doctor I found out I had three broken bones. They said that they were really bad and I was in a cast for about seven weeks. Then I started riding again and that's why I didn't do anything this weekend. This is actually the first Sunday race I haven't made the main at as A Pro ever. I'm a double A Pro now but I raced single A today. They told me it was my last time though so now I have to race Pete (Loncarevich) and Greg Hill and those guys. So I'll be a double A Pro now and I don't know what that means. That means they're bigger and faster and dumber, that's what they are. BMX pros aren't smart. BMXers in general aren't smart."

What do you consider yourself?
Chris: "I guess I'm a BMXer. I'm not really awesome at anything, you know what I mean? You take someone like Greg Hill or Mike King, he's awesome at BMX but really that's all he's good at. Well I'm not awesome at racing and I'm not awesome at street riding, I'm just kind of..."
Voice: "You proved that you're not awesome at street riding last night!"
Chris: "I'm allright but I'm just not awesome. I'm not like Craig Campbell or someone."

So what are you awesome at?
Chris: "I don't know, I'm awesome at doing all kinds of things. I'm a good salesman. Someday I might put that to work."
Voice again: "You're a good scrounge."
Chris: "Yeah, I'm a good scrounge."

What kind of music influences you? What kind do you enjoy? Do you get into rap music or something?
Chris: "I've been rhyming a lot lately, so I guess I'm getting into

rap. Ah, I don't know, I listen to anything, I don't care. It makes absolutely no difference to me. Everyone says I listen to gay music. Spike thinks I listen to gay music. But the reason why he says that is because my tape box, it's like a hair dryer box or something, is filled with all these tapes that my friends gave to me so they're all pretty lame. I have like Eagles tapes and I have all kinds of 'no good' tapes. Paul Simon tapes, Whittney Houston tapes, I have just about as bad as it gets. But they were all for free so that's why it's bad. If I were to buy tapes I think they would be better. I think they would be pretty cool, like The Red Hot Chilly Peppers and The Cure and The Cult and kind of stuff like that. I might just throw the whole box away, that's what I might do. That might be smart. It's so bad it's famous. I sent a copy of it, I just laid it on the copy machine and sent it to some guy in Texas who has a 'zine because he had heard how bad it was. I did buy one tape though, but it fooled me because I thought it was going to be good. It was called The Robert Cray Band or something and I heard a review on the radio for it and I thought it was going to be hot and I had ten bucks at the time so I bought it and it turns out to be some fuckin' jazz tape or something. There's this song on it called 'Don't Be Afraid of the Dark', it's like a beer commercial or something. My tape box is no good."

Do you feel you're at a disadvantage because you don't have a major bike sponsorship?

Chris: "No, it wouldn't make me better or anything. I think I have a different attitude than all these other guys. They get on the gate and they're like, 'Ah, I'M GONNA WIN, I'M GONNA WIN' and I'm on the gate and I'm just like 'I gotta make twenty bucks (laughter)!' No, that's why I turned pro because I just need the money. Like this weekend I got fifth in my semis both days and I didn't make the main either days. I didn't make one fucking penny and now look where I'm left--In the back of a fucking trailer selling shit (LAUGHTER)."

END.

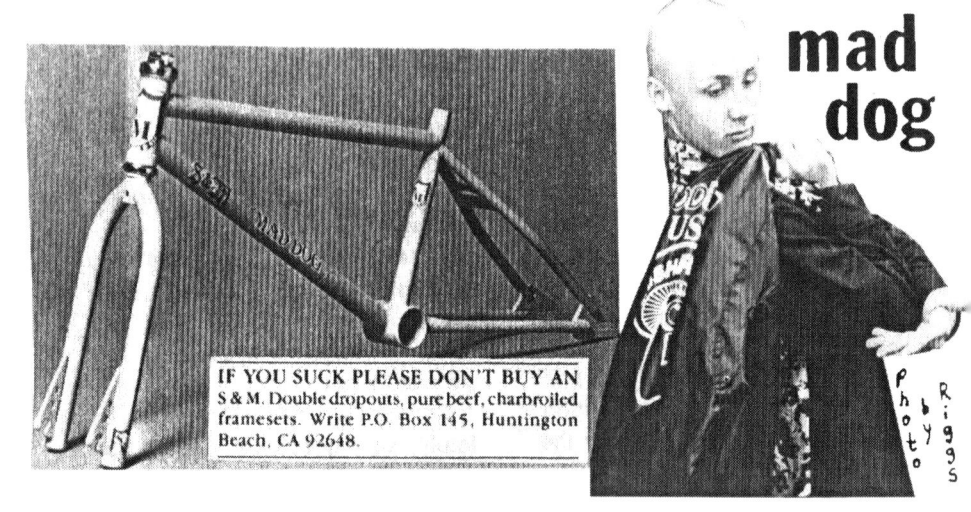

mad dog

IF YOU SUCK PLEASE DON'T BUY AN S&M. Double dropouts, pure beef, charbroiled framesets. Write P.O. Box 145, Huntington Beach, CA 92648.

photo R. iggs

Be dazzled by the fanciful antics of this radman, John Huddleston. He's a mover.

Photo by Spike

DORKIN' 3

Eaton not liking this bent axle too much.

Dorkin' III is done and ready for mass consumption. See the superstars of freestyle explode from your screen. A good many unknowns dice it up and dork it, too. Sound man Lungmustard made sure the soundtrack'll knock yer friggin' socks off. Good quality comedy here, chickens. $20 postage paid from K. Jones or Eaton. Trend is supposed to stock it soon.

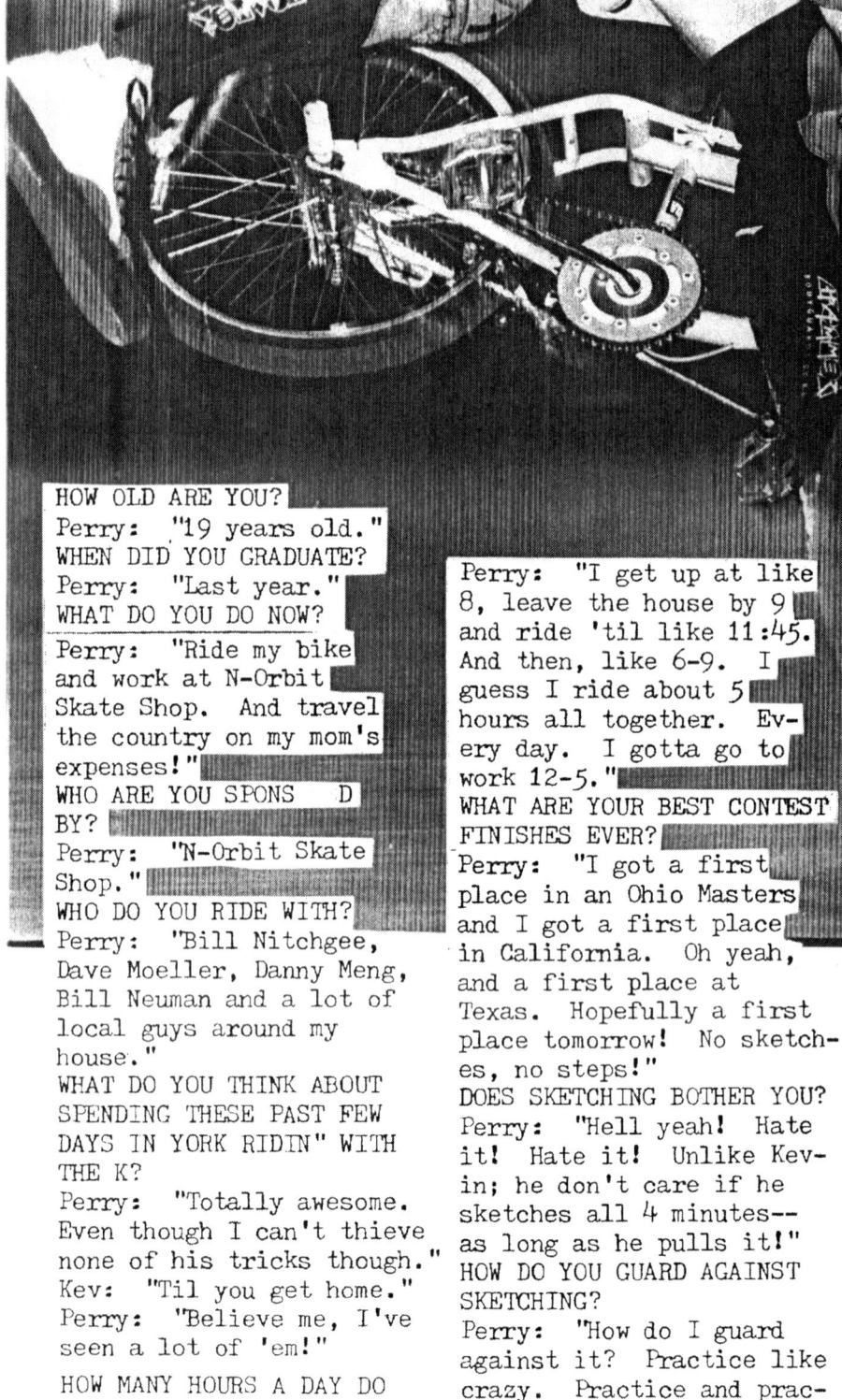

HOW OLD ARE YOU?
Perry: "19 years old."
WHEN DID YOU GRADUATE?
Perry: "Last year."
WHAT DO YOU DO NOW?
Perry: "Ride my bike and work at N-Orbit Skate Shop. And travel the country on my mom's expenses!"
WHO ARE YOU SPONS D BY?
Perry: "N-Orbit Skate Shop."
WHO DO YOU RIDE WITH?
Perry: "Bill Nitchgee, Dave Moeller, Danny Meng, Bill Neuman and a lot of local guys around my house."
WHAT DO YOU THINK ABOUT SPENDING THESE PAST FEW DAYS IN YORK RIDIN" WITH THE K?
Perry: "Totally awesome. Even though I can't thieve none of his tricks though."
Kev: "Til you get home."
Perry: "Believe me, I've seen a lot of 'em!"
HOW MANY HOURS A DAY DO YOU PRACTICE?

Perry: "I get up at like 8, leave the house by 9 and ride 'til like 11:45. And then, like 6-9. I guess I ride about 5 hours all together. Every day. I gotta go to work 12-5."
WHAT ARE YOUR BEST CONTEST FINISHES EVER?
Perry: "I got a first place in an Ohio Masters and I got a first place in California. Oh yeah, and a first place at Texas. Hopefully a first place tomorrow! No sketches, no steps!"
DOES SKETCHING BOTHER YOU?
Perry: "Hell yeah! Hate it! Hate it! Unlike Kevin; he don't care if he sketches all 4 minutes-- as long as he pulls it!"
HOW DO YOU GUARD AGAINST SKETCHING?
Perry: "How do I guard against it? Practice like crazy. Practice and practice and practice 'til you

Photo by Spike

got it so wired it's not even funny. That's how the Midwest is--no sketches and no steps. Unlike you people in Pennsylvania-- you don't care!"
HOW LONG HAVE YOU BEEN RIDING?
Perry: "For 4 years all together. About 2 and a half on flat, the other 2 on ramp."
HOW DO YOU PRACTICE?
Perry: "Sometimes I use visualization. I picture me hitting my tricks perfect with no sketches."
Kev: "No steps."
Perry: "No steps. I go out and try to do it how I picture it."

WHAT ABOUT MAXWELL MALTZ'S "PSYCHOCYBERNETICS?"
Perry: "Yeah, that's this book I started to read just to get psyched up."
DID YOU EVER READ IT BEFORE?
Perry: "No. I've had it like half a year and I'm only on page 32 or somethin'. I only read it when I'm totally bored or on a Greyhound bus."
WHAT RIDERS INFLUENCE YOU THE MOST?
Perry: "Well, it's obvious--Kevin Jones is one of 'em 'cause he influences everybody. Danny Meng, Bill Neuman. That's about it really. Lots of undergrounders that come out and totally jam. Keep me on my toes."
HOW MUCH AIR PRESSURE DO YOU RUN?
Perry: "I use around 115 in the front and about 100 in the back."
WHY IS YOUR BIKE SO SOLID?
Perry: "'Cause I TOTALLY keep it dialed in! Unlike Kevin Jones with his uncentered front brake, bars WAY too far forward--he kills like 2 brand new GT frames 'cause he doesn't put washers on the rear drop-outs!"
HOW MUCH LONGER DO YOU THINK YOU'LL KEEP RIDING AND WHAT ARE YOUR GOALS?
Perry: "At least 5 years and I wanna turn pro someday. Next year possibly, if I feel I'm ready. *

GT

4130 CRO-MOLY

HUNTINGTON BEACH, CA

1989 team

Other page: Joe Johnson, his knee, and Gary Pollak admiring him from not-so-afar. GT's hairy chested rampsters. Photos by Giberson. This page: The man who thinks he can still wear Life's A Beach shorts and Aggro Rag t-shirts. John Doenut...er um uh Kevin Jones.

Photo by Eaton

Photo by Spike

Contrary to contemporary belief Jason Geoffrey is cruising this BACKWARDS in the above photo by Spike Jonze. But he really IS styling his hair in the shot at left taken by Maverick.

GT·BMX

Quality American-made BMX frames and forks

Photograph by Guy-B

pete

more HOODtees...

Jamie models the latest in Plywood Hood t-shirt technology. Designed by Dale Mitzel himself, the shirts have the new huge PH design on the back and the fairly famous small circle insignia on the front. They're printed on 50/50 tees with one color, resulting in one snazzy outfit component. Blue and grey is the color combo Dale has made so far.

From Trend Bike Source and the pen of Greg Neal comes this jewel of a shirt. Dorsal side features the 2-color "Ride in Peace" Hoods art with the ventral side emblazoned with the bold Trend logo. A milestone must-have! Contact Trend for ordering information.

As for Dale's deal, available at a contest or show near you. Maybe.

obtain.

Elephant gliding at their fave spot. Lakeland's Dave.

PSYCHO HOWD

Hood, Howdy has learned fakie wall rides. Kabong.

The Florida Legend getting a good bite of air.

FL

Howdy "Chip" Riggs workin' his Trick Star like a chainsaw. He claims this is a gas on tightly bundled cardboard.

"Lakeland Dave" they call him. An obscure dude-- and proud of it!

Helicoptering off a berm is Riggs. The boy knows style.

Art an[d]
words b[y]
Scott
Towne

Ream jo[b]
by
Super BM[X]

Every time I go on a long trip, or a short trip with someone wreckless at the wheel (Spike Jonze comes to mind right away), I always consider the possibility of crash and burn—taking the big dive...dying. When you think about it, there are so many great things that you take for granted: Friends, family, riding...living. Whenever the plane would get shakey, or Spike would let go of the wheel to get something out of the back seat, I think of my wife, my future (or lack thereof) and everything I haven't done yet—it really makes me want to do everything right now, while I still have the chance. Getting mad, sitting around, arguing with someone over some petty item—what a waste of time. The next time I start to get pissed off working on some beater Huffy at the shop, I'm going to Snuffy's track and stretching a no-hander so far that it hurts. I've been wimping out on those for far too long.

LARRY WALKED INTO A FENCE.

UGH!

INTERVIEW: craig G.

1987

Photo: Steve Giberson

1989

1985

Daily: "We're here with Craig Grasso at a street contest in Woodward, PA and we're gonna have an open interview."
Craig: "Hello, I am Craig. The tape you are about to experience is a very special one. It is a subliminal persuasion recording. I got one of those tapes at my house, man. Self-confidence tape. It's hot. I listen to it all the time."
Daily: "Is it waves breaking on the shore?"
Craig: "But it has guitar in it too! And also on the other side is self-hypnosis. It's rad, man--you can hypnotise yourself.
Daily: "Does it build up your self-confidence?"
Craig: "I think. I think that's why I've been doing better."
Maverick: "You ever let anyone else listen to it?"
Craig: "Yeah. Craig Campbell's listened to it a couple times and he liked it."
Maverick: "Is that what happened to his hair?"
Craig: "Yeah. He went crazy."
Daily: "When was the last time you flatlanded?"

Craig: "Fuck. Bloody aaaaaaages ago... (laughs) No! Um...well the last time was with R.L. and Pete Kearney down at the beach. I was doin' bar rides. That's flatland I think. Yeah."
Maverick: "Who's your favorite ridin' buddy?"
Craig: "Shit. By faaaar--Barry Manilow. Man, I ride with that fucker all the time (laughter). He's hot. He always gets me goin'."
Maverick: "Does he do the tricks that make the whole world ride (laughter)?"
Craig: "Yeah. That's my buddy."
Daily: "Tell us more about your job testing heart rate machines."
Craig: "Well, the name of it's...Oooooh! Hipper! That was Brett Hernandez, man. That fucker went down. He rides for GT, I think that's why (laughter)."
Daily: "No--Dyno."
Craig: "Oh, Dyno. Sorry...Dyno. What the hell was I talkin' about? Heart rate machines? Allright, the place is called Brettwood and the lady that works there is called Kimberly Stein and she is WELL good lookin'. Anyways, there's these things called OKI Datas. You hook someone up to these machines and it tests the heart rate and it makes sure that it's hearting at the right rate. It's 60 beats per minute--I think everyone knows the proper heart rate."
Daily: "And you test these?"
Craig: "Yeah, I test 'em and make sure they're all printing right and I gotta program in the date and program what exact...(the crowd yells) They're prescribed for different people so you gotta put their name and the date and the time they had it done."
Daily: "What're the hottest models of heart rate machines out right now?"
Craig: "Um, let's see...I'd say OKI Datas are really good. Um, A-2000's are really good. I don't know. I just test 'em. I know those two are ones we carry. Oh, I'm staying in D.C. for three weeks."
Daily: "Why are you staying in D.C. for three weeks?"
Craig: "Because I wanna hang out with all these people--all my friends. I'll name 'em off: Scooby, Nubby, Spike, Brian's gonna be there. All these guys- Greg, Rodney, the posse's there. Wendy, that's a good reason to go."
Maverick: "Aren't you worried about the crime rate there? Like one person gets killed there every eight hours?"
Craig: "(In disbelief) Nooooo..."
Maverick: "Yeah. Only go out in the streets for seven hours at a time and you'll be safe."
(Much crowd response is generated to Kevin Martin's announcement that the Great class is about to start.)
Craig: "Is this the Good class?"
Maverick: "No, Great. That's Voelker."
Craig: "No, is this the first rider?"
Maverick: "Yeah."
Craig: "Hey man, I gotta go 'cause it's the first rider. Hold on, I'll ride across the place and see if it's my class now..."

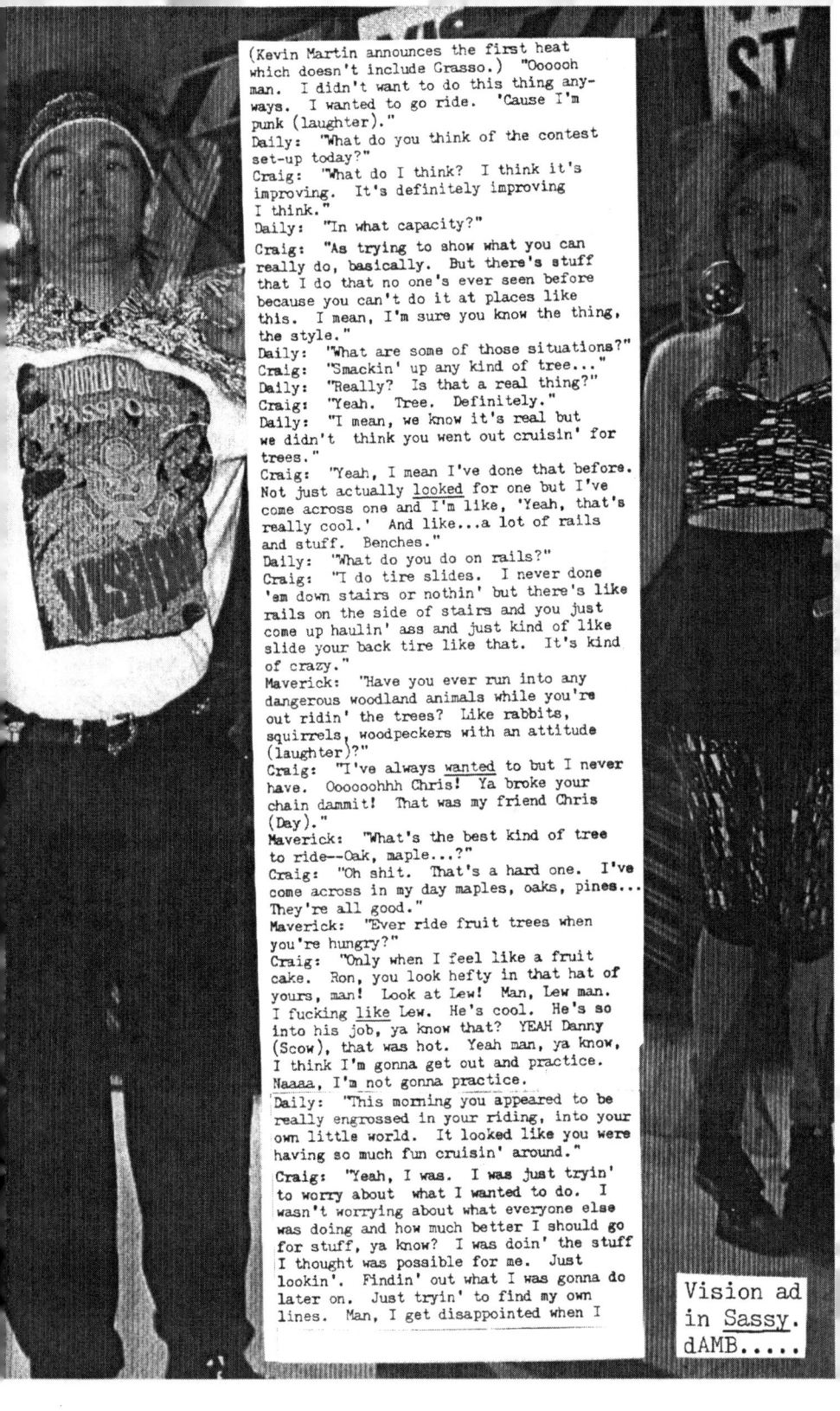

(Kevin Martin announces the first heat which doesn't include Grasso.) "Oooooh man. I didn't want to do this thing anyways. I wanted to go ride. 'Cause I'm punk (laughter)."
Daily: "What do you think of the contest set-up today?"
Craig: "What do I think? I think it's improving. It's definitely improving I think."
Daily: "In what capacity?"
Craig: "As trying to show what you can really do, basically. But there's stuff that I do that no one's ever seen before because you can't do it at places like this. I mean, I'm sure you know the thing, the style."
Daily: "What are some of those situations?"
Craig: "Smackin' up any kind of tree..."
Daily: "Really? Is that a real thing?"
Craig: "Yeah. Tree. Definitely."
Daily: "I mean, we know it's real but we didn't think you went out cruisin' for trees."
Craig: "Yeah, I mean I've done that before. Not just actually looked for one but I've come across one and I'm like, 'Yeah, that's really cool.' And like...a lot of rails and stuff. Benches."
Daily: "What do you do on rails?"
Craig: "I do tire slides. I never done 'em down stairs or nothin' but there's like rails on the side of stairs and you just come up haulin' ass and just kind of like slide your back tire like that. It's kind of crazy."
Maverick: "Have you ever run into any dangerous woodland animals while you're out ridin' the trees? Like rabbits, squirrels, woodpeckers with an attitude (laughter)?"
Craig: "I've always wanted to but I never have. Ooooooohhh Chris! Ya broke your chain dammit! That was my friend Chris (Day)."
Maverick: "What's the best kind of tree to ride--Oak, maple...?"
Craig: "Oh shit. That's a hard one. I've come across in my day maples, oaks, pines... They're all good."
Maverick: "Ever ride fruit trees when you're hungry?"
Craig: "Only when I feel like a fruit cake. Ron, you look hefty in that hat of yours, man! Look at Lew! Man, Lew man. I fucking like Lew. He's cool. He's so into his job, ya know that? YEAH Danny (Scow), that was hot. Yeah man, ya know, I think I'm gonna get out and practice. Naaaa, I'm not gonna practice.
Daily: "This morning you appeared to be really engrossed in your riding, into your own little world. It looked like you were having so much fun cruisin' around."
Craig: "Yeah, I was. I was just tryin' to worry about what I wanted to do. I wasn't worrying about what everyone else was doing and how much better I should go for stuff, ya know? I was doin' the stuff I thought was possible for me. Just lookin'. Findin' out what I was gonna do later on. Just tryin' to find my own lines. Man, I get disappointed when I

Vision ad in Sassy. dAMB.....

see people ride. It just makes me go 'Fuck, man.' Because it's so good, ya know? It's like I wanna be doing the same shit but..."
Daily: "You also wanna be doing different stuff, right?"
Craig: "Yeah. Well, I shouldn't say I wanna be doin' the same shit. (Pause) I can respect it. I can respect their riding so it's like 'I KNOW that was hard man.' I'm psyched. I'm stoked to be here."

Daily: "OK, what about your band and your music? Do you play drums?"
Craig: "Yeah. I play drums. I'm no Neil Peart or nothin' but I can hit some stuff. While I was in D.C. I got together with this band and we made a jam. It was like a mix between Butthole Surfers and Dolly Parton. Man it was hardcore--just madness.
Daily: "Do you sing?"
Craig: "Yeah. I do sing a little bit but I don't make that my main thing. I like to play drums. Maybe someday I'll be doin' everything myself."
Daily: "Have you ever heard R.L. play drums?"
Craig: "Yeah, he's really good. He's a lot better than me, I'll give him that much."
Daily: "Didn't you used to play guitar?"
Craig: "Yeah, still do."
Daily: "Keyboards?"
Craig: "No, I traded my keyboard for a car. Some guy really liked it so..."
(Mega yelling from the crowd.)
Daily: "You're not worried about not bein' out there warmin' up?"
Craig: "If I pulled it off earlier in practice I can pull it off during my run, ya know? But I'm gonna go out there. Yeah, I'm gonna go out right now. Just catch me back, man."

Daily: "OK!"
(Grasso does not "qualify" to the finals and is sitting on his bike not looking sad as I approach him later on...)
Daily: "What do you think about not makin' the cut?"
Craig: "Not makin' the cut? It's cool..."
Daily: "Every guy that made the cut was like a crazy guy. A jumper."
Craig: "Yeah, a jumper. That's all I gotta say. That's cool though. I sold $170 worth of shit. I got money."
McGoo: "(Laughing hard) 'I sold $170 worth of shit!' What'd you sell--stickers, t-shirts?"
Craig: "Yeah. I'm psyched."
Brett Hernandez: "What am I doin' wrong? I didn't sell 50¢ worth of stuff (laughter)!"
Craig: "Get stuff from McGoo and sell it. That's the only way to make money, man."
Brett: "I didn't know there was that much to be made!"
McGoo: "(Walking away) I can't believe Grasso picked up 170 bucks this weekend sellin' shit...!"
Daily: "What about your artwork? Like your jacket here, your work in that club?"
Craig: "All my art stuff is goin' good. A lot of people are psyched with it. I never knew I had the talent until I started doin' it. I think dreams help alot with it. I dream about a lot of weird shit."
Daily: "What about your bikes? Ozone."
Craig: "Ozone bikes--I don't even know if they're comin' out to tell you the truth, man. That was some hype thing. They're worryin' about GT and Haro and all that shit. Fuck that."
(Wilkerson rides up...)
Ron: "Sorry you didn't make it."
Craig: "No problem. I sucked anyways..."

1987

Videopic by Eaton

THE CURE
DISINTEGRATION

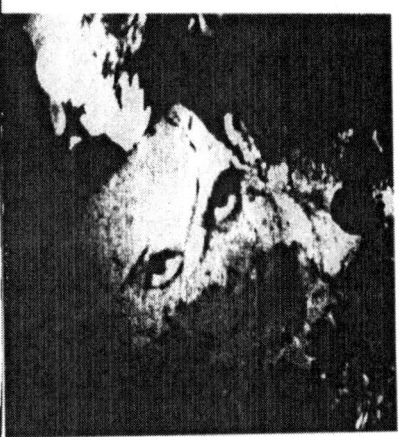

Robert Smith's entrophic persona seeps undiluted into every nook and cranny of "Disintegration." The 12 track album takes a most fearful headlong plunge into the turbulent innerworld of cunning love and emotional meltdown. The Cure has submerged again...deep and dark as ever.

"Prayers For Rain" lashes out at doubt in well-orchestrated festering futility. The resonant pounding of Boris carries the song like a Japanese death march. "The Same Deep Water As You" owes its entrancing bleakness to Smith's echo-laden vocals.

Their single "Fascination Street" features an ornate blossoming structure culminating in some rhythmic lyrics.

Perhaps the most noteworthy piece of the album is the title track: "Disintegration." The anguished but forceful voice of Smith's is backed by a plane of thick sound which moves fast and hard. The words are typically Smith:

"now that i know that i'm breaking to pieces i'll pull out my heart and i'll feed it to anyone crying for sympathy crocodiles cry for the love of the crowd and the three cheers from everyone dropping through sky through the glass of the roof through the roof of your mouth through the mouth of your eye through the eye of the needle it's easier for me to get closer to heaven than ever feel whole again ..."

It is prescribed in the liner notes: THIS MUSIC HAS BEEN MIXED TO BE PLAYED LOUD SO TURN IT UP.

Simply shattering.

HIGGINSART

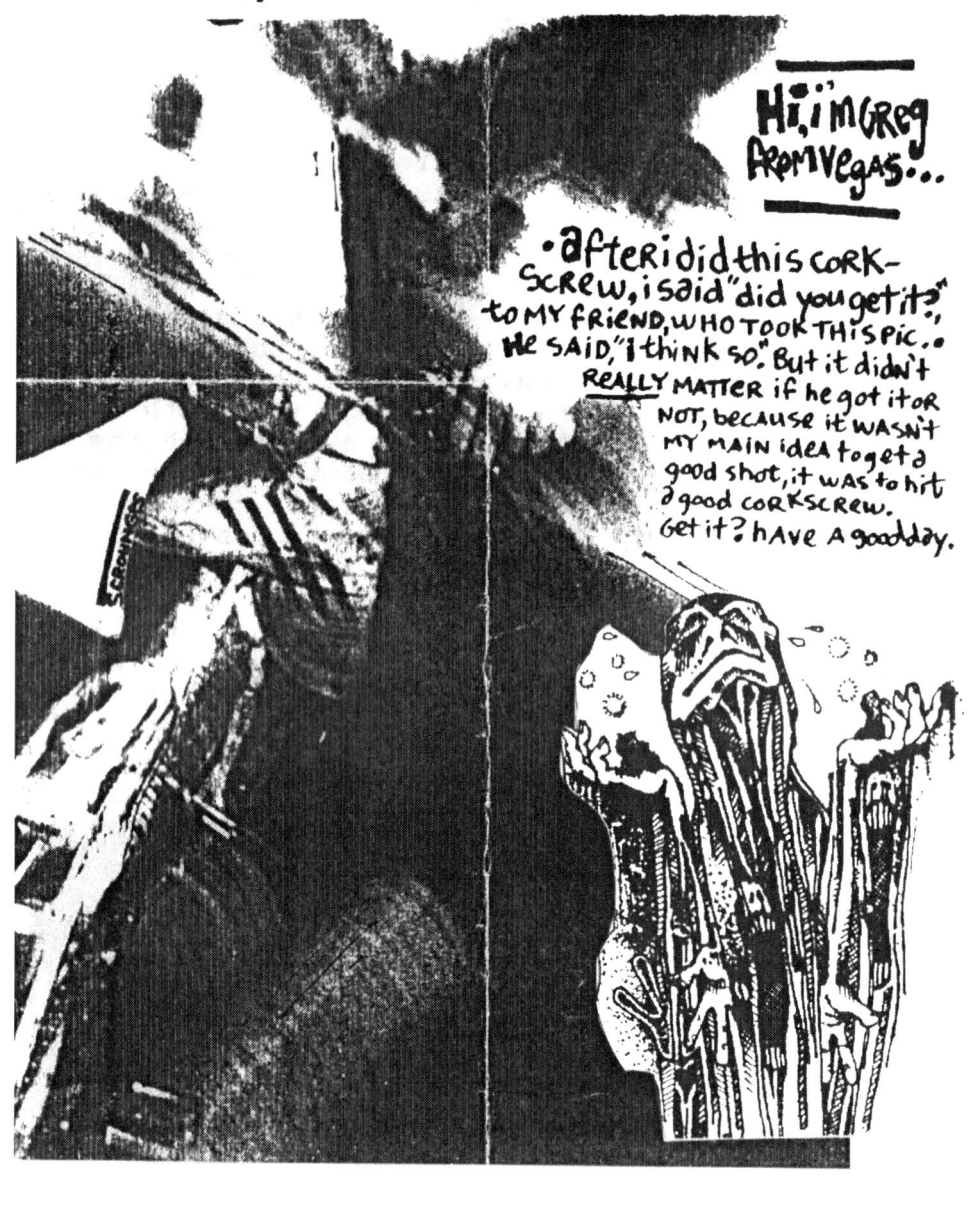

Hi, i'm Greg from Vegas...

• after i did this corkscrew, i said "did you get it?" to my friend, who took this pic. He said, "i think so." But it didn't REALLY matter if he got it or not, because it wasn't my main idea to get a good shot, it was to hit a good corkscrew. Get it? Have a good day.

His renderings are obviously the work of a highly imaginative and skilled individual. Their spontaneity is drawn from the same deep well his riding is. He started Team Scrounge. He rips at flat and street. "Funny" describes his personality. You can TRY to describe his art. Ladies and gentlemen, would you please welcome....Greg Higgins!

THINK POSITIVE
trend
SOURCE
TRENDIEST!
AGGRO RAG
FREESTYLE MAG!
greg

a public service message from...

Scrounges:

♥ I...

idiot.

bikes before babes.

me & my freinds, we are buds, if you don't like one, you don't like all, if you like one, you like us all. that's how it is now scrape.

·SCROUNGES·

QUIP O' THE CENTURY:

Perry Mervar: "Man, you guys do so much more than ride!"

Left: "It's the eye of the tiger, it's the king of the strike..." DM
Top Left: No handed rail slide. Jones pulls these every time, no lie.
Above: Bowling alley local and prospective half pipe owner Tommy Wales caught in a friendly exchange with a desk clerk.

AGGRO RAG FREESTYLE MAG!

HOODS go BOWLING

Pictures by Maverick.

At Right: The K bombs one down the lane in a blur of power and concentration. Bottom Right: Dale unleashes a backspin on the waxy floorboards of lane 2. The manager was happy about this one. Below: The Jammer puckers up and shows perfect form.

marty stoyer

Reading this mini-interview of Marty Stoyer may lead you to believe he is full of scorn and contempt. Not true. Marty is just a pensive sort of youth that goes about paving his own way. His broad sense of humor attracts him like a magnet to stick sword fights, strangers in airports and large cucumbers at salad bars.

<u>Marty, are you ready for the interview?</u> "Yes I am." <u>What've you been doing with your life lately?</u> "I have a job at a bike shop. And ridin' and tryin' to stay outta trouble I guess." <u>What's the name of the bike shop?</u> "Nester's Full Cycle Bike Shop." <u>Are you still sponsored by Schwinn?</u> "Yeah." <u>Do you get your bikes through the shop or do they send 'em straight to you?</u> "Straight to me. They're pretty jewish but...(laughter) they still get here. You gotta order like 3 months ahead of time." <u>Do you like the bike? Are you happy with it?</u> "No. It's too long and the drop-outs cut your sneakers. And it has shitty components." <u>Did you say that to Schwinn?</u> "Yeah." <u>What did they say?</u> "They don't care. They hate us." <u>Who's on the team? You and Jim Johnson?</u> "Yeah." <u>Does Jim still ride a lot?</u> "He skates more than he rides now. But he like just rides for shows and stuff. We have a show next weekend in Wisconsin at some fish festival." <u>What are your favorite, main tricks?</u> "Backpack-- a trick I'm workin' on now. It's upside down... you're kinda in the caboose position but you're kickin' backwards. Your foot's on the other side. Raggedy Ann, which is a no handed, no footed version of Ronnie Handerson squeaks." <u>Tell us more about your burnt hand tricks.</u> "Well, one hot day I had a pair of JT gloves. We were just foolin' around and I tried to do regular squeakers with my hand. I fell over and almost hit my head.

So I was thinkin' of a better way and I was doin' Squeakerson and I put my hand down and scratched it. As time progressed I just learned how to squeak with it." *Did you make it up?* "Yeah. I did it at that Ohio contest two years ago. *What was the last contest you entered?* "Arizona." *Why?* "Too expensive." *Doesn't Schwinn pay?* "Yeah, just for big ones. I'm too lazy to get a routine together. I don't like contests that much because all it is is a bunch of idiots bitin' your tricks. I'd rather just have my tricks for people I like to ride with and myself." *Not many people bite your tricks because they're so hard and unusual. Too much of a pain in the ass to learn.* "(Laughs) Yeah. It's not really worth it to learn 'em." *What are your goals?* "I think my main goal is to keep freestyle fresh. Not to become like a sucker--like all the other kids sold out and just bite their tricks. I know I'll never do that. That's what freestyle was all about, you know? Kids forgot about what the origin was. Now they think it's bein' the greatest at the 'in' tricks. But there should be no 'in' tricks. Like, your own trick should be great forever. I mean, if you make up a trick then it'll be great forever. As long as no one else bites it. That's why people are killin' it (freestyle)." *Why do you think it's getting like that?* "I don't know. I think the kids are too lazy. They're gettin' too into contests--winnin' winnin' winnin'. People just do whiplashes and stuff." (Ian Clemens) "I know, I don't even think they learn basics anymore. They just go right to the popular tricks. And then they *can't* make up anything else because they don't know any other tricks to derive 'em from." (Marty) "Most of the kids nowadays haven't been in it long enough to even know what it's about. They don't even KNOW you can make up a trick. They wouldn't even think of it." *How much longer can freestyle keep goin'?* "It'll go on for a couple more years but it's gonna have to change. At this rate it'll die by the end of the summer. Unless people start realizin' what it's all about." *What did you do with that cucumber you had?* "Played hacky sack for awhile then it broke apart and I threw it at some kid." *

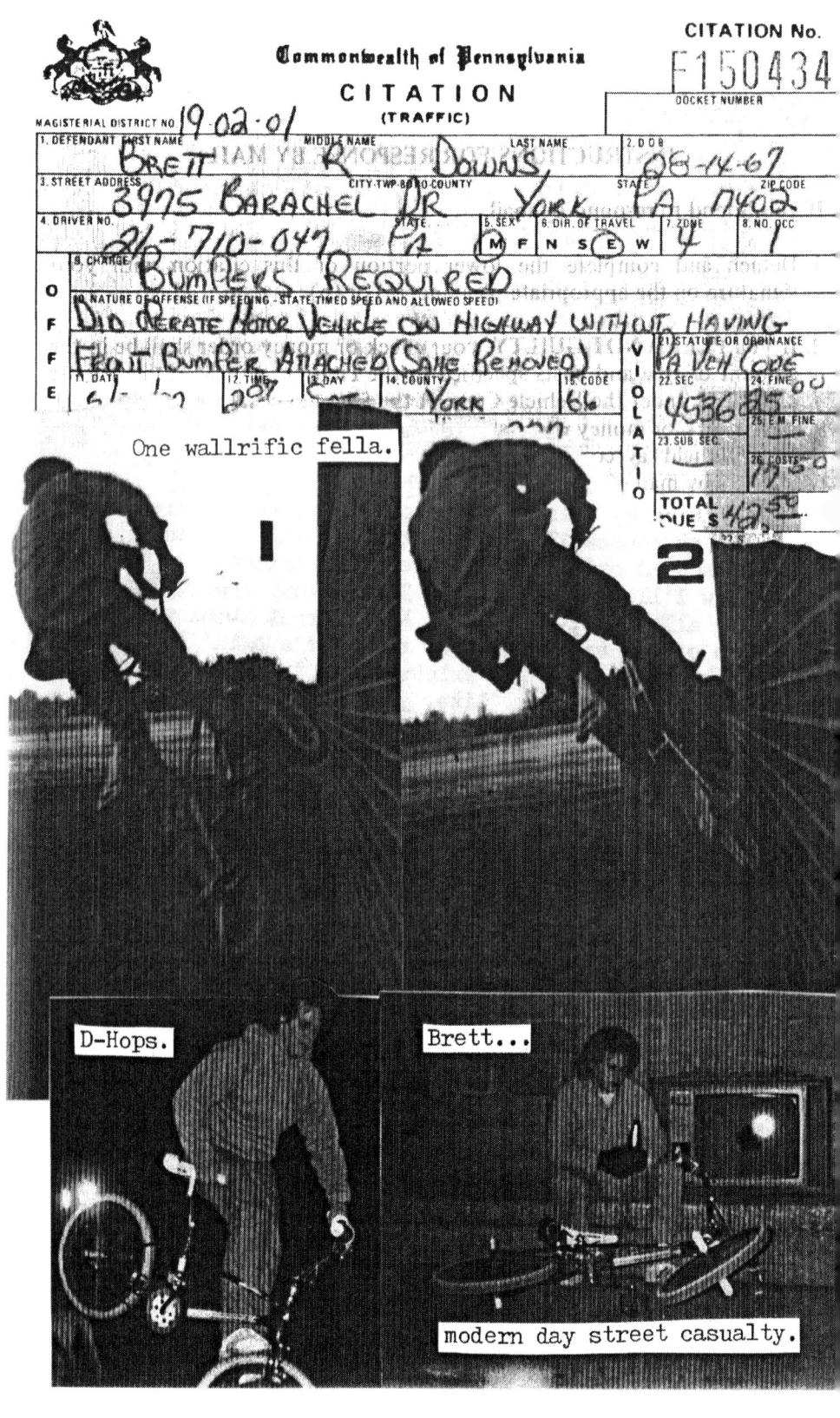

Commonwealth of Pennsylvania
CITATION
(TRAFFIC)

CITATION No. F150434

MAGISTERIAL DISTRICT NO. 19-02-01

1. DEFENDANT FIRST NAME: Brett   MIDDLE NAME: R   LAST NAME: Downs
2. D.O.B: 08-14-67
3. STREET ADDRESS: 3975 Barachel Dr   CITY: York   STATE: PA   ZIP: 17402
4. DRIVER NO: 26-710-047   STATE: PA   5. SEX: M   6. DIR. OF TRAVEL: E   7. ZONE: 4   8. NO. OCC: 1
9. CHARGE: Bumpers Required
10. NATURE OF OFFENSE: Did Operate Motor Vehicle on Highway Without Having Front Bumper Attached (Same Removed)
11. DATE: 61-1-2   12. TIME: 207   14. COUNTY: York   15. CODE: 66
21. STATUTE OR ORDINANCE: PA Veh Code
22. SEC: 4536.25

One wallrific fella.

1

2

D-Hops.

Brett...

modern day street casualty.

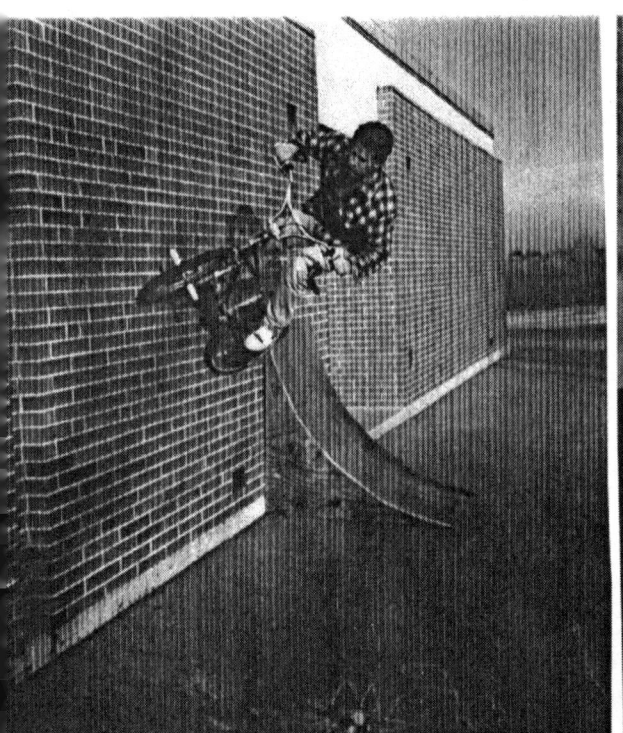

This is the wall ride that finally broke the camel's back. Rear wheel annihilation already in progress.

Plywood Hoods, 1st show. York Rod and Custom 1985. Mav.

Lungbastard can really be a buddy sometimes. Look at him gingerly move the front cable out of the way so Brett can get monster leverage.

Dorkin' III's Best Actor Travis Trimmer as he appeared on the front page of <u>The York Daily Record</u>.

Here Travis makes a fool out of this curb in broad daylight.

"O.K. NICK"

DAVE FOX
back in the day.

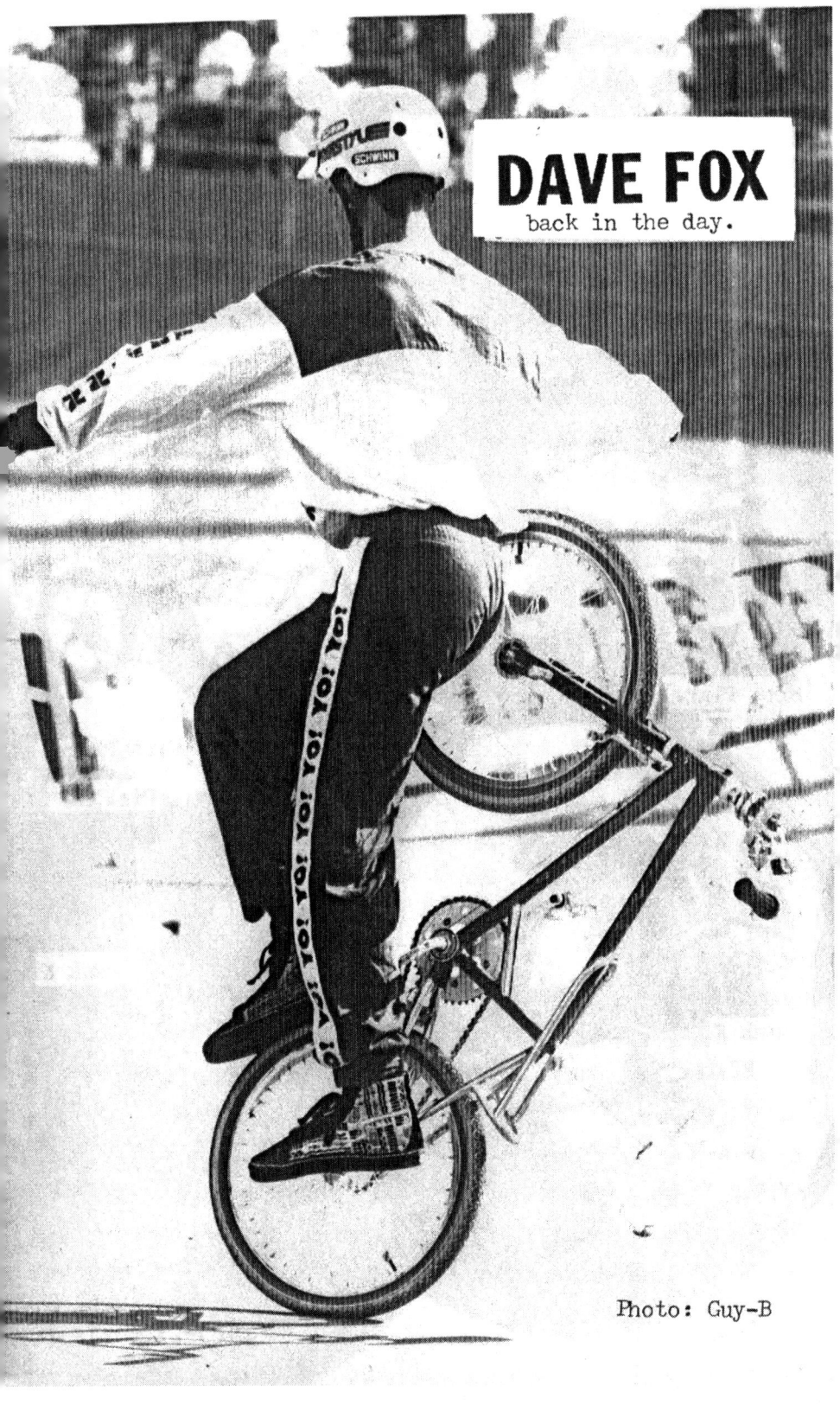

Photo: Guy-B

West Germany
Actchung!

Matt Pingel
Pic: FK

Matt Pingel
Pic: FK

Frank K
Pic: MP

Frank K
Pic: MP

idge

Greg Neal's Top 5 Summer Activities:

#1) Disassembling lawn sprinklers
#2) Renting out a warehouse and selling illegal National Hockey League products
#3) Water proofing egg slicers
#4) Making sure elementary school world maps stay in good shape
#5) Writing to dorks

Ho' the press!! Scope on this CLASSIC Pit shot of Kevano Jones reversing a ghost ride Jose Yanez flip into leaves. Suicide.

Greg Neal

RASTA DUFFY

TREND

P.O. BOX 201778 AUSTIN, TX 78720-1778

Latin Dance Rhythms with
TREND
The best BIKE SOURCE
CALL: (512) 338-4466

ABORO
RAG
FREESTYLE MAG!

c/o Mike Daily
3778 Cayuga Lane
York, PA 17402

STATE COLLEGE
ELKS
COUNTRY CLUB
B.P.O.E. 1600

From: Daniel W
To: Mike Daily
Subject:
Date: Mon, 22 Aug 2011

Hello there Mr. Daily,

Just a short note to let you know that there are some of us in Sweden who are really anticipating the arrival of the AR-book. Enclosed you will find some documentation of our last contact, about 22 years ago.

/Daniel W

3778 Cayuga Lane
York, PA 17402
US-A

Danielson,

Thanks for your kind words about Aggro Rag! I appreciate your support and enthusiasm. Glad you liked it. I'm sure you read FREESTYLIN' regularly. Well, at the beginning of the new year I'll be working for GO: The Rider's Manual as Associate Editor. I'm stoked — California is a rad place. That means A. Rag production will taper off. Hopefully I can do one more issue before I move to CA. If so, you'll get it. I'm sending you our brand new shirt and some past publications I've done. Hope you enjoy the stuff! Thank you for the pics. Keep riding over there.

Your friend,
Mike Daily

PLYWOOD HOODS

KEVIN JONES:

"The memory I have of this moment is going into that hotel room[16] and Eaton pulling out a cassette tape of the RAW (Relax And Win) positive mental attitude life-coaching motivational tape made specifically to help BMX riders win races. He drew the shades, turned down the lights and all the Hoods laid out on beds and the floor, listening to that fuckin' thing for 20 minutes. I was tripping and laughing at the same time." —**Lew**

[16] Wayne, NJ.

THE MAN.
THE INTERVIEW.

by Mike Daily

Kevin Jones quit BMX to break? Mind-boggling. Mind-boggling at the time. The guy had always been our "go-to" for glimpses of greatness. Go to The Pit[17] and watch him do tabletops. Go to The Quarry behind Burger King and bear witness to clicked Leary's.[18] Go to Thunderdohm and get our minds blown. Each successive time we saw him, he had a new bike with all the latest parts. And new tricks. He made our jaws drop at Dunkin' Donuts, Argento's Pizza and Best Products. We asked him questions and he wouldn't answer them. He made strange noises that sounded like video games sound effects and rode away, whistling. He wouldn't leave the scene—he'd ride. It was like we were riding with him. Kevin Jones. Kevin Scott Jones.[19]

York, PA, had a booming BMX scene in the early '80s. Be that as it was—and as good as Kevin Jones and Mark Eaton were—they got so into breakdancing, they no longer even owned bikes. They sold 'em to buy rolls of linoleum. And shag carpeting for underneath it. They never went anywhere without a can of Pledge[20] stowed in someone's sweatshirt or windbreaker. They chose "The Cardboard Lords" as their group name. They set a deadline and crammed for the final exam: "You can't be in The Cardboard Lords unless you can do three windmills by June 30, 1984."[21]

The Cardboard Lords set out to become the best breakers in the York metro area. They didn't know of—or see on TV—anyone who could do more headspins than Kevin. (He could do 30, hands-free.) He also wowed club crowds doing hands-clasped-behind-his-back windmills, and by taking off his hoodie while spinning. By the end of their run in May '85, The Cardboard Lords were winning every breakdance battle and competition they entered in York, Harrisburg, Baltimore and Philly.[22] Then, breakin' died. It died because guys weren't keeping up with it. Most couldn't keep up with it. Some had become too good—too unreal *great* at it. Breakin' had become intimidating. It had become too competitive.

---

[17] Defunct dirt jumping zone—now a parking lot where annual York Jams are held.

[18] Diamond Back Pro BMX racer Harry Leary's signature jump: He kicked out the back end, turned the handlebars 180 degrees and leaned off to the side, kind of like an X-up Crews—the Crews made popular by Redline Pro John Crews.

[19] Kevin Scott Jones was born on May 12, 1967. Pro skateboarder Tony Hawk (Anthony Frank Hawk) shares the same birthday as Kevin. Kevin was born a year earlier than Tony.

[20] Furniture polish. Aerosol.

[21] The crew became: Kevin Jones, Mark Eaton, Mark Wales, Barry Markle, Jake Sires, Jamie McKulik and Dale Mitzel.

[22] The Cardboard Lords never competed in New York City.

The same kind of crash happened in freestyle BMX at the end of '88. Hell, by the end of summer. Skyway Recreational Products—factory sponsor of Kevin Jones, Craig Campbell and Eddie Roman[23]—was one of several major manufacturers forced to drop (or downsize) their team rosters. Many riders returned from tours and received business letters stating, in effect, the companies could no longer afford to support them. Freestyle bike sales had dropped, hard.

A year prior to The Crash, Skyway had rushed to sign Kevin after his second place finish in 19 & Over Expert at Round 3 of the AFA Masters series held May 2, 1987, in Austin, Texas. Kevin had busted out trolley, his head-tube-straddling, no-handed scuff that he got into from backwards peg picker; uptight wheelie, his upside down backwards wheelie in tight circles while turning the cranks by hand[24]; standing room only, his standing-upright backwards infinity roll[25]; elephant glide, his sitting-on-the-crossbar-while-letting-the-back-end-of-the-bike-swing-around foot-drag-scuff; and then—after he had run out of time, unfortunately—locomotive, the backyard-like progression of his tag sanity hops (Kev had actually coasted the locomotive a few seconds without scuffing, then pulled it off).

Lew reported in the September '87 issue of *Freestylin'*:

"Kevin Jones got the crowd louder during his run than anyone else the whole weekend, including the pros. Every trick he did looked impossible yet was wired. He had a style so fresh it's gonna take even the best guys a few months to catch up. He did one of those runs that left every man, woman, and child in the arena stunned. He got second place."

Haro's Rick Moliterno—ever the man to beat in 19 & Over Expert—got first. Kevin later told Spike Jonze for *Freestylin'* (August '89): ""I would have been satisfied if I'd have made the top ten, and then I got second. I didn't know why there was all the controversy about it…[Rick] beating me. I was just glad to get second, plus I got sponsored. That's all I really wanted to do anyways was get sponsored. I never really cared about getting first."

Newly sponsored by Skyway, Kevin lost to Rick again at Round 4 of the AFA Masters Series held in Columbus, Ohio. That win was all Rick needed to clinch both 19 & Over Expert Flatland and Overall (Flat + Ramps) titles for the year, so Rick didn't even attend the next AFA Masters in Wayne, New Jersey. (Kevin won the class in NJ, but touched a lot during his routine.)

Rick Moliterno announced he was turning pro for '88. He told *Freestylin'*: "I'm 100 percent ready for pro now. At the end of last year everybody thought I was gonna turn pro, but I didn't feel like I was ready, but now I am. For SURE."

Rick did shows with Dave Voelker in France the same weekend the '87 AFA Masters Finals went on in SoCal.

Kevin pulled a perfect run[26] for first place.

---

[23] Don't forget to prank call Eddie Roman.

[24] Later became known as crank-a-roni.

[25] Kevin had added a radiator hose clamp to the chain stay of his Master so his foot wouldn't slip off.

[26] No sketches, no steps.

September 28, 1986, in Long Island, New York, Kevin Jones entered his first AFA Masters contest. He'd equipped his CW California Freestyle with a homemade locking brake lever[27] that worked better than anything on the market—even on six-strut Skyway Tuff Wheel mags. He'd lock it to do his tag sanity and flea collar hops—the latter a reversed, step-through-the-frame variation of Ceppie Maes' antrider. His power-move hang glider boomerang[28] earned much respect. Rick Moliterno saw the trick and quipped, "The man don't joke about boomerangs." *Aggro Rag 7* reported that Kevin "managed to tie CW's Greg Kove[29] in 16 & Over Expert Flatland *even with a completely blown run*."[30] With all due respect today to Greg Kove, it was a subtle way of saying, "This guy is terrible! How is this guy sponsored?" Seeing stars ride in real life was a motivator—lame, rad, didn't matter. Independent riders and teams everywhere were feeling: "Wow, we've got a shot at this!" This was a significant slice of what made freestylin' on bikes such good times: "The Dream" of getting sponsored by some company "out there" seemed within reach to most anyone who rode.

Kevin rolled out another 100% original routine—this time soundtracked by a mixtape song from the movie, *Wild Style* (1982)—at the second AFA Masters contest he attended, the '86 Finals at the Velodrome in SoCal. Kev pulled stall lawnmower to reverse peg picker to K picker (backwards pedal picker) to chicken hook switch, and busted out his uptight wheelie as the run-ender. He tied Chris Day for 11th place.

We had heard NorCal undergrounder Tim Treacy had been doing a brakeless, foot-on-the-back-tire scuffing trick he called "the backyard". Tim eventually received magazine coverage[31] for it in the May '87 issue of *Freestylin'* (the issue came out several weeks before the Austin AFA Masters were happening). It was the world's first look at the trick and the new technique. Kevin Jones was astounded. He recalls: "I remember just seein' the foot—the tire scuff—and I thought that was crazy. It didn't make any sense. It seemed like such a skill. We heard about it and realized, like: 'Whoa, you can actually move the back wheel and push it like that—different than squeaking and kicking.'"

[27] Kevin removed a wire loop from a mop that was hanging in his garage, drilled a hole in his brake lever and added the loop to the lever. He used a rubber band to hold the loop in place. The rubber band made the lever spring back when he unlocked the brake.

[28] Pat Romano style.

[29] Greg Kove once rode to a dance tune mixed by his uncle. *Freestylin'* noted "it had snatches of dialog from a TV interview with Woody [Itson] and Martin [Aparijo] mixed in with the music."

[30] Italics mine.

[31] Full page color photo by Windy Osborn.

Aware that the back tire could be scuffed as well as the front, Kevin developed his first scuffing move, the locomotive, while holding onto the I-beam along the ceiling of his parent's garage. He planned to do it as his final trick in Austin. Kevin was learning trolley at the same time that Aaron Dull was figuring out the same trick riding with Tim Treacy in San Francisco (Aaron called it "the puppet"). Aaron's "stick bitch"—bars backwards, holding the left front peg, scuffing the back tire from the side, with the bike spinning in circles—and Kevin's caboose was another instance of their synchronicity. Same tricks, different names, done on opposite sides of the country.

Mark Eaton

Scuffing became all the rage. Even Jason Parkes was doing it…sort of. (Jason mixed scuffing with squeaking, and a sequence of the combination[32] appeared in the July '87 *Freestylin'*.) Rolling tricks were on the verge of surging onto the scene. The only forward-rolling trick pulled[33] at the Finals in November '86 was the forward side glide by Adam Jung from Hawaii. Mark Eaton remembers[34]: "Yeah, he was the only one and not many people saw him doing it. I saw it and it burned in my head. It was the inspiration for the steamroller. I learned steamrollers in mid-January and then the whiplash came immediately after."

All weekend long in Austin, Mark Eaton was in "fast-forward" mode. He was doing steam rollers and whiplashes at speed, and a variety of his homespun[35] combos. *Freestylin'* (September '87) ran a photo of him doing a bar hop, seat-grab, squeakerson-type variant of Kevin's elephant glide, introducing him as: "Fellow Plywood Hood and counterpart of the K, Mark 'Lungmustard' Eaton." Soon after the contest, Kevin signed a contract to represent Skyway. Mark wanted to ride for a living like Kevin was going to—*get paid*

---

[32] Backwards scuff-squeaker with one foot on the top tube—precursor to corkscrew.

[33] "I didn't go very far, but I pulled it."—Adam Jung, *Aggro Rag* 13, (August 2012).

[34] What is this? A Pepperidge Farms commercial?

[35] Literally (homespun). Many were perfected down in his basement.

so he could avoid having to work the pre-sunrise Roadway truck loading/unloading shift that Kevin had shared with Dale Mitzel. Mark declined a co-sponsorship offer from Haro, holding out for a better ride from Revcore. The Revcore deal never materialized, though. Lung felt strung along and burned by Revcore's Product Manager[36] at the time. On the commentary track for *Dorkin' in York: The Complete DVD Collection: The Birth of Independent BMX Videos*, Mark has no abiding love for the hardware: "I was ridin' for Revcore at the time and I'll go on record by saying that was one of the worst frames I've ever ridden, and I'm mad to this day that I rode that bike. I still have that frame, but it definitely wasn't good—by any means."

That summer, Maryland resident Spike Jonze received his first official assignment for Wizard Publications, Inc. Prior to his drive out west to Torrance, CA, Spike was asked to go to York, PA, to interview us for a feature story ("Life, Liberty, and the Pursuit of the Plywood Hoods"). As we led him and co-photographer Bob Stukey[37] from location to location to shoot for the article, Spike skated full blast through York like it was a street-style course. Spike's black and white photo of Mark stretching a "joy twist"[38] appeared on the cover of the October '87 *Freestylin'*.

During Spike's interview, Kevin commented on how he felt being factory sponsored: "Yeah, I'm psyched," he said. "Now I have to ride hard to prove myself."

Jones will talk. Or "Jonesy", as flatlander and close friend Leif Valin calls him.[39] True, I interviewed Jonesy for *Freestylyin': Generation F; 1984-1989 (2009)*. Now the time had arrived to conduct "THE MAN. THE INTERVIEW." which I had announced back in the eleventh issue of *Aggro Rag* (August '88) was "Coming Soon…" Ha.

From the time Kevin Jones retired his pink-Tuffed neon green Haro Master in Summer '87 (when he received his first Skyway Street Beat) to the end of Summer '88 (when Skyway ceased sponsorship less than a month after tour was over), he *had* ridden hard—hard enough to innovate hang-5, no-handed hang-5,[40] forward elbow glide, opposite-way whiplashes, rope-a-roni , John Doenut[41] and more (more than he can remember). He'd invented phenomenal ways to roll into trolley (death truck) and caboose (dump truck)—crowning achievements of the era. He did death truck *into* dump truck, pretty much for one reason and one reason only: *because it was hard*, like JFK explaining why we were sending men to the moon. Intense. The "press conference" for that one, by the way (death into dump) was *Dorkin' III* (June '89).

[36] "Hollywood" Mike Miranda.
[37] Hadji's brother.
[38] Can can rivet.
[39] Nice. Nice.
[40] No-handed hang-5[40]? Yoops. No-handed hang-5 was a "fidge trick" that Kevin did in one of the early *Dorkin'* videos. He'd bolted a brake lever onto his forks and tied a rope from the lever to the handlebars to pull it off. It was shot tight so no one could see the rope. He later learned the trick by turning the bars backwards and bracing his knees against the bars.
[41] Reverse tailwhips to freak squeak holding the seat behind him, scuffing clockwise in circles.

Post-Skyway, Kevin rode GT bikes throughout filming for *Dorkin' III*. GT Bicycles had hooked up him with a full factory sponsorship. After Jonesy missed a booked flight to do shows in July '89—pulled a "no show, no call", basically—he was terminated. GT's Team Manager[42] couldn't believe it. Mark Eaton could: "Kev could *so* care less," he says. "He needed a root canal on a tooth, and he just didn't want to go do it." The TM allegedly told Mrs. Jones by phone: "I want you to know his career is ruined." (Mrs. Jones believed him.)

GT got its money's worth out of him, considering that *Dorkin' III* contained Kevin's hardest, most accomplished riding to date: hitchhiker, backpacker, cross-footed hitchhiker to backwards backpacker, backwards forward side glide, etc. After riding for 2-Hip/Wilkerson Airlines for nine months, Kevin actually returned to riding GT/Dyno products without being paid or flowed to do so in *Dorkin' IV* (October '90). Canadian Hood Chase Gouin rode a chrome Dyno frame with GT forks in *Dorkin' IV*, his debut as a Plywood Hood. Chase is absent from *Aggro Rag Freestyle Mag! Plywood Hoods Zines '84-'89: The Complete Collection* because by the time he'd arrived on the York scene—eager to find his P.U. (Purpose in the Universe)—I'd already moved to Southern California to work for Wizard. He and Kev endeavored to learn "All Four" of every trick they were doing: regular-footed, opposite-footed, cross-footed regular, cross-footed opposite. They went on to master every conceivable variation of every trick they did in the early '90s.

Dorkin' in York (May '88), *Dorkin' II* (November '88) and *Dorkin' III* video tapes were absolutely mandatory indie media items to buy, watch over and over again, and bite from. Er, "be inspired by." Pros Martin Aparijo and Woody Itson—both of whom were breakdancers themselves (Major Chain Breakers, sponsored by Vans)—learned locomotive and other "K" creations: Martin had locomotive glides wired, and Woody did caboose and reverse trolley (pedal picker position). No one was doing backwards whiplashes faster and further than Dennis McCoy, who took cues from Lungmustard and Kev to make flatland more dope and dangerous than ever.

---

[42] Shaun Buckley.

Dennis had invented "G-string"—G-turn to rolling tailwhips—often linked to funky chicken and/or hyperspastic front yard. (No surprise when Kevin named DMC as his all-time favorite rider in *American Freestyler*).

Top amateurs incorporated Hoods styles as well: South Bay's Chris Day ruled at one- and no-handed rope-a-roni and forward rope-a-roni with aggression. Florida freethinker Gerry Smith owned rollback tailwhiplash to forward rope-a-roni to Smith decade. Hoosier Perry Mervar cruised super-smooth hitchhikers. New Yorker Joe Gruttola coasted two-footed locomotives (F-glide). PA homeboy Gary Pollak said he was "tired of rolling tricks" in the July '89 *Freestylin'*, but Pinky's G-strings, forward side glides and backwards whiplashes spoke otherwise. Street riding was "in", but the BMX freestyle industry was "on the outs", sales-wise. Same article, same issue, *Freestylin'* asked, "How do you see street riding? Will it be 'out' in a year or two?" Brett Hernandez gave what has turned out to be the most visionary reply: "It seems like in street skate contests, they'll mix freestyle skating tricks with street tricks in their runs. Maybe that'll be what happens in freestyle now, too. Doing flatland tricks while you're doing a run in a street contest. There's tons of stuff you could do…a hang five up onto a curb, then roll off…combining the two sports. I don't know."

Kevin Scott Jones will talk about this—how flatland moves he made up a quarter of a century ago are now the staples of modern street riding—in "THE MAN. THE INTERVIEW." He'll also address the origin of scuffing, basketball sneakers of the '80s/'90s, why he waited so long to turn Pro, how he feels about contemporary flat, why he's stopped trying to make up new tricks, what bike frames he's designed and what his "dream job" would be…or is already.

Mike Daily: First question: The great George Gallo from New York asks: "Does it bother you that everyone has lifted your tricks?"

Kevin Jones: [Laughs.] No, it doesn't bother me. I mean, it probably did, you know, like early—in the *real* early days—more like if it was a month after I just did the trick, and then I saw everybody do it. That kind of bugged me at the time, because I was tryin' to compete and tryin' to be able to do an original contest run every so often. But it started gettin' harder and harder and harder to do that, because then I didn't stand out any more—because maybe a month later, there's like 20 guys doin' the trick that I did the month before. It just made it kind of blend in again. Over the long term though, No. It's awesome.

George Gallo

George adds: "I know what he would say because he's humble, but everyone would want to ask that question, I believe."

I definitely used to hate it quite a way back, but at the current time I never think about that at all.

What are the top three main tricks that he's referring to?

Well, the hitchhiker and the backpacker, and all the little subtleties of those. Those were like the two main ones. And…uh… well, of course, there's the hang-5. That's one that pretty much every single person does. Those would be the top three: the hitchhiker, the backpacker and the hang-5.

What year was the hitchhiker and the backpacker?

I'm thinkin' the hitchhiker was at the very end of '88. That was like November or December of '88. And then at the beginning of '89—maybe February—I did the backpacker. By that point, I had done both of them probably like 500 times each. I practiced it really hard right after I learned it. By the time I did the hitchhiker maybe like 200 times, I had decided I wanted to do the backpacker and then I just tried to catch up with that—accomplish as much as I could in a short amount of time.

What about hang-5? When was that?

I don't have an exact month for that. I'm tryin' to think what bike I woulda been on to do it. I don't know if it was '87 still, or early '88. I don't remember much about that—the particular month or anything.

What's really interesting about that is when you go to a skatepark now, so many street kids who really don't have much foundation in flatland are doing hang-5 and hang nothings—no brakes on the bikes—as part of their skatepark riding.

Yeah.

It's almost more popular than manuals, I noticed. What do you remember about the feeling of first doing the hang-5 and hang nothing?

The hang-5 was cool but it wasn't like a big deal, really. It was like, whatever. Peg wheelies were already out so it was kind of like the peg wheelie, more or less. Kind of like a fiddle trick. Because back then when we did peg wheelies, it wasn't like we were really doin' a trick. It was just like a starting point, or something you'd do to do something else. Or just something to do. It's pretty much how the hang-5 was. I mean, it was a trick, but if you just did that, it wasn't like you really did anything. It would be like, OK: You're gonna do hang-5, you're gonna go forward and then go into something. You know? So I don't think of it as a big trick. It didn't take long. I did it pretty much instantly once I decided to do it. There wasn't practice involved—maybe a couple minutes of thinkin' about it and tryin' it and there it was: I was already doin' it as far as I wanted to, by then.

Were you doin' it as fast as you wanted to? Could you go full speed?

Over maybe like five minutes, I went faster and faster and faster until I was going at a medium speed, like on a slant down a hill. I didn't go at full-speed-pedal or anything on the first day, but it didn't take much longer.

Are you noticing how popular that is right now?

What, the hang-5?

Yeah.

Oh, yeah. It's everywhere you look. Yeah, just like you said: streeters and everybody do it a lot. I still do it. Probably every single time I go out ridin', I do it at some point. I possibly do it a hundred times in one day, for all I know. I change it up though. Like, I'll try it—do it—into something else, or do it out of something. I just make it different somehow.

Luke Strahota from here in Portland, Oregon, asks: "What are some trick names you thought of that never got used?"

[Laughs.] Trick names that I thought of and never got used? I don't think there were any. I think for every one, there was a trick.

What would come first: the trick, or the name of the trick?

Oh, it depends. Sometimes the name would be there first. You'd just have a crazy idea for a name, and then it'd be like: "Alright, now you gotta do the trick." Other times, you'd wait and something about the trick would just pop into your mind as you were trying to describe it. You'd be like: "Oh, I got this trick," and you'd just kind of put it together in your mind, like: "Oh, OK, I'll just call it this." It just fits. There was never really a whole lot of thought into any of it—it sort of just happens. You're never sittin' there goin': "Oh yeah, I really need the name for this trick." By that point, you would already just say something to everyone or somebody else might just put the name on there for you— just describing what they saw you doing. Joe Gruttola named the death truck.

Yeah, he mentioned that when I interviewed him. You called one trick the caboose and on the West Coast they called it the stick bitch.

Yep. Stick bitch.

Was Tim Treacy the first guy you saw scuffing?

That's what I remember, yeah. Unless it was Oleg [Koenings] doin' the crossfooted stick b. I forget what that trick was called. The side squeak? What the heck was that called?

Insanity roll, I think.

That was kind of a scuffing technique. Slightly different though: using not the length of the foot, but sideways and just like kind of using the brake. Sorta like a brake squeak—like an Eaton-style scuff.

Interesting.

That might even have been before Tim Treacy. I don't know.

Yeah, I think that was before.

Then I think when Tim Treacy did it, there was no brake whatsoever. It was just straight-up scuffing.

On a bike with Tuff Wheels.

Yeah. I'd like to see that picture again. I always wonder about that. Seems so odd.

Brett [Downs] from Hollywood, PA, asks: "I don't have any questions for him that I don't know the answer to, but ask him about *Aggro Rag* and how the scene in York impacted him." What do you remember about *Aggro Rag*?

"Aaaaggro Raaaag Freeeeestyle Maaaag…" [Laughs.] *Aggro Rag* was awesome. It was the magazine that showed us riding. It was cool to have a place to see our pictures—just see it and have other people see it. It was cool that you got us our first sponsors like the ODI Mushroom grips and the Yoo-Hoo and the [Flying Feet] shoe store where I got the discount. That seemed like the best time, back then. Everything was totally new. It was really awesome to get it out there. It was awesome that other people actually saw the *Aggro Rags*. And then of course that started the whole explosion of the little zines of BMX. Everything I remember about it was awesome— I know that much.

Thanks. Greg Higgins from Las Vegas— now living in Portland—asks: "Over the course of the past 20 years with fatherhood and other vocations and interests coming into play, do you see a pattern emerge that drives you to approach other variables in the same way you do your riding?"

The only thing I can think right off is just how much patience it takes to go for what you want to do, and how you're gonna get there. From riding, you see how hard it is and how much time and effort it takes to do what you want to do, and it's kind of the same for everything else: I make little plans in the same way as I would for riding. For certain tricks or a contest, I would need a plan—a riding plan—of how I was gonna piece together the practice and get there. And I kind of use that same deal with everything else that I do. I have a lot of patience for things than I would otherwise, I guess.

Roger D. Ford asks: "How's the family and have you been taking care of yourself?"

Roger! [Laughs.] The family is awesome and—yep—I'm takin' care of myself. I quit smokin' and I don't drink. It's not like I won't drink, but somehow I don't end up doing it very often. I'm still ridin' as much as I can. I exercise and I eat pretty well, as well. I cut out—for the most part, I cut out—a lot of the junk food. But, I mean, I still eat the Tasty Cakes and Martin's chips when I get the chance. Yeah, everything's good: The family's great and I feel really good. I'd like to make to 100.

Here's a question from Scott Towne in Michigan. He asks: "How did it feel as an amateur to have the entire Pro class shaking in their Vision Street Wears that you were redefining the entire activity of flatland BMX?"

[Laughs.] I don't know. It probably was different than people would think, because my mindset wasn't…uh…I wasn't thinkin' about that so much. I wasn't even really aware of that. I don't really know what to say about that one. I mean, I was just tryin' to do my thing. It was different, you know? It was like being in my own little world—in my mind—just tryin' to do my tricks and tryin' to ride. I wasn't noticing that as much as maybe other people were. And then when I would hear about it, I'd just be like: "Oh, yeah," but kind of not really pay much attention to it.

I have a question for you from Maurice Meyer—

Yeah!

—from San Francisco. Maurice says: "I guess I'd ask him about contests and shows—the business side—and how it affected his riding, and how his perspectives changed over time. And why did he wait so long to go Pro? (Thanks, by the way!) And how does he feel about the state of freestyle—specifically, flatland?" OK, starting with Drob's first question, let's go from '84—from the first Plywood Hoods shows that we did—through '89. How did your perspectives change over time?

In the early days when the contests were awesome—you know, '84, '85 and '86—it was just somethin' to do: You would hurry up and try to practice really hard to learn the stuff so you could do it quick. With the contests back then, it became almost like a challenge to try to hurry up and learn some good stuff to do and try to get it down, and have a reason to practice it over and over and over—whereas if there weren't the little contests in the early times, we probably wouldn't have tried to dial the stuff in as much, and we would have just kind of done it for fun and moved on. The shows at that same time felt awesome. That was great. We got to show what we were doing and possibly try to get people into it. I don't know if it really did so much back then, but I guess that was our hope: to get more people doin' it. I just kind of did the shows wherever; with whoever. At a later time—after being sponsored—it was more like the business side. It seems like I kind of had to do it and it felt like I should do it, but it wasn't really necessarily what my idea of what I wanted to do to make a living was. But it was sort of a way to make some money, which bought more time to try to ride. Money wasn't really a big factor, but there was maybe enough to keep me going to where I could ride the whole summer instead of work. Well, I kind of missed the whole…I mean, it was never at that point where there was a lot of money.

Why did you wait so long to go Pro?

I don't know. It sounds weird to me for it to be put that way—that it seemed as though I waited long. I thought it was really fast, myself. I probably would have never really entered Pro—or turned Pro—until many years after the first time that I did when I was riding for GT. Skyway wanted me to compete in Pro. I would have never really thought about it if they didn't mention it. And then the contest series too, as well… like if you won so many Expert competitions, they said you'd have to move up to Pro. I probably never would have just entered Pro. I don't know what I would have done, but I can't see that I would ever have just turned on my own.

One thing I find interesting is that the Pro class was keeping an eye on you and noticing what you were doing, and a couple of the main guys ended up learning a lot of the tricks. I'm thinking of Martin [Aparijo], Woody [Itson] and R.L. [Osborn]. Did you notice that? They were doin' a lot of the stuff. They had it down.

Oh, yeah. They were doin' the locomotives and stick b—the caboose or whatever—and then later the hitchhiker. Yeah, I totally noticed that.

I heard that you and Chase [Gouin] wrote to Nike in 1990 just to get shoes, and they weren't into it.

Yeah. With Jerry Uy's help, I was tryin' to get us on Nike and they just said, No. All-out. They didn't want anything to do with BMX.

You would have been stoked to get even the current production-type shoes at that time, right? Nothing special.

Yeah—regular basketball shoes—because we were payin' for 'em and at that point they were like $80 to $100 for the best ones. I was buyin' $100 pairs of sneaks once a month. That was a lot of money back then. I wouldn't spend $100 a month now, but I guess it seemed more important back then to have shoes that worked. With the endless ridin' on little pegs, it was almost impossible to do it all day on a flimsy shoe, you know?

Yeah.

It just hurt too much.

Do you remember what the best model was?

I wasn't so stuck on any one kind. I just really liked the hi-top feature and stiff soles. That was all I ever looked for. I don't remember the names of 'em or anything. They changed a whole lot. I never got too hooked on one kind because by the time you really liked one, then maybe they didn't make it anymore. It was a pain in the butt just lookin' for 'em, and they were so expensive. It seems crazy. What would that be equal to now? Like $200!

[Laughs.] You went through a pair a month?

Yeah. That's ridin' every single day for ten hours—most of a whole day.

That's another thing I've been thinking about: I've been trying to comprehend the concept of someone riding that much every day. And you did it—day in and day out.

Oh, yeah. For so many years. Minus the sleep thing and maybe tack on an hour and a half over that, the rest of the time was pretty much ridin' like ten to 12 hours at a time. Of course, you're not constantly doin' it. You know, you stop for a couple minutes here, you go get a drink…it adds up. But without any major break, I could go ten hours for sure. I would just ride and ride and ride. I would just keep doin' it and keep doin' it. It seems crazy now. I mean, now I don't get burned out, because I *can't*. I can't ride that much so it's fun. I could ride hard six hours one day and then the next day, there's no way. The body just can't do it. It kind of works out because that way I don't get burned out—in my mind as well—if I'm not overdoin' it.

How do you feel about the current state of freestyle? And specifically, flatland? What became the most marginal part of the sport—flatland—is now a core, connected group of worldwide riders who are so dedicated. Internet talk shows like *FlatWebTV*…that's so cool to see.

The modern state doesn't seem any different to me. People always ask about that. I don't know. I guess I just don't see it. To me, it seems the same. I mean, it obviously seems like there's way more people doin' it throughout the world. Like, you got the Japanese riders and they have their own kind of style, for the most part. Now it doesn't seem a whole lot different, other than there's just way more people doin' it. There's still all the old people—they're still riding. And I don't factor them out. There's not a whole lot that aren't riding. I mean, there's more that are riding than aren't riding, somehow or another. They might not be riding contests or anything, but they still have the 20" bike and they still do tricks. To me, that is the scene still: the whole scene. It's not just like the new scene. It seems like it's coming back around. People just kind of re-appeared, sort of—like a lot of old school people—over the last five years or so. They're still goin'. They're still there, still doin' it. It's like people thought they were long gone and done, and now they're back.

In the *Freestylin'* book, you said about freestyle: "It's very strange and different—specifically flatland freestyle. It's so different. People don't really understand it. And the riders don't want to change it, they just want to do it." Can you say anything more about that?

Change it for the public, or try to make it more popular? Yeah, that just never seems to work. I mean, I don't really know how that would work out. It's just fun to do—just tryin' to do tricks that you like and not really care. I don't think of it in terms of entertainment for the average person. That'd be too weird. There's no point for that. There's other forms of bike riding where you could do it differently—do it as a show or an act. The flatland seems like it's more about actually what you're doin' with the bike and the tricks themselves, and maybe even your own personal idea of what you're tryin' to do. For me, I don't ever think about what somebody else is thinkin' about what I'm doin'. I'm never even concerned about it. That doesn't even factor in. The only thing I'm thinkin' about is whether I like doin' it, or whether it feels good doin' it a certain way.

Do you still set goals for yourself? Are you still makin' up tricks?

Uh…I abandoned the whole idea of tryin' to think about makin' up new tricks. It just seemed kind of hard to think about. I mean, they just happen, you know? I don't really think about it or anything. All of a sudden you just did it a different way after tryin' a variety of ways, and it sorta just happens on its own. Almost every time that I try to force tricks, it definitely didn't seem to work, so I just kind of stopped tryin' that. But if you put enough time in…you know, you gotta leave the room open. The way that they usually happen is by not tryin' to over-practice. Like if you just sat there and you're like: "OK, I'm gonna do this, and it's gonna start like this and it's gonna end like this…"—and then you do that ten times—then there's no room for anything else to happen in-between. I might just have an idea of how I'm gonna start something, and then just go from there and do it and see what happens. That's usually when a lot of the new ones happen. But a lot of times they disappear, because you don't remember them. I know there's a lot of tricks that I've done that if I saw it, I wouldn't even know that I did it. Like if I saw somebody else do it—not knowing that in real life, I had already done it. It's just weird.

[Laughs.] Can you think of an example of that?

Not really, right at the minute. But I know when I'm ridin', sometimes just certain things happen and I'm like: "OK, I know that never happened before. That felt really good. It was a different technique, and it made something else happen…" But by the time you get to the end and ride away, you forget about it. It's strange. It's kind of hard to explain. For the most part, it's not so much like a visual thing. Somebody standin' there watchin' might not even have noticed something different happening. It's just sometimes, something else works that you might not even have thought would even work. Or maybe you didn't even try it really—it was just like the instinct that you did at the moment. You just did something and then: "Wow, that made it work differently." And now that made it possible.

Yeah.

Kind of like the modern pumping. Nobody was pumping too much, and now there's not anything that people don't pump. So at some point, somebody invented the pumping. They might have just used it to save it a little bit, or thousands of people might have done it a little bit over a long time to kind of save themselves from messin' up.

Over time, it evolves. I guess that's kind of like how the thing is that I'm tryin' to explain. It's like that, but maybe I won't see the end result for many more years. When the little pieces and little techniques work a little bit, I feel them and I know that they're there—and I know that I'll be able to stumble across them in the future as well—and maybe eventually they'll lead to something good and I can do it consistently.

My friend cirebo in Portland asks: "How many frames have you designed, and what are the most drastic changes you made between them through the evolution of the tricks and styles of riding?"

There's not a whole lot of frames. There was the Level frame: We had the chainstays dropped down lower so you could have a small sprocket and still have the brake down below. And then also at the time, we had the ultra-low seat stays so there was tons and tons of scuffing room. It was really low—as low as the really low ones now—and you could do tire decades. That was pretty much a good feature back then: all that clearance and space between the tire and seat stays. There was, of course, the Big Daddy. There wasn't a whole lot of features other than being over-strong and extra heavy-duty. That was kind of like the main idea there, because prior to that I was just gettin' tired of readjusting the frame every so often—trying to find a new one because they would crack. I'd ride for five or six weeks and crack the frame, then I had to find something else...and then crack it again. I just wanted to have something that I could not think about it for a year: just have a frame, get it all dialed in and be done with it. And know that that's what I was gonna be ridin'. So that was more or less just a super heavy-duty thing. And now the Strowler: It's just pretty much a simple frame.

It is quite a bit streamlined compared to the Big Daddy.

Oh, yeah. The original Big Daddy was almost seven and a half pounds for just the frame. It was 50% heavier than a Strowler. The Strowler has new tubing—smaller diameter—and there are more cutouts in the right places, for weight. Weight was not even a consideration at the point of the Big Daddy. Nobody even knew what the weight was. Nobody even asked. At that point, it didn't even matter. We didn't weigh our bikes when we had our Haros and CWs and all that. We never knew what it was.

"What would be your dream job?" asks Raymond J. Schlechtweg Jr. from Pennsylvania.

My dream job? Damn...I don't know. I don't work, so I don't know.

[Laughs.]

Well, it wouldn't be ridin' my bike to make a living. It wouldn't be that. I really don't know. I don't have a dream job. Avoiding havin' a job is my dream, but—

And are you doing that? Do you have to work?

Oh, no: I don't have any job whatsoever. And I don't plan on having one any time soon. Maybe at some point I'll want a job. If I did have a dream job, I probably would try to do it. I think about it maybe once a year really hard for a little while like: "OK, what could I do? Is there something I want to do?" But nothing comes to mind and I don't bother.

"Daily's gonzo acid drop of *Rad* meets *Breaking Bad*." —**Lazy Fascist**

Moon Babes of Bicycle City
NOVEL (2014)

Next year, Portland's Lazy Fascist Press will publish *Moon Babes of Bicycle City*, a lyrical novel about the demented Moon family—Rod, Chatauqua and daughters named Suzue, Araya and Ukai—and their attempts to survive in a bike clubs-ravaged New Mexico town where cars have been outlawed and the terrain is a world like no other.

Lazy Fascist Press, 2014

MOON BABES OF BICYCLE CITY

South of Roswell, north of Hope, east of an Apache reservation, west of Dexter and Lake Arthur lies Bicycle City, New Mexico.

Mike Daily

1st sentence was published as a broadside by 48th Street Press in Caracas, Venezuela.

MORE MEDIA

"Underground classic." —**Global-Flat.com**

***Aggro Rag Freestyle Mag! The Hip-Hop Issue* Number 13**
ZINE (2012)

For the first issue of my zine *Aggro Rag* to appear since '89, I interviewed 15 of the most innovative flatlanders from the fluorescent era of freestyle. Twenty-three years later, what are these guys thinking? What *were* they thinking? Finding out felt a bit gonzo at times, but it was something I had to do. Each copy of this limited edition of 500 is signed by Plywood Hoods Brett Downs, Mark Eaton, Kevin Jones, Jamie McKulik, Dale Mitzel and me, Mike Daily. Covers are individually autographed in gold paint pen ink by Intrikat, Chad Johnston. "Aggro Rag Freestyle Mag!" ink stamps make each copy unique.

Stovepiper Books Media, 2012
5 ½" x 8 ½"
68 Pages

"The essential prose on Steve Richmond." —**Todd Moore**

Gagaku Meat: The Steve Richmond Story
BIOGRAPHY (2009)

First published in Holland, my biography about Santa Monica "Meat Poet" Steve Richmond (1941-2009) features our personal correspondence, exclusive photos, new poems, bibliography highlights, and additional insights from Richmond's friends and small press publishers.

Stovepiper Books Media, 2009
8" x 10 ¼"
32 Pages

"*ALARM* is a fantastically real account of life as we know it—and especially succeeds at uncovering the humor and magic of our most normal days working, loving, and living." —**Craig Finn,** The Hold Steady

ALARM
NOVEL + 2CD SET (2007)

A man and a woman in Southern California's San Fernando Valley wrangle with relationship concerns in the immediate aftermath of the 9/11 terrorist attacks. The drugs don't work. The pubs don't work. The moonlight drives don't work. The books don't work. The movies don't work. The records that used to work don't work. *He* doesn't work. Mick O'Grady is at a point in his life where he doesn't know whether he should get a three-month trial subscription to *The Christian Science Monitor* or twelve issues of *Leg Show* and a calendar. He keeps moving.

Stovepiper Books Media, 2007
5 ¼" x 7"
212 Pages

"Mike Daily packs so many stylistic smash cuts into *Valley*, MTV dulls by comparison." —***Ray Gun Magazine***

Valley
NOVEL (1998)

Drifting through his days in a haze while attempting to make sense of numerous mysteries unraveling before him—from the oddball people he meets to the mysterious margin scribblings, receipts and photos he happens upon in used books by his favorite authors—BMX magazine editor and college student Mick O'Grady examines love, literature and random road signs he sees in the San Fernando Valley.[43]

Designed and published by Andy Jenkins/Bend Press, 1998
5 ½" x 8 ½"
224 Pages

"I look forward to *Stovepiper*. The main thing is to do what you want to do and to publish what makes you feel good. Maybe better than good."
—**Charles Bukowski** in a letter to Mike Daily

STOVEPiPER
ANTHOLOGY (1994)

Poems by Greg Barbera, David Barker, Charles Bukowski, Neeli Cherkovski, Ana Christy, Jim DeWitt, Keith Dodson, Douglas Goodwin, Alan Kaufman, Marvin Malone, Bill Shields, Mark Weber and Jeff Weddle; fiction by Hugh Brown Shu and Merle Tofer; excerpt from *Beggars in Paradise* by Irving Stettner; illustrations by Bukowski, Greg Higgins, Bad Otis Link and Joseph Solman; and Steve Richmond's 33-poem center section, *The Poets Are All Liars* with paintings by Andy Jenkins.

Stovepiper Books, 1994
5" x 8"
144 Pages

STOVEPIPER
BOOKS MEDIA
http://stovepiperbooks.com

---
[43] A suburb of Los Angeles.

443